The

SECRETS

of

MY LIFE

D1707703

The

SECRETS

of

MY LIFE

VINTNER, PRISONER, SOLDIER, SPY

P E T E R   M .   F .   S I C H E L

Archway Publishing books may be ordered
through booksellers or by contacting:

Archway Publishing
1663 Liberty Drive
Bloomington, IN 47403
www.archwaypublishing.com
1 (888) 242-5904

ISBN: 978-1-4808-2406-5 (sc)
ISBN: 978-1-4808-2407-2 (e)

Library of Congress Control Number: 2015920317

Print information available on the last page.

Archway Publishing rev. date: 1/6/2016

In memory of Alexandra Sichel,
and with gratitude to Stella Sichel

CONTENTS

PART 3: BEING A WINE MERCHANT, WINE
GROWER, AND WINE PERSONALITY

INTRODUCTION

Ich träum als Kind mich zurück,
Und schüttle mein greises Haupt;
Wie sucht ihr mich heim, ihr Bilder,
Die lang ich vergessen geglaubt?

I grew up in Germany and England, and the poems and songs I learned as a child stayed with me all my life, particularly the above-quoted Adalbert von Chamisso poem:

> I dream of my childhood, and shake my
>   gray head,
> The pictures I thought long forgotten still
>   haunt me.

We all have stories to tell about our lives, stories that interest primarily our children and close friends. If a life was lived in so-called interesting times and spent doing interesting things, it might interest a larger audience.

Who knows—maybe my life is of wider interest. It has been a long journey, blessed by a happy childhood in Germany, at that time a far-from-happy land. What a difference a loving family can make in a society in ferment. My story includes escapes, one well planned to avoid a dangerous future and one from the advancing German armies. I was fortunate to be able to come to America shortly before the United States joined World War II. I served in the American military, the Office of Strategic Services (OSS), and the CIA, and finally I joined my family's wine business and worked in it for almost fifty years.

The loss of a treasured, brilliant child to cancer at fifty was the saddest incident in an otherwise happy life.

It is not easy to put all this to paper—to decide what to tell and what to leave out. Having written the book, I wonder whether there are chapters that would have been better left out and others that might have been written more realistically, told in greater detail to reflect how I felt about the incidents that I considered worthy of mention.

Maybe I will write a second and more focused version, but being over ninety-three, I would like to get this memoir published, warts and all.

I have learned some lessons—the greatest, no doubt, being that we too often do not leave well enough alone. Societies and people have to evolve because forced evolution leads to trouble. I am sad about the paranoia and plain hate that inform our politics and so much of our society. I abhor the confrontational attitude that gives no room for tolerance.

I have learned to look forward and not backward: the missed opportunities and the mistakes I have made cannot be changed. Hopefully, I learned from them, but to worry about them makes no sense. My story includes decisions I had to make to live with my conscience. In some cases I chose to walk away rather than be involved in what I thought was wrong. In other cases I took issue, but my voice neither was heard nor made much of a difference.

In most of my life, I was an observer rather than a doer. Being an intelligence officer gives you some insight into what motivates the policy makers but does not give you the right to interfere in matters of state. You serve the goddess of truth and find out that many policy makers would rather be guided by their own prejudices and ideologies than the truth.

Every life is a lesson to be lived, and I hope you will find some interest in some episodes from mine.

I finished the manuscript of this book in 2012 and sent it off to my publisher. He came back and asked me to get clearance from the CIA for the chapters dealing with my life in the agency. It had never occurred to me that discussion of my service in the CIA more than fifty years ago needed clearance, yet the publisher refused to go ahead without such clearance.

In due course I submitted the portion of the book that dealt with my seventeen years with the OSS and CIA to the CIA for clearance, and to my surprise I was told that certain parts of my book could not be published, since they dealt with incidents that the CIA had never acknowledged. In spite of some of these incidents having been written up in other books and newspaper reports, the CIA insisted that unless the agency had acknowledged an incident, it was at best speculative if written up by people who had no "official" knowledge.

There ensued a long series of correspondence and face-to-face meetings, which would not resolve the CIA's insistence on my dropping the mention of certain incidents for security reasons. In the meantime I became older every day, my friends became more anxious to see what I had written, and I was faced with the possibility of never seeing the book in print in my own lifetime.

I finally compromised and decided to edit the book to retain facts that I could mention. The CIA also finally allowed me to mention matters that were previously blacked out. This enabled me to write about my CIA career in a way that made sense.

In any case, I felt all along that the more important part of the story is my youth in Germany and the complicated relationship of German Jews to Germany. I was fortunate to have two or even three German "periods" in my life—the first as a child growing up during the world financial crisis of the Great Depression and the Nazi takeover, in the 1920s and early '30s, and the second as an intelligence officer in World War II, recruiting Germans to be sent back into Germany as spies. I was stationed in Berlin after the war for almost seven years, reporting both on East Germany and on the Russian presence in East Germany. My third and final association with Germany was as an owner and executive in a wine business that enabled me to deal with and get to know Germans at multiple levels of a complicatedly structured society.

I think the greatest pleasure in writing my memoirs is the knowledge you acquire by doing the necessary research. It forces you to read up on history that you were not taught and to search for dates to correctly anchor your story, and like all research, it ends up involving a lot of reading, which, though not essential to your book, is inspired by information you came across while researching specific incidents on which you feel the urge to follow up.

I never would have read, among other books, two massive biographies of Bismarck or a number of books by Ian Kershaw, Joachim Fest, and Sebastian Haffner, let alone the long book on George Kennan by John Lewis Gaddis or the *History of Germany* by Golon Mann, without the urge to know more than I really had to know to write this book. My reading turned out to be an education I felt I needed to help me understand how all this tragedy was possible. Needless to say, this reading gave me a lot of facts but never gave me an answer. I do feel that there is a direct relationship leading from Luther to Bismarck to Hitler but have found no one as yet who agrees with me. I am too old now to pursue that line of argument in a more learned way.

I hope that reading this book will lead you, like me, to seek other sources to help inform you about a period in world history that we should try to understand more, since some of the lessons, like the severity of the Treaty of Versailles, might well encourage us not to repeat the mistakes of yesterday.

The world I describe is a world that does not exist anymore. It was before the computer, before the Internet, before cell phones, before twenty-four-hour newscasts. The one lesson I have learned from being in the machinery of international politics is that trying to interfere in other countries to impose one's own ideology or method of statecraft is bound to fail. Not only that, but it also will bring results often worse than letting a society evolve by itself to find solutions closer to our ideals.

PART 1

Youth, 1922–41

CHAPTER ONE

My Family Roots

My great-grandfather Herz was the first member of our family to carry a family name. Prior to the end of the eighteenth century, most Jews were known by their given names and patronymics—the first name of the person, which in my case is Peter, and the first name of the person's father, followed by the indication of a difference in generation. In my case, this name would be Peter Eugenson (Peter, the son of Eugen). As the Jews were liberated from restrictions—one of the benefits of the French conquest of the left bank of the Rhine—they were asked to assume family names. Herz changed his first name to Hermann and picked the name of Sichel, which means half-moon or sickle in German.

The family had been, from the early part of the eighteenth century, merchants living in Sprendlingen, a small town about equidistant from Mainz and Bingen, in the Grand Duchy of Hessia. (At that time, before the establishment of Germany as a single country in 1871, Germany was ruled by many dukedoms and principalities and a few kingdoms, such as Prussia, Saxony, and Bavaria.) The family sold the produce of the backcountry of Rheinhessen to the nearby market cities. In the early 1800s, the main product they sold was wool. With the arrival of the steam engine, however, they increasingly made their money by buying wine and selling it in bulk to wine merchants. This business became so important that my great-grandfather Hermann, with three of his sons, left Sprendlingen in the middle of the 1800s and established a wine business in Mainz. The oldest son, Adolf Sichel—my great-great-uncle—stayed in Sprendlingen to maintain contact with grape growers and winemakers.

Mainz, which was founded by the Romans as a fort on the left bank of the Rhine, is the principal commercial and cultural center of the region. It is close to where the river Main joins the great river. It was a bulwark defending the Roman Empire from the tribes that lived on the other side of the Rhine. It had an important role in the Holy Roman Empire, being one of the city-states that elected the emperor. Its cathedral to this day dominates the city, as do many other beautiful churches. It was ruled for centuries by *Kurfürsten*, dukes who were both the temporal and religious rulers, and to this day the bishop of Mainz is an important part of the Catholic hierarchy. Mainz is also the city where Gutenberg invented the printing press.

I know a fair amount of my father Eugen Sichel's family history. When the Nazis threw my cousin Lucian Loeb out of his civil service job in 1933 because he was Jewish, my father and our cousins asked him to research the Sichel family history while he was waiting for his visa for England. Since Lucian had served as a senior official in the interior ministry of the State of Hessia, he knew where to find the records of the past.

In his research, Lucian found birth, death, and marriage records, as well as legal documents, including marriage contracts. Some of these were in French since the left bank of the Rhine was annexed by the French after the 1789 French Revolution. He also found synagogue records attesting to my ancestors' active participation in the Jewish community. He even found records of a small foundation that my great-grandfather Herz had established with his brothers to provide for the dowries and support of their sisters. He unearthed the details of the murder of one of my ancestors, who was waylaid after claiming the award for a lottery's winning ticket. The murderers were duly caught, tried, and executed.

The middle of the nineteenth century was an exciting time for enterprising businessmen. The sudden shrinking of the world—due to trains and steamboats—made travel and commerce easier. Except for three comparatively short wars involving Prussia against Denmark, Austria, and France, it was a period of peace and of increasing free trade. There were no restrictions on travel. The only countries that required a passport for entry were Russia and the United States. Gold coins, which were minted by all the major states, made it almost as easy to move from one country to another as it is today in the eurozone.

The three young men who moved to Mainz with their father Hermann and incorporated their company in 1857, Joseph, Ferdinand, and Julius, were hardworking and enterprising. Mainz, an old, historic city, assumed greater importance as a hub of commerce in the middle of the nineteenth century. The brothers built three apartment houses on the Kaiserstrasse, the main residential street, in a new part of town. Behind these three apartment buildings was a large courtyard, enclosed by a three-story office building. This was the headquarters of their rapidly expanding business. Under the courtyard and under the three apartment buildings they dug deep cellars for the storing and aging of wine.

Each one of the three sons moved into one floor of the apartment buildings, and they rented the rest of the floors. When I grew up, we lived in one of the apartment buildings, and my father and his cousins, by now the third generation, went across the courtyard each morning to their office and returned for lunch to their apartments each day, often with business guests. These buildings stood until they were destroyed in an air raid in World War II, just a few years after we left them. When I returned as an officer the day Mainz fell to the US Seventh Army in the spring of 1945, they were in ruin, but luckily the wine cellars were untouched and full of wine. I was able to have the US military government protect the property as an Allied property, which saved the wines until the legal details had been worked out to return the property to the family.

The family's business grew quickly, not only selling wine in Germany but also increasingly exporting it to other countries. Their trade with England became so important that they established an import company there in 1896 and another import company in New York at about the same time.

In the meantime they had started to import wine from France. This became an important part of their business, so they established their own company in Bordeaux, Sichel & Co., which also supplied their affiliated import companies in London and New York. To run these companies they fell back on members of the family, including cousins and in one case a son-in-law, a son of a Danish banker, who changed his name to Sichel and took over the management of the London import company and the supervision of the house in Bordeaux.

The period between 1871, after the Prussian-French war, and 1914 was a period of expanding wealth and expanding world trade. The partners, and ultimately their sons, saw tremendous opportunities and took advantage of them. Not only were their current markets growing, but new markets also were opening up, and an increasing part of the population in non-wine-producing countries started to drink wine.

In due course the three sons who had moved to Mainz with their father were followed by their oldest sons in owning and managing the business. The members of this next generation were ideally suited to each other, hard-working and enterprising as well. Each one was different in his own way. The senior partner was Hermann, who was actually the son of Adolf, who had stayed behind to supply the wine but was an equal partner with his brothers. Hermann was a diplomat and well versed in finance. He was the one who put all money in wine during the inflation and made sure that the company did not suffer during that period. He also became a pillar of the various associations of wine growers and wine merchants in Germany. Hermann was also the partner we went to when we had bad marks or had done something wrong. He always helped to put it right. He was calm and wise and knew how to talk to children.

The other two partners, besides my father Eugen, were Charles and Franz. My uncle Charles was a born salesman, a man who could not live without selling and, if possible, selling to the largest and most important accounts. He was fluent in English and French and spent most of his time in England building that most important market. He ultimately became a British citizen and immigrated during World War II to the United States, where he continued as a star salesman.

His younger brother Franz was entirely different. Blond and blue-eyed, he was reserved but also gifted to the same degree as his brother in his ability to speak English and French. He was considerably more sophisticated. He was not supposed to be a partner in the family business. The family had an unwritten rule that only one son from each branch could join the business. They had seen too many family businesses fail because too many members of the family depended on it for their livelihood.

Franz was trained in the business, but it was understood that he would seek his life elsewhere. After he came back from World War I, however, he proposed to his cousins that they establish a spirits import division and that he would set it up and run it. In a short time Franz established Sichel Marken Import Gesellschaft, or SMIG as we called it, in Berlin and was able to get such world brands as Black & White scotch, Gordon's gin, Rémy Martin cognac, Cointreau, and other world spirits brands for exclusive distribution in Germany.

In many ways Franz was a visionary. He saw many business opportunities in postwar Germany, including investment in private railroads, which would have enriched the family enormously. When he and two of his partners ended up in the United States during World War II, he volunteered to leave their small import company, saying that it could not support three partners. With another creative German-Jewish wine merchant, Alfred Fromm, he bought a small import and wine- and spirit-marketing company, Picker Linz, which had the sales and marketing rights to the Christian Brothers wines. The Christian Brothers had established a winery in the Napa Valley in the 1880s to produce sacramental wines and continued to produce them throughout the Prohibition area. After repeal they also produced wine for the general market, with the profits being used to support the missions of the Christian Brothers. When Franz Sichel and Alfred Fromm bought Picker Linz, almost all of the Christian Brothers wines were fortified wines being sold as sherry, port, and various other designations. At that time there was more fortified wine being consumed in the United States than table wines. Franz and Alfred were instrumental in teaching the Christian Brothers how to make table wines and bottle them. They created a successful wine business jointly with them. Then as federal restrictions enacted during the war limited the use of cereals for spirits—which reduced the distilling of whiskey and neutral spirits and limited the availability of spirits—Franz brought the Christian Brothers into the brandy business, buying distillates from the government, from grapes that the government had purchased to support the price of the fruit. He was instrumental in creating the large and highly successful Christian Brothers Brandy. In later life he would tell me, "Peter, the greatest gift would be to wake up in the morning and look at the world as if you had never been there before."

By 1914 the Sichels had a thriving business in German and French wines not only in Germany, England, and the United States but also throughout most of North and Central Europe, as well as in Russia and other parts of the world. An Oslo-based Sichel salesman, a Norwegian by the name of Hoeltermann, traveled twice a year to the East and West Coasts of South America to work on these emerging markets. When I took over our family wine business in the 1960s, some of the same importers who had been working with this salesman before the war were still buying wines from us.

World War I destroyed this thriving business. The family found themselves on opposing sides during the war, and the British cousins retained the ownership of the London and Bordeaux companies, but the German participation was seized by the Allies. It took a second world war to bring the family together again. I have never quite understood what happened to the two sides of the family after World War I. My cousins were not very forthcoming about what happened, but I did find out that there was an attempt to bring the family together after the war, but it failed, both because the German part wanted to dominate the business and because one of the German partners behaved dishonestly, which prevented any understanding until after World War II. By that time everyone had been on the same side during the war, and economic conditions made it desirable to have but one Sichel wine business.

CHAPTER TWO

Earliest Memories

I was born on September 12, 1922. I was the first Sichel to be born in a hospital, breaking the tradition of home births in the family. My mother had experienced a difficult birth with my sister Ruth, who was born on ~~December 25, 1920~~. My mother was suffering at the time of my birth from jaundice and preferred to give birth in a hospital.

My earliest memories go back to the airy, cheerful apartment on the Kaiserstrasse, in a building built by my grandfather. In the courtyard, which was partially covered by a glass roof to protect the workers in inclement weather, there were empty barrels and wooden packing cases, rubber hoses to pump wine into and out of the cellar, and full barrels and packed wooden cases awaiting their dispatch to the four corners of the earth. We children were warned never to play among the barrels and packing cases and were told about other children who had lost their lives or been badly hurt by doing so. We ignored the warnings and with our friends played hide-and-seek and many other games among the mountains of barrels and cases, without ever having an accident.

I can truly say that I grew up in the wine business. Not only were we children, when we did not have school, asked to bring my father his sandwiches of sausage and cheese across the courtyard to his office at ten o'clock, but our mother sent us across the courtyard to the chief clerk to ask for money, which the chief clerk usually gave us with the comment "What? Again?" I assume that each cousin drew money as he needed it and that at the end of the year there was an accounting.

Our apartment had four bedrooms, a living room, a "salon" next to the living room where we received guests, a bathroom, two toilets quite separate from the bathroom, and one bedroom. This one bedroom was used as a guest room but also as a place to assemble the laundry, darn our socks, iron our clothes, and generally maintain us in good shape. The rest of the apartment consisted of a large kitchen with an enormous coal stove, which not only was used for cooking but also provided hot water for the rest of the apartment. Since there was only one bathroom, and we usually bathed no more than twice a week, each bedroom had a sink with cold and hot water for our toilet in the morning and evening. Each room had a tile stove, which kept us warm during the winter. These were replaced by central heating in the late 1920s or early '30s after my father made a killing in the stock market.

On warm, sunny days we took our breakfast, and sometimes our lunch, on the balcony overlooking the broad boulevard that was the Kaiserstrasse. Otherwise, we would eat in the dining room, the only room that Papa had not permitted Mama to change when, in 1920, she moved in. Whereas she had redecorated the rest of the apartment with light wallpaper and curtains, as well as small, pretty furniture, the dining room had heavy, carved wooden furniture and dark, decorated wallpaper. It was altogether heavy and very much a throwback to the late 1890s, when solidity spelled security. A large British painting of a cow hung on the wall, and one day Ruth started arguing with me about who of us two would inherit the painting. Papa overheard us and said, "Who knows if any one of you will inherit it? Who knows what the future will bring?" Indeed, the Nazis auctioned it, and I was never ever able to retrieve it after the war.

There were two or three young maids, usually daughters of vintners, who worked to earn their dowry. Their bedrooms were on the fifth floor of the apartment building. In addition there was Kättchen, our cook, who had been my grandfather's cook before and was the undisputed ruler of the domestic staff. She, like most of our domestic servants, was a pious Catholic. My father sent her to Rome during a holy year as a reward for her many years of loyal service.

When Kättchen finally retired in 1930 with a pension my father provided, she still would join us on birthdays and Christmas and bring cakes and cookies. She was very much a member of the family who told us children tales we never heard from our parents. We adored her, and she is the one who taught me some of the basics of cooking. She would put me on the immense kitchen table and teach me how to make mayonnaise, hollandaise, béchamel, and all the other tricks of her trade. We children were permitted in the kitchen when my parents entertained and could try the dishes as they were assembled. The stove always had a huge stockpot, which served as a base for many of the delicious soups that not only were served before most meals but also were provided to beggars who came to the back door. My mother believed that beggars should be fed rather than paid. So during the harsh winters of the Depression, there were always some strangers eating their soup and a thick slice of black bread with sausage on the rear landing, where a small table and stools were set up.

The family's happy domestic arrangement with young vintners' daughters, who were forever in good humor and were treated like daughters by my mother, changed on September 15, 1935. The Nazis passed a series of laws that included the "law of purity." It decreed that no Jewish household could employ Gentiles younger than forty-five years of age, to prevent *Rassenschande*, literally the shame of miscegenation. Another law took away all political and civil rights of Jews and decreed that the Nazi swastika flag was coequal with the flag of Germany and was to be flown at all times with the national German flag. We were forced to let our maids go and hire a butler and some rather dour but perfectly nice elderly domestic servants. The house was still run perfectly, but the singing and fun had gone out of it. It was a mirror image of what was happening in Germany as a whole. Funnily, the butler was a former civil servant who wanted training to emigrate and find a job as a butler in England. He was good-looking and charming, and we adored him. He was usually mistaken for another guest when we entertained, both by looks and by his speech and familiar manner; he was more like one of us than a domestic servant. But then butlers usually are. When he finally found a job as a butler in England, we were sorry to see him go.

I was a sickly child. Before my seventh birthday, I had contracted every child's disease except whooping cough. This was before every child was given preventive shots. I had in succession mumps, measles, German measles, and everything else you can think of. Then in 1929, I caught scarlet fever and had a mastoidectomy—a surgical procedure to remove an infected bone behind the ear—after which I never was sick again. Up until that procedure, however, I was not only a sickly child but also underweight. I had no appetite and was forever exhorted to eat. It was inconceivable to Papa that one of his children did not like to eat. Everything was tried: raw eggs mixed with port, little sandwiches of anchovies, just about everything that was supposed to feed a boy and give him appetite. After I finally recovered from scarlet fever, I suddenly developed an appetite, gained weight, and never had the problem again. So maybe Papa was right: a full and plentiful diet was the key to health and happiness.

A strict routine governed our lives. We all assembled for breakfast shortly after seven in the morning. Breakfast was always a plentiful repast, consisting of fruit, hot rolls, sausages, cheese, soft-boiled eggs, jams, and honey, with coffee for the grown-ups and milk for us children. We children were often sent to the corner grocery store to fetch milk, which was ladled into the tin containers we brought from home. We also fetched eggs, selected from a pyramid of freshly laid eggs, and butter cut from an enormous mountain of freshly made butter. This was before packaging made shopping such a boring pastime. I remember an argument I had with my father when I asked him to give me money to pay for the butter and milk. I could not get it into my head that our name was good for the credit the shop would extend to us. This was a world where you bought your groceries in specialty stores: your sausage at the butcher, who would give us kids a piece of hot *Fleischwurst* (a sort of baloney, but much better), and the hot rolls at the baker, who also baked the cakes and tarts that our cook prepared, their ovens being so much better suited to do so. There were butchers who specialized in game and wild birds and, of course, fish stores that sold not only fish from the sea and rivers but also some prepared and smoked fish dishes. All these stores were within a five- to ten-minute walk from our front door, and this was prior to the existence of the plastic bag. We never went out to shop without a solid cloth bag or basket to bring back the groceries, a custom I have readopted in recent years.

We ate most of our meals at home. The main meal was lunch, where relatives who were visiting often joined us. At times my father also brought customers who happened to be visiting. There was a certain routine to our menu. Monday's lunch was usually a thick soup with sausages, such as lentil or bean soup, a dish that could be prepared beforehand, because Monday was laundry day. This was before washing machines. There was a laundry room in the courtyard, where the maids would wash the laundry by beating it against a washboard and afterward hang it up to dry and then bring it back to be ironed in the spare bedroom. Other days we had spinach with fried eggs, pot roast, and other meats with vegetables, and every Friday we had fish. Our daily dessert was fruit, except for Friday, when we invariably had a dessert such as a pudding or tart. This was the reward for eating fish and being careful with the bones. We also were encouraged not to speak during Friday's lunch and to concentrate on the fish bones.

Current affairs were openly discussed during those meals, as well as any other newsworthy subjects. We children were included in the discussion and were listened to. We discussed many subjects and often had to consult encyclopedias to resolve arguments. In later life I maintained that I had learned more at my parents' table than I had ever learned in school. This was a period of frequent national elections, as well as great public disturbances. Our parents would patiently explain the different policies of the parties running for office as well as the character of their leaders. Their distrust of such people as Chancellor von Papen and others who thought they could make a deal with the Nazis was for a time a recurring subject. This was also a period when the Separatists, the people who had strived to have our part of Germany become part of France after World War I, were physically abused and at times murdered as traitors. Our parents described their point of view dispassionately, pointing out that they had a right to their opinion.

I often think of my parents. I think of them in the context of being a parent myself and wonder what my children think of me and how our relationship could profit from my understanding of the relationship I had with my parents. I reflect on the changes in my parents' outlook and relationships as they went through the nightmare of two emigrations. They tried to adjust to the different cultures in the countries that had given them shelter. Above all, I think about the feeling of security I have almost always had: being able to sleep without a feeling of worry and insecurity. But I have also experienced crises in my life, times I slept fitfully while worrying about problems. My parents must have had constant worries after 1933 that bedeviled their existence.

CHAPTER THREE

My Parents

Papa, as my father was addressed and whose name was Eugen Hermann Theodor Sichel, was born in 1881. Except during World War I, when he was in the army, he lived with his parents until they died, and he continued to live in the same apartment where he was born until he had to leave Germany in 1938. As far back as I can remember him, he was always overweight, and as far as I can remember, he never did anything about it. He was a fine-looking man and full of good humor. He was also hardworking both in his business and in the various cultural and charitable endeavors ~~he got involved in.~~ He was a superb host and an upstanding citizen.

(My father and mother could not have been more different in personality and emotional makeup.) My father was sentimental, romantic, and always close to tears or to outbursts of temper, which quickly passed. These fits of temper often resulted in the slamming of doors or other physical manifestations of anger. Indeed, this was a generation that showed their temper; all my father's cousins, the four partners of the family's wine business, possessed big tempers.

My father was a man of insatiable thirst for acquisition of knowledge, be it history or natural science. Though he never went to university, he had learned Latin and Greek in gymnasium (the equivalent of high school) and had read classics in both languages, including the New Testament in Greek. He studied subjects of interest to him until the end of his life.

When I was young, and that would include the first seventeen years of my life, I regarded my father as a man of authority and wisdom: the unquestioned head of the family who knew what was best for me. He was tall and stout, and though always overweight, he carried himself well, being both impressive and elegant. He had lost his hair early in life and maintained that this was the result of having to wear a steel helmet in World War I. Since he saw no action in that war, I always wondered whether this claim of his was true.

Papa talked about the things that happened in his life and the things that interested him. He discussed how he had nearly died during World War I because of a gall bladder operation that had gone wrong and how the Catholic nurses had nursed him back to health. This devotion had impressed him so much, he often recounted, that for a while he played with the idea of converting to Catholicism.

Eugen was the youngest child of Ferdinand and his wife Jenny, née Wolff. He was pretty well forced to go into business as the only son of a partner in a prosperous business. Although I believe my father's inclination and interests lay elsewhere, this was an age where only a few rebelled against the plans of their parents. Throughout his entire life, he cultivated a serious and all-absorbing interest in the natural sciences, besides his inquiry into many other fields of knowledge, and would have preferred an academic career. Under the circumstances, he made the best of it. Once the decision had been made that he would join the family business, he devoted himself to it fully and without reservations. He took his duties seriously, becoming initially a good taster and salesman and, ultimately, an excellent administrator of an increasingly successful international wine business.

In cultural terms, my father could be described as the perfect German: law-abiding to a fault, generous, courteous, and helpful wherever possible. He had few prejudices and none that affected his relationships with others. He was social in every way, enjoying company, conversation, and getting to know foreign lands and their culture.

He had a great sense of family and reached out not only to his two sisters and their progeny but also to the endless cousins he had from the twenty or so odd sisters and brothers of his parents. There was always a Wolff (Papa's mother Jenny, a former Wolff, had ten brothers and sisters) or Sichel cousin visiting us, and my father would spend many a night sitting at his desk to write letters to his family and friends. This was a generation that still believed in letter writing, one that still kept careful records of everyone's birthday or other family celebrations of note. My father had the most beautiful handwriting I have ever encountered. When he noted something confidential, he invariably noted it in Greek.

He was also a great trencherman, eating eggs and sausages and cheese in the morning and again in mid-morning. He enjoyed every meal to the fullest and was convinced that a full, rich diet was the key to health and happiness. As a result he was, as noted previously, always overweight and suffered from high blood pressure. I do not know when my father started to have problems with high blood pressure, but it must have been around his fiftieth birthday, which was in 1931 (he spent this birthday with Mama in Paris, where they bought a lovely service of Limoges, which the Nazis seized when we left Germany and which I traced after the war and got back). I have often wondered if the medical profession at that time equated high blood pressure with diet and weight. As a result of his blood pressure, however, we never cooked with salt, so that medical connection was, already then, public knowledge.

My father harbored a sense of entitlement, which I found annoying, even when I was very young. That sense of entitlement was evident in his complaining when he was not invited to certain parties or functions, when members of his family or friends did not ask him to participate in outings, and much worse, in his expectations of what his children owed him. After my mother died, he felt that my sister should live with him and spend her life looking after him. This destroyed his relationship to my sister, who ended up with that same sense of entitlement.

I often wondered where this sense of entitlement came from. I have observed it in many Germans and many

German-Jewish refugees. It might go back to the fact that the German citizen, more than any other, lived in a highly structured society that provided certain benefits and security, as well as a sense of belonging. Once that structure was destroyed, as a result of inflation and the world financial crisis, a general personal insecurity—a malaise—took over, a sense of being lost. It created anxiety and an urge to once more belong and be cared for.

On being joined once more to a family, social class, or stronger outside group, the expectation called for inclusion in whatever activity that family or group was engaged in. I remember vividly when my father complained that his cousin never asked him to take a drive in his new Cadillac; I questioned him why he should, to which he answered, "It is his duty." I was flabbergasted by the answer but dropped the subject. I had similar experiences with my sister, who presumed that certain people owed her certain courtesies, again with little logic to her complaints. When I returned to Germany after the war, I was amazed that many of my new acquaintances and friends, mostly highly intelligent and successful people, also had a sense of entitlement, and I concluded that it must be part of the German makeup.

On a personal level, in an effort to explain his sense of insecurity, Papa told us that his mother, Jenny, had been sickly and had died young. Papa recalled that she had been a very difficult woman who had made his father's life difficult. On top of that, Jenny had never given Papa the love and attention a child expects from his mother. The relationship with his father, however, seemed to have been a good one, but it could never replace the love he lacked from his mother. In the final analysis, I believe that Papa's insecurity stemmed both from the lack of a loving mother and from his having to work in a profession for which he initially had no enthusiasm.

For these reasons, both my sister and my father needed to be reassured that they were loved. My father was the youngest of three children and his parents' only son. There was another somewhat curious facet of my father's character: he had an extraordinary fear of microbes invading his body. He washed his hands after reading the newspaper and after handling money, both of which he was convinced were full of dirt and microbes. If flatware fell to the floor, it had to be washed, not just polished with a napkin, and God forbid that food should fall; it would immediately be thrown away as dangerous, and no washing would eliminate the threat.

He also was a great moralist. Honesty was his faith, and God forbid if we were found to have lied or dissembled. I remember to this day his telling me that he saw it written on my forehead that I had told him a lie. I still today feel it written on my forehead, though I gave up lying in my teens. He explained to me that lying required an enormous memory to remember the lies, a logic that I accepted without reservations.

All through my childhood my father talked about what he could not afford. It was really quite ridiculous since it extended to such things as upbraiding my mother for serving chicken during the week, a dish he thought should be reserved for Sunday in the true sense of the

French monarch Henry IV. His constant complaint was that we could not afford this. It convinced my sister that we were really poor and that sending us to England to school was a major sacrifice.

In the same manner, we did not install central heating since presumably my father believed that we could not afford it. However, when he made a killing on the stock exchange in Phillips stock, he suddenly decided that he could afford it and had it installed in the late 1920s. However, some of the tile stoves were not removed because my father never quite trusted the central heating.

He could, however, be a great deal of fun. Though my sister and I resented that our holidays, or vacations, required a careful study of the appropriate Baedeker guidebook prior to our arrival wherever we were going, be it Venice or another city of great culture, we did profit from the discipline and could make fun of our obligatory studies. He enjoyed culture in any form and was a great teacher who patiently taught us to appreciate art, music, architecture, and all the things that make life beautiful.

Even in the most stressful moments together, my father was ever the educator: After we escaped France in 1941 and waited for three weeks in Lisbon to catch the ship to the United States, we were dragged to every cultural monument and forced to read up on the cultural and political history of Portugal. Though we resented it at the time, it stirred in me, at least, a lifetime curiosity about cultural and historical knowledge quite similar to my father's.

My father was fifty-two when the Nazis took over, and his world collapsed rapidly, chiefly because he could not believe what was happening. Here he had given all his loyalty to Germany, and suddenly he was rejected, like being rejected by a lover. My father could never believe it, even when he was finally forced to accept it. From being a loyal, law-abiding citizen, as well as a prominent member of the community, he had to face rejection.

In 1938, when our family had settled in France, after my parents had escaped from Germany, he insisted that we speak only French while we lived in France and then mainly English after our arrival in the United States. During this time, he developed a strong hate for the Germans, not necessarily for things German or for Germany, but for the people who had put Hitler in power and had caused all the misery and death.

This hate ultimately became such a preoccupation that I insisted that he come to Germany in 1947. I spent two weeks with him, first in Berlin and then in Mainz and its environs. He met old friends and old associates and saw the enormous destruction and the suffering of the population. After two weeks he understood that the country had paid a price, and he buried his hate.

He had always suffered from high blood pressure and retired in 1946, spending the rest of his life reading, visiting museums and lectures, and attending concerts and the opera. He lived with Ruth in the apartment we moved to in Kew Gardens in 1941, easily accessible by public transport, where friends and relatives visited him. Ruth went to Adelphi College and subsequently took a job as a sales lady in a department store, like so many other refugees. His sister Margaret had moved to an apartment close to his after her husband died in Cuba and had experienced no difficulty joining her son in New York. They met almost daily at five o'clock for *Kaffee und Kuchen*, the old German tradition of drinking a cup of coffee with a piece of cake at the end of the afternoon. Margaret had a key to the apartment and found him one afternoon dead in his bed when she arrived. He had died during his afternoon nap.

So as I grew up, Papa remained the undisputed figure of authority and the fount of all knowledge. He set the tone of the family, while my mother ran the house and provided the setting for a happy home life.

In contrast to Papa's hot temper and fiery outbursts, Mama was totally different emotionally—she was always calm. I never saw her lose her temper or raise her voice. She was a beautiful woman, but who does not consider one's mother a beautiful woman? She always looked a little sad or serious, and all the photos of her show that. She combined a great joy of life, particularly when she was with her children, with an insightful pessimism about the society and era we lived in. She had experienced the sudden death of her father when she was fifteen and shortly thereafter the war, in which she saw the horrors while working in a hospital for the wounded. She described in detail witnessing Germany's enthusiasm to go to war in 1914—the mass, militaristic hysteria that led, in her words, to the destruction of a generation.

Mama, whose name was Franziska Luisa Loeb, was sixteen years younger than Papa, but in bearing and outlook she was the more mature of the two. She had been engaged to marry a man she loved, who unfortunately was killed shortly before the end of the war. Mama was one of the daughters of Max Loeb, the lawyer for the Sichel companies, and no doubt Papa had known her most of his life. How their marriage came about was never discussed, and for Mama it may well have been a reaction to her losing her fiancé. She had warmth, a quality that made her loved by everyone in the family. She had few if any prejudices and accepted people as they were. When a cousin of Papa came out as a lesbian, it was Mama who went out of her way to show her friendship and ensure that she was accepted, or maybe tolerated, by the rest of the family. It must be admitted that our family, being true German *Bürgers*, was not particularly tolerant of people who behaved or dressed or acted differently from the accepted norm of their class, so her tolerant attitude about such affairs was particularly notable.

This was part of the German middle class's preoccupation with *Kinderstube*, which freely translated means "children's room" and would be more appropriately called "nursery." But in its figurative sense, it has to do with then-accepted norms of deportment and behavior, which must adhere to standards that are not defined but that are supposed to be known to everyone in a class. Such standards included how you ate with fork and knife, how you dressed for various occasions, who greeted whom first when meeting in the street, how to bow, and all the intricate customs of everyday life. Overall, *Kinderstube* is similar to the Japanese *bushido* code of conduct, and people are judged as having, or not having, *Kinderstube.* This preoccupation with behavior extends also to how people live in their homes, to the extent that after the war I heard people criticizing their neighbors for various infractions of the norm. The preoccupation often results in people almost spying on their neighbors, to find fault with their behavior.

This—almost spying on your neighbors—is part of a much larger national characteristic, which I can only describe as "every German is a policeman." There is a strong ethic of conformity and obedience to the law. It manifests itself in no one ever crossing the street against a red light and citizens vocally upbraiding anyone who dares to do so. It is encouraged by a society that has strictly outlined what is permitted and insisting that what is not is forbidden. It is also a regimented society that has strict rules regarding when shops can be open and when shops can put their merchandise on sale. And it is a society that has largely prevented discounting and considers itself extremely honest. Yet at the same time, it is a society that by and large distrusts its neighbors and feels secure only through utmost vigilance. (Angela Merkel, Germany's present-day chancellor, ran up against these social values as she wrestled, along with her European counterparts, to address the economic crisis in Greece and elsewhere.)

Mama came from a politically conscious home. Her father, Max Loeb, had been active in liberal politics. He knew and worked with young Theodor Heuss, who eventually became Germany's first postwar president (1949–59). During the period between the wars, most of the liberal politicians were anti-Prussian, as were most *Bürgers* in our part of Germany. They resented the aggressive militaristic Prussian policies. Mama never forgot World War I and its terrible toll. She thought all wars were unnecessary. She understood that Hitler was determined to start a war of conquest, having read his plans in *Mein Kampf*. She also sadly realized that the war against Hitler was inevitable, difficult, and the only way for civilization to survive. She had no illusions of how difficult it was going to be, forever warning my father that the French would collapse from the first German onslaught.

Mama started worrying early about the Nazis and instead of reading the *Frankfurter Zeitung*, the liberal national newspaper everyone of her class read (somewhat like us reading the *New York Times* now), read the *Voelkischer Beobachter*, the organ of the Nazi Party, and *Mein Kampf*, Hitler's book outlining his worldview and plans. She was convinced that the Nazis posed a mortal threat to Jews and to civil liberties. She also was convinced that their propaganda outlined what they planned for Germany and that they would triumph, not shirking from murder and intimidation. She understood their appeal to the romantic soul of the Germans.

My father's denial of the darkening social, political, and religious situation within Germany through the 1930s, combined with my mother's more realistic assessments of the threats we all faced as Jews, certainly had an important bearing on my own feelings while being raised in a German-Jewish household. And without doubt, these feelings and remembrances are worth examining in detail, especially as they influenced my subsequent actions (and choices) prior to, during, and after World War II.

As the Nazis consolidated their power, Mama warned Papa that they would succeed and that we had to leave Germany before the Nazis destroyed us. She was convinced that all Jews would be killed and that the Middle Ages had returned. It did not destroy her but put a heavy burden on her, which she was able to handle only by taking up petit point. Keeping her hands busy and concentrating on complex designs was her means of steadying her nerves. She ultimately replaced the worn-out petit point on all our old Louis XVI chairs.

My mother was forever sensitive to the misery surrounding her. She would never pass a beggar on the street without giving him a few coins, and when my father asked whether he was really in need, she would reply that some of them no doubt were and merited our generosity. I am equally driven today, and now my wife, Stella, has replaced my father as the cynic.

Overall, the relationship between Mama and Papa was a happy one, and I never saw major discord between the two. Even Mama's harping that we must leave Germany did not seem to annoy Papa. He thought her anxiety was overdone but was willing to live with it. Papa depended enormously on Mama's steady hand, both socially and in the immediate home. She was a good *Hausfrau* in the true sense of the word and ran a smooth and happy home. This left Papa to worry about his business, feeling secure in his home. He was totally devastated when Mama suddenly died at the age of forty-six in New York in March 1943, from a burst appendix. He truly was not able to even boil an egg, but the loneliness came not solely from the loss of a wife who had provided a smooth-running happy household, but from the loss of a partner who had understood him and supported him with all his insecurities and fears.

Papa encouraged us all to eat heartily. He came from a generation brought up to believe that a plentiful diet guaranteed a healthy life. Mama did not share Papa's enthusiasm for large meals and in spite of entreaties often left her eggs uneaten, her rolls untouched. She had a horror of becoming fat; she said that nothing was uglier than a fat woman. A stream of American shelter and women's magazines, sent by her sisters in America, informed her about a balanced, healthy diet. As we grew up, we saw muesli added to the breakfast table. The sausage sandwiches, which we took to school for the ten o'clock break, were replaced by peanut butter sandwiches. Mama ultimately dieted one day a week, only eating fruit and drinking water on that day. Mama never argued for her diet preferences, and except for replacing our sausage sandwiches with peanut butter, she did not impose on us a restricted or healthier diet than Papa believed in.

She was the best mother one could ask for. She tried to spend as much time as possible with us children, in spite of our having a governess, or better, a *Kinderfräulein*, whose function was to look after us when our parents could not, help with our homework, deliver us to parties at friends' houses, and make sure that we were properly washed and dressed. We hated our *Kinderfräulein*, and it turned out that the last one we had was a member of the

Nazi Party, so we were right to hate her. Her name was Emmy, and we wrote each year to Father Christmas to get rid of her. We ultimately succeeded.

We owned or leased, jointly with Uncle Herrmann and his wife Marie, a piece of land within easy walking distance from home where we grew flowers and vegetables. This is a popular custom in German cities that survives to this day. They are called *Schrebergarten*, and when you enter a German city by train, you will find them on the outskirts of most cities. Each of us children had a designated plot of land, which was to be cultivated according to our wishes. We had a small hut on the land, which was enclosed by a fence. I hated having to work my plot and always grew vegetables, considering my sister's cultivation of beautiful flowers a waste of land. To make things worse, our aunt Marie, who had a green thumb, forever upbraided us children for being lazy gardeners, which we were.

Every spring in our youth, Mama went with us to our garden and helped us plant, weed, and put it in shape so that Aunt Marie could not make nasty remarks about our gardening. She would sit in the evening with us at the piano and teach us songs or strum her guitar and sing them for us to learn. She took us on outings, and her happiest times were either with us children or with her three sisters, who adored each other and were each other's best friends all their lives. They laughed and chatted with each other as if they were still young girls without worries and responsibilities.

I can understand her sunny personality in spite of her

great worries and pessimism. I share this character trait. I am generally a very happy person, and though I am often extremely pessimistic about such things as the economy, the conduct of foreign affairs by our government, and many other matters, this does not affect my generally sunny disposition. I guess the pessimism comes from the brain and the spirit from the heart.

CHAPTER FOUR

My Sister Ruth

Ruth was born on December 26, 1920, about twenty-one months before I was born. My first memories of her are from when we had adjoining bedrooms at 28 Kaiserstrasse, where my bedroom was in our house, number 28, but hers was in the next house, number 30. My father had appropriated a room in the apartment of the next-door house to be able to accommodate his family. There was a fire door between Ruth's room and mine, which usually was not closed. We used both our rooms for playing with our toys and receiving our friends when they visited.

From early childhood Ruth was afraid of the dark and afraid of being alone. Nightlights solved the first fear; the second was solved by a mechanical bird Papa gave her to accompany her wherever she went, including the toilet.

Ruth was a beautiful girl with curls and a pretty face, a real doll, but she was also charming and kind and adored by everyone in the family. She adored Papa, who in turn adored her. She was without doubt the favorite child.

Though our relationship was peaceful most of the time, I remember her beating me with drumsticks until my nose bled and I ran away to my parents. I do not remember the cause for this outburst, but it no doubt was a matter of jealousy. It was the only aggressive encounter we ever had. We must have resolved whatever the problem was, and we lived in harmony from then on.

Unlike me, Ruth was an obedient child, trying to please her parents and everyone else. She was a good student, did her homework, and after attending a private primary school went to the all-girls Höhere Mädchenschule, the best high school for girls in Mainz. She made friends easily and swam with all of us in the Rhine, using the protected areas, which was mandatory. She learned to play tennis, but like me, she never played it really well. She skated with all of us in winter and did better than I did, since I was afraid of the hard falls that inevitably would come due to my never feeling safe on skates.

We lived in harmony together, shared laughs and secrets, and were part of a happy family. As she grew up in the late 1920s and early '30s, she, like I, became more conscious of the world around her. The difference between her outlook and mine was her belief that everything Papa said was God's truth. She believed that we could not afford chicken except on Sunday, that we could not afford central heating, and all the other allusions Papa made to our supposedly stretched finances. I always argued with her that the appearances contradicted Papa, but she would not buy that argument. This prevented her from being as comfortable as I was living in our family, worrying forever about whether she and we could afford one thing or another, sometimes to quite ridiculous degrees.

The transfer to a school in England and thus the abandonment of her friends in Mainz came at a sensitive time in her life. She was fourteen going on fifteen, so she suffered both from going through puberty and from being torn from the friendships and companionships that gave her life structure and security. She had never established the kind of relationship with her parents that could supply this security: admiration and love from her father was not adequate, and maybe the reluctance of children to communicate with their parents prevented a deeper relationship with Mama.

Fortunately, the crisis of changing language, culture, and school was quickly resolved when she found that her school in England, Moira Hose in Eastbourne, was sensitive to all her problems. In addition she quickly found friends as loving and hospitable as the ones she had left. Not only did her best friend, Rosemary Lane, become a lifetime friend, but Rosemary's parents adopted me and became friends with my parents, visiting us in Germany.

Ruth was anxious to please, pretty, and well mannered, and in Germany, she was good in school and popular with her schoolmates. But with all the fun we had as children, there was always a slight reserve in her. She suffered from strange fears all her life, shyness she found difficult to hide, and a love of her father that later turned to rebellion, when he wanted her to live with him after Mama died.

Ruth really suffered from our flight and double emigration (first to England and later, in 1939 via France, to the United States; see next chapter) even more than Papa. When war broke out, and she could not go back to England to her friends and the new life she had built, she developed anorexia nervosa, which at that time was little known but fortunately was successfully handled. Later in life she developed a benign brain tumor, which was successfully removed. Though she went to college, she never quite found a place in America and ended up marrying a former German military police captain who had served in the Wehrmacht and had been captured by the Russians and spent five years in a POW camp in Russia. He was the brother-in-law of Ruth's best friend in Germany. Having a sister in America, he immigrated to America after his release from Russia, afraid that the Russians would march into Western Europe, and he would once more be under Russian domination.

They were two lonely people who did not quite fit into the society they lived in but who found some degree of happiness with each other. Whatever else he lacked, he looked after her well. Alas, Ruth died young at the age of fifty-seven, after going through a horrific encounter with cancer. Oddly enough, except for a very short time when she worked in a department store ~~to make money,~~ she never worked. The sisters of Mama, who loved us both, left her some money when they died. This, along with the little money Papa left us, a small German pension her husband had, and a job I arranged for her husband, enabled her to live a comfortable life. We saw each other regularly, and she enjoyed my children as they grew up. In spite of all that, there was always some distance between us. One reason was her feeling of entitlement. She felt that since I had successfully rebuilt the family business, I should share my success with her. Her husband was convinced that we hated him because he was German, and we were Jewish. It was a complicated and frustrating relationship.

CHAPTER FIVE

My Extended Family

My maternal grandmother was the only one of my grandparents I knew; all of the others died before my birth. We called her Oma, the popular name in German for a grandmother. Her maiden name was Katharina Levi. She was the widow of my grandfather, Max Loeb, a highly successful lawyer who had paid off his father's debts after the latter went into bankruptcy in a failed newspaper venture. My grandfather was involved not only in the Jewish community in Mainz but also in politics, in the latter quite prominently. He came from Worms, the oldest Jewish settlement in Germany, and from a family that was deeply religious, with rabbis in their ancestry. He had grown up with close ties to his grandparents, who initially had lived in the country, but who moved to Worms as they became old. He died at the age of fifty from cancer of the stomach, which had not been correctly diagnosed. He dictated a memoir in the last weeks of his life, which shows his strong interest in the Jewish community and his fight against anti-Semitism, as well as his interest in politics.

Oma was the daughter of a money lender by the name of David Levi. My mother's grandfather Levi was a kind and generous man, according to my mother. He came from Kirschheimbolande, a small market town some twenty-five miles southeast of Mainz. He had moved to Mainz in his old age to be close to his children and grandchildren, having been widowed early. My mother and her sisters were close to him and related that he wore a wig, which was so well made that they found out about it only when they once stormed into his bedroom to extend their birthday wishes and found the old gentleman wearing a knit cap in bed with the wig on a stand nearby.

Though Oma died when I was barely six years old, I remember her extremely well. She could not have been more than five feet tall and was one of the sweetest persons I have ever known. She lived in a house in the old part of town, on a square called the Ballplatz, opposite a Catholic girls' school. Both her house and the school are still there today. When I was growing up, the old part of town did not have electricity; both the streetlights and the lights in the houses were lit by gas. A man lit the streetlights every evening. Tiled stoves, some of them quite elaborate and beautiful, heated the rooms. When we children visited, there was always a smell of apples baking and chestnuts roasting in the stoves. Sometimes when our parents entertained, we spent the night at her house on the Ballplatz. Oma also took us to the central market on the square in front of the cathedral, where the farmers of the region offered their vegetables, fruits, cheeses, and meats, as well as fish from the rivers around Mainz, including the Rhine.

At that time there were still salmon in the Rhine, which I believe are coming slowly back since the cleaning of the river. Once, Oma bought us a fish that we proudly carried in a little bucket home. Oma was quite deaf and had a large old-fashioned hearing aid that looked somewhat like the old advertisements for RCA Victor. She also had diabetes, which accounted for her early death, at barely sixty-five.

When Papa married Mama, Oma asked Papa to visit her prior to the wedding. When he arrived, she had spread all her stocks and bonds on the dining room table and asked him to pick whatever he wanted as Mama's dowry. According to Papa, he did not touch anything and told her that Mama was dowry enough.

We were very sad when Oma died. I was taken to her funeral, but Mama and Ruth stayed at home because it was not considered proper for women to go to a Jewish funeral at that time. After the funeral, Ruth and I tried to get our parents to move into Oma's house on the Ballplatz, so much more like a home than our modern apartment in the new part of town. Alas, the house was sold, and when I came back to Mainz during the war, it had become a *Bierstube*, though now it is again a private residence. I still dream of the house on the Ballplatz, eighty years after I was in it last. It still holds a strange fascination. In my dreams I investigate the rooms, which we rarely saw, where my grandfather had his practice. It is as fascinating in my dreams as it was in my childhood.

My father had two sisters, my aunt Margarete Mayer-Alberti, who was married to a judge in Saarbrücken, and my aunt Nanna Mayer-Alberti, who had wed an industrialist in Coblenz. The two sisters had married two brothers. We used to visit Nanna regularly. She kept a superb house, with a great cook and many servants. She had chickens to provide fresh eggs for her husband and guests in the morning. Her garden was well kept, and her tennis court was a delight to us children, who loved to visit her over the weekend, just one hundred kilometers from Mainz. I loved Aunt Nanna, for her down-to-earth attitude, her many wonderful stories, and her sheer pleasure in life. Her husband, Willy, had a roving eye, and whenever caught by her, he would give Nanna wonderful jewelry to make up for his infidelities. Willy died in the early 1930s of cancer, being an inveterate smoker. My mother returned from Coblenz one evening, and I was already in bed but not asleep. She kissed me and told me that Uncle Willy had died, and for the first time, I understood what death meant and felt a great sadness. Willy was fun and knew how to talk to us and amuse us, and we loved him.

Nanna was still in Germany during Kristallnacht in November 1938: her wonderful house was vandalized; her furniture, glasses, and dishes were thrown out of the window; and her son was arrested and put in a concentration camp by the Nazis. He was ultimately released, and she spent the rest of her life in a rented room in Newcastle, England, where her son William (renamed from Wilhelm) established a successful business. After the war she came to visit me for two weeks every year, in Berlin or Washington or wherever I was. In planning our days and nights, we tried to live as we had in the past. She was the closest link to my father's immediate family, and she provided me with a link to the past, which I had lost because of the early death of my parents.

My father's mother had ten brothers and sisters, and his father, three brothers and four sisters, so there were plenty of cousins scattered all over Europe and America. In one way or another, these cousins and their children kept in touch with one another and formed a strong family tribe. They often spent their holidays together, corresponded with one another, and enjoyed each other's company. This strong family loyalty and feeling has come down to my generation and the generation of my children, even though we are now talking about cousins twice removed, with considerable age differences even within one generation. The fact that for many years some of them shared a business strengthened these ties. These ties became important when all members of the family finally fled Germany and had this strong family network to help them find refuge in a world increasingly closed to refugees.

We had strong ties not only to the cousins of my father who were my father's partners, and who were all "uncles" as far as we were concerned, but also to their sisters, who were not associated with the business, and to their husbands. So we ended up with a whole slew of uncles and aunts, both real and honorific. Some of them became close members of our immediate family and had considerable influence on our lives.

We children visited aunts and uncles on important days such as Easter and New Year's Day, to extend our best wishes to them. It was a pure formality since usually they did not receive us, so we left our calling cards with our best wishes. The ritual called for them to pretend that they were not at home, to make our task of visiting all our relatives that much easier. We often walked on the promenade along the Rhine with our parents on Sundays and holidays, greeting other *Bürgers* engaged in the same ceremonial exercise.

We had dozens of relatives in Mainz, Wiesbaden, Darmstadt, Frankfurt, and Mannheim, all cities of considerable importance and cultural weight within an hour's drive at most from Mainz—and some, like Wiesbaden, a great deal closer. Though we lived in Mainz, we participated to some extent in the cultural and social life of some of these other cities, went to the theater or opera there, and were close to our relatives who lived there.

When my grandmother Loeb died in 1928, her youngest daughter, Bertel, twenty-three years old at that time and a student at Frankfurt University, moved into our house and became part of our closer family. She was eight years younger than my mother and had grown up in the unsettled times of the postwar period, suffering both from the lack of a father, who had died when she was seven, and from having a mother who was loving but incapable of understanding the world of the 1920s. It was from her that we learned the latest jazz music and popular songs, and she really was like an older sister to us. This was not so strange, seeing that she herself was one of four sisters, the oldest being sixteen years older than she. She was a beautiful and kind addition to our household when she was not away at school or, later, being trained in Dachau to become a landscape architect. She developed some emotional problems and came back to live with us and underwent an analysis with Max Friedemann, who would become her husband. It was in our apartment in Mainz that they celebrated their marriage in 1935, and ultimately, Uncle Max became one of the important influences in my life.

Max Friedemann came from a prominent Jewish family in Berlin. He initially studied mathematics but realized that he would not be outstanding in the field and switched to medicine. He was born in 1881, just like my father, and was twenty-four years older than Bertel. After studying medicine, he studied psychotherapy under Jung and knew Freud but did not adhere to either of their schools. He ran a clinic in the mountains outside Frankfurt until he had to leave in 1938, being offered a temporary research position in Cambridge. He was a man of many talents with a wonderfully even temperament and a thirst for knowledge that encompassed many fields. He also was a great musician who played the second fiddle in a quartet of doctors in New York. Alas, when he turned ninety, the other members of the quartet had died, so we gave him a piano for his ninetieth birthday, and he continued, until a few days before he died at the age of ninety-seven, to play it.

Max was in many ways the father I did not have in my mature years. I consider myself lucky to have had him *in loco parentis* up to my fifty-sixth year; he was wise, well read in both literature and science, and enormously knowledgeable about music, and he combined a joie de vivre with an appreciation of everything beautiful, including women. He and Bertel had an ideal marriage, and Bertel worried what would happen to her when Max died. Alas, Bertel predeceased Max, a tragic result of her heavy smoking in youth and later life.

After Bertel's death I would go to concerts and opera with Max, have him join us for dinner, and quite frequently join him in one of the few German pastry shops that were left on Eighty-Sixth Street in New York, where they served *Kaffee und Kuchen* at four or five o'clock in the afternoon. He was a man with whom I could discuss everything, be it personal problems, the mysteries of the heart and body, or cultural or philosophical questions, and gain an insight into the thoughts of a wise man on many subjects. We discussed the question of there being or not being a God. He could not believe that there would not be a higher being, though as a scientist he could not explain it. We discussed death, of which he was not afraid, though, like all of us, he dreaded dying if it involved pain. Luckily, he was in good health up to one week before he died at ninety-seven. He remains for me a warm and wise memory, a man who provided the guidance my father was never able to give me. He exuded a quiet confidence and strength that I have rarely seen, a man perfectly at peace with himself.

Mother's Three Sisters

It is as well to discuss here also my mother's other sisters. The oldest, Melly, a redheaded beauty, had been close to her father and probably was her father's intellectual equal. She was eight years older than my mother, who was also eight years older again than Bertel, the youngest. In 1911 Melly married John Simon, a German-Jewish American and an entrepreneur who was involved in helping Germany evade the Allied blockade during World War I. As an entrepreneur, he was rich one day, broke the next. He also had a roving eye, and the marriage broke up some time in the 1920s. Melly then studied medicine and ultimately became a teacher and worked as a psychiatric social worker at the Payne Whitney Clinic at New York Hospital. She was involved in many good causes, and it was through her friendship with Ben Cohen, one of the members of Roosevelt's brain trust, that she was able to get us special immigration visas in 1941.

She was not only the oldest sister but also the one to whom the others looked for advice and counsel, and she exercised this function for my sister and me long after my mother died. She had a wide circle of friends and acquaintances and after retiring from Payne Whitney worked for a number of years at the Johns Hopkins University in Baltimore, Maryland. She occupied a singular position among the Loeb family members, many of whom ended up in the United States and were helped both in finding jobs and in finding wise counsel from her.

During World War I, when she was still presumably happily married, she lived in grand style in New York. When the war wore on, she had her younger sister Sophie, a couple of years her junior, join her in New York to get her out of Germany and the war. Sophie, another redhead, petite and beautiful, was very musical; she had a beautiful voice and wanted to be a singer. Her father did not permit her to go "on the stage," as the saying goes. She did, however, sing with groups and choruses and even solo in oratorios, and it was said in the family that she had performed with Toscanini. Sophie enjoyed the social whirl in New York and ultimately married a New Yorker of Swiss Hungarian extraction, Eugene Bascho. He initially had been in the liquor business, but when Prohibition came, he went into the cotton business and lived for a while in Memphis. When Sophie finally agreed to marry him, after Eugene had asked for her hand from her mother, traveling especially to Europe in 1921 to do so, she moved to Memphis, Tennessee.

Sophie lived as a Southern belle for a while, and Eugene learned to spit out his chewing tobacco, but it must not have been easy. Finally, Eugene bought himself a seat on the Cotton Exchange in New York and moved north, buying a house in Long Island and ultimately a lovely house in Westport, Connecticut. Unfortunately, Eugene loved dogs and gardening, whereas Sophie loved to travel. Somehow she gave up the idea of travel. But she made up somewhat for her lack of travel when her husband died. Sophie, who lived to ninety-five, was barely five feet and thin as a rail, but full of spirit and a rare sense of humor. I have never seen anyone as quick with repartee. She was a woman who in many ways meant as much to me as did Max. She was increasingly a part of our lives as she got older, treating us as if we were her children. She was kind and generous and good company, appreciating music and theater, good conversation, and good food. She ate an egg every morning for breakfast and kept her house until she died at the age of ninety-five, spending her winters in New York with a companion.

When she reached her late eighties, I noticed that she seemed to be not quite "with it" at times. I went to see her doctor and asked whether anything was the matter. He told me that she visited him frequently to complain about little pains and other problems, but he could not find anything the matter with her, and he had prescribed valium to calm her down. I asked him to cut out all medicine that was not required and replace the valium with a vitamin. Sophie became lively within a few weeks and continued to be so until a year before she died. Unfortunately, Monica, the companion who had been with her for many years, developed terminal cancer. Sophie insisted on looking after her, though she must have been close to ninety at the time. She said, "Monica has looked after me all these years; I must look after her now that she needs me more than I need her." She, like all the sisters of my mother, was motivated by a rare sense of decency, knowing what she must do under all circumstances.

The four sisters, so very different from one another, were each other's best friends, and nothing made them happier than being together. Since none of them, except my mother, had children, we found ourselves, after my parents' early deaths, with three substitute parents who gave us counsel and love and the feeling of security that comes from knowing that whatever happens, someone will be standing by to help.

CHAPTER SIX

My German Education

I was sent to a Montessori school a couple of years before I entered grade school. I must have been four. I remember it as a happy time, and it probably prepared me emotionally for grade school. The grade school, which I entered in April 1929, was the Leibnitz Volksschule. I was one of more than fifty students in my class. The fathers of a lot of the other boys were unemployed, and they often lacked the sandwich we all wolfed down at ten o'clock. Mama gave each of us two sandwiches and taught us to share our ten o'clock snack.

This was at the beginning of the world economic crisis, beginning with the crash of Wall Street in October 1929. I graduated from grade school in April 1932, a year earlier than I should have, because I jumped a class. The Leibnitz school was two blocks from home, and even at the age of six, I walked there by myself. My best friend at school was the son of a messenger employed by my father, by the name of Bundschuh. My friend's mother used to come and clean our house, in spite of three maids and a cook whom we employed full-time. I always had the feeling that my mother employed her because the Bundschuhs needed the additional income.

I found school easy, if somewhat boring. Ruth had gone to a private school, which I visited a number of times and for some reason did not like. I had been scheduled to go there as well, but due to my vocal dislike, I was sent to a public primary school. In my first year in school, my sister came down with scarlet fever during the summer holidays. This was three months after my school year started in April 1929. I was still out of school in fall 1929, still being a possible source of infection, and then I too came down with scarlet fever. So I was out a full three months while my fellow students learned their ABCs and their basic calculation tables.

So Mama took it upon herself to teach me to read, write, and understand my numbers. Since I was a curious child, she decided that the easiest way for me to learn to read was to read aloud the names of shops, the public posted notices, and the like. She succeeded to such an extent that to this day I read aloud what I see along the road. My youngest daughter tells me jokingly that she hates my mother for having implanted that habit in me.

It must have been around the time of my graduation and admission to the gymnasium that I became conscious of the political strife in the streets of Mainz. The battles were fought both in the streets and at the ballot box, between the uniformed militias of the Communists, Socialists, and Nazis and other rightist parties. There were marches with flags and songs, which usually ended in pitched battles, with many wounded and at times some dead. It was very similar to the parades and battles in Ulster in recent history: men possessed by hate and looking for violence to release their frustration. There were frequent demonstrations with speakers and posters plastered on many walls full of hate and threats. We were implored to stay away from the parades and demonstrations and to avoid being caught in the frequent battles.

I entered the Humanistische Gymnasium on April 1, 1932, and left it in the spring of 1935, that period encompassing the takeover by the Nazis and the imposition of Hitler's dictatorship. These three periods— peaceful and economic well-being prior to 1929, economic hard times from 1929 to 1932, and finally, the imposition of the Nazi dictatorship—mark the three clear periods of my youth.

I had to pass an exam to be admitted to the Humanistische Gymnasium, a school that taught the classics, Latin, and Greek and that was considered a must for anyone who intended to study law, the sciences, or medicine or to become a priest. It was also considered the school of choice for those seeking a humanistic education.

The atmosphere was completely different from the *Volksschule*. The teachers were, by and large, highly motivated and made our instruction interesting. They were able to motivate us to learn and study. Though there was a considerable amount of discipline, there was no pettiness about it, and they motivated us through an appeal to our common sense. We were treated in many cases as if we were older and more responsible than we were.

The other students, coming mainly from families in the professions or from landowning families whose sons were going into the sciences or the church, were also a great deal more varied and interesting than my fellow *Volksschule* students. Their background also guaranteed a higher degree of courtesy and kindness. This must have accounted for the fact that during the three years I was there during the Nazi time, I was never in any way addressed or singled out as a Jew, though no doubt everyone knew that I, along with a number of other boys, was Jewish. The very fact that we took Jewish religious instructions, while other boys were instructed in the Catholic or Lutheran faith, made our Jewish faith obvious. I look back fondly on my gymnasium years, though they did not provide the variety and choice of selection I enjoyed in my public school in England.

Around Christmas 1934, my parents told my sister Ruth and me that we would go to England after Easter 1935 and continue our schooling there in two separate boarding schools in Eastbourne. They also did not want us to learn English prior to going there, being afraid that we would acquire an accent we would never be able to shed. By that time they had made up their minds to leave Germany and were anxious that at least their children be prepared for their later life outside Germany. The fact that the family had a company in England, as well as cousins who could look after us, made this decision a lot easier. I rather welcomed the adventure, particularly since I had suffered recently the great disappointment of my best friend being forbidden to see me. It was a lot more difficult for my sister, who was two years older and reluctant to leave her friends behind. Her friends, fortunately, either were daughters of parents who were opposed to the Nazis or were Jewish. Because she was a lot shyer and more subject to restrictions imposed on girls, who could not roam around as freely as boys, it took longer for her to form friendships. These friendships, however, once formed, seemed in many ways as strong as, if not stronger than, the friendships I made. So it was difficult for Ruth to sever these friendships in Germany, even though she would be able to take them up again during her holidays, as well as correspond with her friends while in England. This, however, was not the same as the daily interaction children have with their friends.

In due course I called on the headmaster of the gymnasium to make my farewell in the spring of 1935. To my surprise he apologized to me that the government had imposed restrictive laws on the Jews, which made my leaving desirable but made him ashamed. It was the second time a teacher had apologized to me. The previous incident involved a teacher coming into a room where pandemonium reigned. He shouted, *"Ist das eine Juddeschule?"* ("Is this a Jewish school?"—a common saying in response to rowdy students). Afterward, he suddenly went red in his face and asked me to see him after class, at which time he apologized for his outburst, which he assured me had nothing to do with his sympathy for his Jewish co-citizens.

CHAPTER SEVEN

History of Germany after World War I

It might be useful for me to give a little background on the social and political scene in Germany following World War I.

The German public went into World War I with enormous enthusiasm; there were initially a number of spectacular German victories in the east, and to a lesser extent in the west, followed by a total stalemate. The Allied blockade resulted in shortages of food and other essentials and caused a lot of suffering. The German government never gave the people a true account of the war, and almost up to the end, the German population thought that they were winning the war. This false optimism later contributed to the myth of a "stab in the back" regarding the call for an armistice when victory seemed close at hand.

On October 28, 1918, German sailors and soldiers mutinied in their garrisons. On November 9, the empire collapsed, the kaiser abdicated and fled to Holland, and a republic was proclaimed. Germany signed an armistice on November 11, 1918, which ended the war. On June 23, 1919, the Treaty of Versailles, drafted by Britain, France, and the United States, was imposed on a protesting German government. On May 11, 1921, the German government, under duress, accepted the Allies' claims for reparations, the amount of which was left open in the peace treaty. The exorbitant amount of reparations claimed by the Western Allies, led by revanchist France, would dominate the political landscape until World War II.

In January 1923, French and Belgian troops occupied the industrial area of the Ruhr in an attempt to force payment of reparations. The local population offered passive resistance, subsidized by the German government. These expenditures led to a rapid escalation of the already steep inflation in Germany, ushering in a traumatic social and economic period of hyperinflation. In August a "Great Coalition" government under Gustav Stresemann ended the passive resistance and eliminated the runaway inflation. The currency reform that stabilized the currency bankrupted many savers, creating a bitter middle class. Inflation, or the threat of it even in its mildest forms, would be a major political factor in German politics from that time to this day.

After the Wall Street crash, Germany could no longer get short-term loans from America and faced complete economic collapse. Unemployment rose to six million, spurring radicalism on the right and left. The premature death of Stresemann deprived Germany of the one statesman who might have provided the necessary leadership in this crisis. The results of a number of elections in the early 1930s made it impossible to form majority coalitions and resulted in a series of weak governments that ruled by presidential decrees. After a series of chancellors appointed by an aging President Hindenburg, Hindenburg appointed Hitler as chancellor on December 2, 1932.

The fire that destroyed the Reichstag building in February 1933 was used to persecute the opposition parties. A further national election gave the Nazis 44 percent of the vote, which enabled them to rule with the Nationalist Party's 8 percent of the vote. With the arrest of the Communist deputies, the Nazis gained a majority in the Reichstag. Then, on March 23, 1932, Hitler forced the Enabling Act through parliament. This act granted full legislative power to the cabinet, without requiring the assent of the Reichstag. It was the formal basis of power for the remainder of Hitler's rule, establishing his dictatorship. In August 1934, President Hindenburg died, and Hitler assumed the dual roles of president and chancellor.

Meanwhile, on the international front, in March 1935 Hitler repudiated the disarmament clauses of the Versailles treaty, and Germany rearmed openly. Then, in September 1935, the Nuremberg Laws deprived Jews of citizenship rights.

In retrospect, there was a moment in 1933 when it might have been possible for Germany to end up a Socialist/Communist-dominated country, not entirely democratic but certainly more democratic than it became

under the Nazis. This did not come to pass for three reasons: (1) the failure of the left to work together, based
on the Communists being ordered by the Soviets not to
work with the Socialists, considering them apostate; (2)
the lack of a charismatic leader on the left who could not
only create a strong alliance but also appeal to the people
at large; and (3) a population who either never believed in
democracy or had lost their faith in it. The unemployed
included not only the proletariat but also the large number of highly educated graduates from universities who
could not find employment and were drawn to the extreme right. Having been brought up with a strong feeling
of entitlement, they had to blame someone for their lack of
employment and success, and the Jews and leftist parties
were obvious targets.

It is hard to imagine today the rage of the unemployed
academicians. They, more than the workers, were the en-
ablers of Hitler. The strong anticommunist ideology of the
Protestant and Catholic churches made them reluctant to
oppose the Nazis, who had learned to divide and conquer.
Pastor Niemöller, an active opponent of the Nazis who
spent most of the war in concentration camps, observed
after the war, when commenting on the attitude of the
religious establishment toward Nazi persecution: "The
Nazis first came for the Socialists and Communists, and
we did nothing. Then they came for the Jews, and we did
nothing; by the time it was our turn, it was too late."

The period until I went to primary school was peaceful, or at least my memory does not bring any unpleasant recollections of that period to the fore, but that may

be because of my age—after all, that period ended when I was six in 1929. The next period remains clear in my mind because it was a period of utter misery: enormous unemployment and beggars everywhere. There may have been a little less public demonstration in Mainz because it was still under French occupation, but I am not even sure about that. There was a feeling of unreality brought about by the French occupation, which limited German political life.

The left bank of the Rhine was occupied after the Versailles treaty, our part by the French, other parts by the British. Initially, the occupation was intended both to prevent a remilitarization of the Rhineland and to ensure that reparations were paid. The occupation was not popular since it was restrictive and always evident. It was the fourth time in modern history that the French had occupied Mainz; the occupation after World War II would be the fifth. Most of the soldiers were black, and there were ten thousand of them, well disciplined. The population regarded them as an insult. There were periodic restrictions, such as curfews, that restricted life and made it more complicated. We had a French colonel billeted in one of my father's apartments who, when he left in 1930, said good-bye to my father (by June 1930, the last of the French soldiers withdrew from the Rhineland). My father told him how glad he was to see him go, whereupon the colonel inquired whether my father, because of the name Sichel, was Jewish (there is a Rabbi Sichel in one of Victor Hugo's novels). When my father told him that indeed he was Jewish, the colonel told my father that the day might well come when he would regret that the French had left the left bank of the Rhine. My parents' relationship with this colonel had been extremely formal up to then: there were no social contacts between the occupying power and the German population, unlike after World War II.

It is worthwhile to describe the pervasive mythology and community environment, for lack of better words, in which I was raised in Germany. There was constant reference made to the harsh and unfair treatment of Germany through the Treaty of Versailles: the exorbitant reparations and the loss of over 13 percent of Germany's territory to its neighbors, as well as the loss of all of its colonies.

However, in our particular circle of friends and family, the blame for the war and the loss of the war was ascribed to the refusal of the Prussian-dominated government to recognize that the war was lost, long before the mutiny of the army and navy late in 1918 forced Germany to ask for an armistice. The government had falsely told the people that Germany was close to winning the war; this was a complete lie. This also made the final collapse and flight of the kaiser that much more of a shock. My parents and their friends also blamed Marshal Hindenburg and his chief of staff General Ludendorff. The general fable that Germany was close to winning the war, but had been given a stab in the back by German traitors, persisted in spite of evidence to the contrary. Germans just could not face the fact that they had been beaten. This was not only the line of the Nazi Party but also a myth believed by a large part of the population. They blamed that stab in the back on the German Communist Party and the left-leaning parties such as the Socialists. The Nazis, in spite of the fact that Socialists had been loyal supporters of the war, advanced these falsehoods. Most notably, the Nazis also blamed the stab in the back on the Jews.

In spite of these obvious indications of German *misère*, there was a general feeling that we Germans were exceptional in every way. Our history and culture and our achievements in science and the arts were singular. The large numbers of Nobel Prizes awarded to German scientists and physicians, as well as Nobel Prizes in other fields, were quoted as proof of the exceptional contribution of Germany to the world. There was always that undercurrent that this was so because we, as Germans, were a chosen race. Our heritage was one of heroes and knights who had been victorious throughout history. We knew the song of the Niebelungen, where Siegfried had slain the dragon; the tale of Friedrich Barbarossa, the emperor of the Holy Roman Empire, who was asleep in a mountain with his red beard growing through a marble table, waiting to wake up when Germany needed him to lead once again; and the accomplishment of Hermann the Cherusker, who had defeated three Roman legions at the epic Battle of Teutoburg Forest. All these tales of heroes of the past were part of the German mythos and were cause for pride to the common men.

We also grew up knowing and singing many folk songs and marching songs, which we sang as we went on organized outings with our school. These marching songs also were strongly influenced by battles and victories and heroes dying for their fatherland. After the Nazis took over, we were marched regularly to the movies, singing increasingly aggressive marching songs and watching films of Nazi heroes murdered by Communists or winning street battles by overwhelming enemies.

Then, too, there was always the hate of the archenemy France in the air: the country that had taken away Alsace-Lorraine, which was rightfully ours. There was also an extreme hate of Poland, for having created the Polish Corridor, which cut off Danzig and East Prussia from the fatherland. These angry emotions and restive geopolitical views were constant preoccupations for the educated, and probably also the less educated, classes.

The Sichels were loyal Germans in spite of their international business, their fluency in English and French, and the considerable time they spent outside of Germany. They had all served in World War I, though only one member of the family, Franz, had seen service at the front, and he had come back as a pacifist. They thought that the Versailles treaty had made it impossible for Germany to get back on its feet and had unfairly penalized the country. Though the family's friendship with France and England never wavered, this was not true of many of their friends and relatives, some of whom hated the French. It is hard today to comprehend the degree of hate and resentment against France and the lack of any effort to eliminate this cancer from the national makeup.

CHAPTER EIGHT

A Traumatic End to a Childhood Friendship

We were happy, busy children. We had loads of friends; some were relatives, and some were classmates and neighbors. There were parties for birthdays and fancy dress parties during Carnival, an important celebration in Mainz. The whole city went mad: Rose Monday and Shrove Tuesday, also known as Mardi Gras, were public holidays. There was a parade with floats, which we watched from our balcony facing the Kaiserstrasse, consuming dozens of jelly doughnuts. These doughnuts were the specialty made for that particular day. The whole population went to town in fancy dress, and there were balls and performances, as well as various clubs that had their own celebrations. Mainz and Cologne are still famous for their Fastnacht, the German word for Mardi Gras, which actually translates as "the night of fasting." Ash Wednesday saw long lines of devoted Catholics exiting church with the ashen crosses on their foreheads, making up for the mad carousing the previous day. We children were told that the church bells had been sent on Mardi Gras to Rome and would not come back again until Easter. Lent started, as elsewhere, with many good intentions, and these were soon forgotten.

I started to play soccer, like every boy, when I was about nine years old. I became obsessed with the sport and would play it for the rest of my youth. I belonged to a club where we played, usually, next to a brick factory. The daughter of the factory owner, Inge Marx, was the first love of my young life. I learned to play tennis but never was very good at it, though I played it most of my life. Swimming turned out to be the only sport in which I excelled, and that was probably because I had learned to swim in the fast current of the Rhine. I was also forced to learn to ride because this skill was regarded as desirable for a young man of my class. I was unfortunate to have as my riding instructor the sergeant who had taught my father to ride in the German Army. He would forever tell me how bad I was and how great a rider my father had been. I never liked riding and never trusted the horse I rode, and fear is hardly the right emotion for riding a horse. Nevertheless, I had to do it and ended up breaking a collarbone in an accident, caused entirely by my fear of the unpredictable horse. I believe at that stage my father understood that riding was not going to be my thing. I mounted a horse again only in later life, to woo my wife. What a man will not do for the love of a good woman.

My friends and I were not wilder than most boys, fought probably no more than others, and enjoyed life as only healthy young children can. Above all, we formed strong friendships. We felt happy, got up early in the morning, and dropped dead-tired into bed at night.

Although I had many friends as a child, by far the closest were two boys: Hans Lang, the son of a judge, and Werner Maurer, the son of the deputy mayor of Mainz, who eventually would be dismissed by the Nazis as unreliable but who would find a job, ultimately, as an executive with the Heidelberger Zementwerke, a major producer of cement. We were inseparable, playing together on the Big Sands in Gonsenheim, a suburb famous for its pine forests and sandy soils, or in each other's homes with our electric trains or toy soldiers.

We would play out, again and again, battles of German soldiers versus French, a never-ending reenactment of the age-old enmity of those two countries. I am sure if my parents had witnessed this, they would have protested, but like most children, we were secretive, suspecting that we were doing something forbidden. There was hardly a free moment when we were not together, and we were sure that this friendship would last all our lives.

Whatever happened around us, it took a long time for us to notice it, but ultimately even we were made conscious that times were changing. An ever-increasing number of my fellow classmates came to school wearing the uniform of the Hitler Youth. At first this did not disturb me because none of my friends were members of the Hitler Youth. This changed suddenly, however, in 1935 when I was twelve. I came home one day and found on our hat rack a Hitler Youth cap. On entering the living room,

I found my friend Hans Lang in a brand-new uniform. It was the last time I saw him. His father was shocked that he had visited me, a Jewish boy, and forbade any more contact with me. His father was a judge and knew that Hans's friendship with a Jew could negatively influence his career.

This sudden loss of a close friend hurt me more than I can describe. Even today, when I think of it, it hurts. I was suddenly deprived of a lifetime friend with whom I had shared all the hopes and dreams a little boy can have. Though Werner Maurer remained a friend while I was still living in Mainz, it was not the same. Werner continued to see Hans, but the threesome was no longer.

When I came back to Mainz after the war, Frau Lang asked me to visit her. Her son had been killed during the war, and she wanted to see me and talk to me. I did not have the courage to see her. I could not guarantee that I would not blame her for that great hurt of my childhood. In retrospect this was unkind because she had lost her only son, and my friends who transmitted her request told me that she had behaved decently during the Nazi time. Regardless, the loss of Hans was the first of the great ruptures that ultimately deprived me of all my boyhood friends. They were all killed, both in Germany and in England. The ones who were left were not that close to my heart. I believe that this disappointment prevented me from ever again forming such close friendships.

To complete this story, Werner Maurer, who had played with toy soldiers with me, ended up in the German marines. He was also killed in the war. His father, an architect by profession, had moved to Heidelberg and was working there as an executive for a large cement company. I ended up in Heidelberg at the end of the war, and I found the Maurers and got in contact with them. They duly invited me for lunch, and they had little changed. Dr. Maurer, with his dueling scars, was still as taciturn and gaunt as before; Mrs. Maurer was still a friendly housewife exuding love and warmth. We sat around the table with one of the other sons, who with another brother had survived the war.

After all the accounts of what had happened to us during the war and emigration, suddenly Dr. Maurer said, "Peter, I cannot understand how you could fight against your German brothers." Here was a highly educated man who had never been a member of the Nazi Party, who had lost his job because he was a Socialist, and he still did not get it.

I patiently explained that the Nazis had set out to murder and exterminate the Jews and that the least I could do was fight them. Mrs. Maurer understood it even before I started explaining. For Dr. Maurer the loss of his son prevented him from understanding or accepting this logic.

CHAPTER NINE

Growing Up Jewish in Germany

In 1879, Heinrich von Treitschke, the famous Berlin historian, published an essay in which he coined the phrase "the Jews are our misfortune." He claimed that mass migration of Jews from the East, who were willing to work harder and cheaper than the Germans, was threatening the labor market. (How familiar this all sounds!) This article was followed by others and caused what was ultimately called the *Berliner Antisemitismusstreit*, literally the anti-Semitic controversy. It was settled by statistical proof that actually the Jewish population had decreased, since most Jews who came from Russia, the Baltic, and Poland moved on further west, mainly to America. But although Treitschke was proven wrong, the harm had been done. From that time, anti-Semitism became socially acceptable in Germany and part of the political and social fabric.

Where we lived in Germany, the Jewish community was homogenous, though there was a small community of Eastern and Orthodox Jews. The latter lived separate from us and the two different Jewish Communities hardly ever crossed paths. We therefore had religious customs and attitudes to the larger society, quite different from the other part of the Jewish community. This was no doubt true in the other cities in Germany where there were sizable Jewish communities.

When I arrived in the USA, I was faced with a much more complex interplay: The so-called "Our Crowd", the German Jews who had emigrated largely in the middle or late 19th century, shared a similar ethos to ours. However there was a much larger Jewish community, largely coming from Eastern Europe and Russia, which had moved up socially, but still retained some of the traditions of their origins. They were more religious and spoke Yiddish, preserving some of the strong feeling of belonging to a community that was happy of its traditions and regarded the outside world potentially unfriendly. Their religious observance, shared stories and cultural traditions were different to mine. It was, for instance, difficult for many of my friends to realize that I had no knowledge of Yiddish. Unlike most of the Jewish immigrants to the United States, who came from Eastern Europe, where Yiddish was their daily language, German Jews spoke German and did not know any Yiddish.

This is not the place to give a learned explanation of what it means to be Jewish. It means many things, but suffice it to say that above all it is not limited to the religion of Judaism. It would be more appropriate to explain it as belonging to a vast and diverse family: a family that is proud to share a religious, cultural, and historic background. Some members of this family might be highly

religious; some may not even believe in God. Yet as a result
of sharing a background that has exposed them to prejudice and discrimination, as well as mass murder, they
identify themselves as part of the Jewish family.

Jews have lived, since their expulsion from their biblical homelands and subsequent expulsions from Spain
and Portugal, in countries with their own strong cultures
and mores, and they readily adopted the customs of their
new homes. Pogroms and discrimination, however, often forced them to migrate again. This imposed a strong
community structure through which they could help each
other. It also often made them retain some of the customs
of their former homes.

A good example is the "ladino" dialect of the Sephardic
Jews of Salonika, still spoken six hundred years after they
were thrown out of Spain, a language all its own and
one little understood by the Ashkenazim of Eastern and
Central Europe—so-called *Ostjuden,* Jews east of present-day Germany—who spoke in various Yiddish dia-
lects, a mixture of Hebrew and medieval German, another
transcultural phenomena. This makes for a vast diversity,
both physically and culturally. Add to this some religious
practices that impose dress codes and lifestyles, and you
find Jewish communities to be more varied than any other
religious or ethnic group. And yet in my experience, Jews
reject being identified as an ethnic group, or for that matter as a race.

Jewish Pride—An Ambivalent Attitude

This pride of being a Jew was not always so, or let us say it was not always overtly felt and stated. It took the evolution of Western society to permit this pride. Many Jews who were exposed to prejudice and discrimination were at times ashamed of being Jews or hid the fact for professional or social reasons—for instance, *conversos*, those Jews forcibly converted to Catholicism in fifteenth- and sixteenth-century Spain. I too hid my Jewishness for a while, during my flight from France. It was a way of survival. I may now be a little too aggressive in telling people I am a Jew, particularly since it is a cultural statement of belonging to a family with outstanding members. It is not necessarily, however, a statement of belief. Like all families, we are ashamed if family members misbehave or become crooks. I can still hear my mother saying, "Did he have to be Jewish?" when she read about a crook being Jewish.

Though most of the aforementioned conversions took place in the latter part of the nineteenth century and the beginning of the twentieth, they did not protect the converted from the Nazi "racial laws," since the Nazis looked at the "race" of the parents and grandparents of each individual. In my own family, when I was growing up, two of my father's cousins had converted to the Protestant faith, and a son of another cousin had joined the Church of England. In every case, these were "social conversions," with a strong indication that these members of my family wanted to distance themselves from their Jewish ancestry. In spite of that, their help to members of the family and other Jewish war refugees was exemplary. But deep down I suspect that they felt embarrassed at being Jewish.

To complicate matters further, I am afraid the assimilated German Jews were quite outspoken about their prejudice toward Jews from the East, the so-called *Ostjuden*— the latter mostly Ashkenazim, it should be noted, just like their German-Jewish critics. This criticism was largely one of social prejudice and fear—fear that eastern Jews' "otherness" would exacerbate anti-Semitism. This same prejudice against Eastern European Jews was shared by "Our Crowd," the German Jews who had come to America in the middle and late eighteenth century and prospered. Funnily enough, the very eastern Jews they despised came originally from Germany, having found shelter in the East. Their subsequent persecution in the East and forced residence in ghettos, however, made for a different cultural and social development than the one of their "coreligionists" who profited from being assimilated into a society that had gone through the Enlightenment.

My father did not share this prejudice. He disciplined me only twice in my childhood. The first time he reprimanded me was when I made nasty remarks about the dress and customs of a Polish-Jewish family who were tenants in one of our apartments. He told me that it was sinful to judge people by their looks, dress, or customs and that more than likely our ancestors at some time in the past had worn the same garments and observed the same rituals. I will never forget the incident. The second time was when I insulted a servant. He told me that it was unfair to insult someone who by his or her position in the household could not reply in kind. My father had civil rights in his personality long before the term was coined.

Though I cannot speak for the total assimilated German-Jewish population in the interwar years—since obviously members of this population varied in their degree of faith and observance of their religion—when I grew up, religious observance was more of a social statement than one of belief and orthodoxy. In my family, I was conscious of being Jewish because we were taken to the synagogue on the Jewish High Holidays and celebrated Hanukkah, and once in a while we went to the synagogue in remembrance of a dead grandparent. We never celebrated the other holidays. We knew the Old Testament and the Haggadah from our religious instructions, but I would attend my first seder only after I arrived in America. Though I studied for and went through the bar mitzvah ceremony in 1935, again it was almost purely a social exercise rather than one reflecting my (and my family's) deep religious commitment to the precepts of the Torah and Jewish law and custom.

There was definitely a stronger observance of our religion after the Nazi takeover. My father, who had rarely gone to the High Holiday services before 1933, felt obliged, in the sense of noblesse oblige, to attend these services beginning around this time. He continued to be agnostic but felt an obligation to show his loyalty to the Jewish community. We suddenly became more conscious of being Jewish, learned about Zionism, and took pride in scientists, artists, and other prominent members of society and history who had been Jewish.

In spite of being more conscious of our Jewish "otherness," we continued to celebrate the Christian holidays, as we (and our Jewish friends and relatives) had always done: mainly Christmas and Easter. Christmas was celebrated with our domestic servants, with whom we exchanged presents, as we did with each other, under a huge Christmas tree with real candles and a bucket of water nearby.

After the exchange of presents, we would sing Christmas carols. On Easter we hid colorful eggs, often finding them in their hiding places long after the holiday. We lived in a Christian society and celebrated their holidays as a matter of cultural conformity, thinking nothing odd about it. We still celebrate them to this day, rather like celebrating the Fourth of July. It has, for most of my family, little to do with belief, but a lot to do with tradition.

Until World War I, all members of my family were Jewish, though only slightly observant and certainly of questionable faith. My father was not a believer. He had never been bar mitzvahed and had no knowledge of Hebrew but had read the Old and New Testaments, the latter in Greek. He actively supported our local synagogue and contributed generously to the Jewish community, but faith was not his thing. He was a son of the Enlightenment, but he paid his due to tradition and was sensitive to the society he lived in. He was the last one to want to offend or shock people. I have no idea of the degree of religious belief or observance of my grandparents Sichel, but I doubt that religion played a large role in their lives. Though no member of the family ever married outside the faith before World War I, this was likely the result of their social circle being largely Jewish. (There is an interesting similarity in the marriage customs of German Jews and French Protestants, where in both cases prominent families married within their faith, their partners being often from far away. In my grandfather's generation some of his sisters married Jewish men from Denmark, the United States, and Brazil. The Protestant families of Bordeaux show a similar pattern). After World War I, however, there were marriages to Christians, as well as divorces. Some members converted to Protestantism, largely, in my opinion, for social reasons. To this day I strongly feel that if you happen to be Jewish, a believer or not, you should not convert unless you discover faith in another religion.

We did have older relatives, however, who were observant. Although this was respected by my family, it in no way encouraged any member of our family to become observant. There was, however, that awe which is usually reserved for the virtuous. I remember going with the half-brother of my grandmother Loeb to the synagogue a number of times and being shocked that most men praying there were old. My mother would at times go to the synagogue on the anniversary of her father's death. We also went, from time to time, with our parents to visit the graves of our grandparents and left little pebbles behind the gravestones, so that the dead would know that we had visited their graves. I don't go to cemeteries anymore, even to visit my parents' graves, considering it pagan.

My maternal grandfather, Max Loeb, who died long before I was born, believed in the Jewish religion and tradition and was observant. He describes in his memoirs, dictated on his deathbed, his problem of finding kosher food during his student days. He kept a kosher household and celebrated all Jewish holidays, though his wife did not keep the kosher household even when they were married and he was away, and she certainly did not keep it during her long years of widowhood.

My mother was a believer, but her observance was limited to the High Holidays. I think her beliefs were more traditionalist and came from a desire to belong rather than from a deeply held faith. There was never any question of being kosher; it was considered a quaint custom in the modern world: after all, the laws had been instituted for safety before food was refrigerated and inspected.

Prior to my bar mitzvah (the Jewish equivalent of the Christian confirmation), I attended religious classes in school in Germany, as did all the other students. There were hours set aside in the school curriculum during which each religious denomination would teach its coreligionists the Bible and details of that denomination's faith. We learned not only biblical Hebrew but also some Modern Hebrew after the Nazis took over, when, for a short period, immigration to Palestine became a possible option. When I later went to school in England, I attended Bible readings of the Old and New Testament and took part in the services in chapel but neither knelt nor said the prayers. Once in Great Britain, I went through a short period of wanting to convert to the Church of England, impressed by a group of young people who were studying to be missionaries, but I quickly gave up the idea when my parents told me that any religion I wanted to belong to was my affair and would meet with their approval. It was a youthful attempt at rebellion, which was wisely recognized by my parents.

I was at best ambivalent about being Jewish. It meant little to me, and I cannot claim that I ever felt a relationship to God. As National Socialist propaganda insinuated itself more and more like a cancer in Germany, I shared with most integrated, assimilated Jewish Germans a certain embarrassment about being Jewish, not knowing whether it was a religion or, as the Nazis claimed, a race. It was on one side obvious that I was perceived by the society I lived in, in some way, as different from the majority. I first resented this and even for a while was a little ashamed of it. I somehow knew that being Jewish was regarded as a bad thing, not quite socially acceptable. But all of this was going on in spite of the fact that I never personally encountered violent acts of anti-Semitism.

A few years later, after having arrived in the United States, I saw that anti-Semitism was also pervasive there, and I became a little aggressive about declaring myself Jewish, even if not asked to declare myself. This was odd since I had not attended a service in a synagogue, except for weddings, funerals, or memorial services, since my thirteenth year. I just felt I had to emphasize who I was and where I came from—all this at a time when I had long recognized that I did not believe that there is a God. I certainly never subscribed to the theory that being Jewish is based on race.

It is obvious that faith and religion, which are two separate things, are a very personal matter, and yet they present a challenge to parents. Should parents introduce their children to religious services or to Sunday school or discuss the subject with their children? In my case, I married a slightly observant Greek Orthodox who believes or follows her religion more out of cultural continuity, but also with some deeply held beliefs. After all, she came from a country that had a "national religion," which was never questioned. Her mother was a traditionalist; her father, a nonbeliever. I left it to my wife to make the "religious decision" concerning our children's upbringing, which resulted in all of them being baptized but none of them ever attending Sunday school. Their observance is limited to Easter service, which is more a cultural celebration, though a religious one. Some of my grandchildren have also been baptized, more from the sense of a traditional cultural celebration; some others have not, since their fathers, like me, are nonbelievers. My children know that I am an atheist, but I am not aggressive about it. I have no ambition to "convert" anyone; if they don't see it for themselves, so be it. In truth, I could not care less what people believe as long as they do not aggressively try to force their beliefs on others.

This is not the place to discuss the unfortunate role of religion in history and the social backwardness it engendered. Having no faith, I find it difficult to understand the faith of others. The hardest thing for me to understand is the perception, of a large part of the religiously observant population, that we are all sinners. Why should that be? Even accepting the necessity of moral and ethical rules in the context of human and international relationships, why should there be a precondition of sin that necessitates forgiveness? It is that part of the religious ethos that I consider repugnant. It is the first step to excessive morality, which often hides bad and antisocial behavior.

Now, looking back through time, in my view the German Jews who did not leave in time, or who left very late, were largely not religious. They were loyal Germans first and Jews second, and that rather reluctantly. They were completely assimilated, they had served enthusiastically in World War I, and they were convinced to the last that their loyalty to the fatherland must be recognized.

For these German Jews, there was no question in their own minds that they were true and patriotic Germans; they could not envision living anywhere other than in their cherished fatherland. To the last they considered German institutions superior to any institutions outside of Germany, even after the Nazis destroyed them. Paul Simon, our family lawyer and a close friend, who left in 1938 after he was no longer able to practice law, settled ultimately in New York, where he became a successful accountant. He lived to a ripe old age and wrote his memoirs shortly before his death. In those memoirs he criticizes the way the law is practiced in the United States, upholding the German practice of law as vastly superior. At the same time, he relates his hate of the French for all that they did to Germany. Perhaps as a result of these bigoted notions, the children he brought up in America never completely adjusted and had an unhappy life. It was difficult enough being a German in the twentieth century; it was almost impossible to imagine and cope with the inescapable tensions of being a Jew *and* a German.

CHAPTER TEN

My English School Years

The German school year started and ended at Easter. So I left the gymnasium at Easter in 1935, after having completed the first three years and having qualified to enter the fourth year. Latin was taught in the first three years, but Greek started only in the fourth. Thus, I never learned Greek, though I could have taken it later in England, where it was a subject of choice, unlike in Germany, where it was mandatory.

My parents had selected, for my sister Ruth and me, two English boarding schools in Eastbourne, on the Sussex coast, a little over an hour from London. The one for my sister was Moira House, a school where she could stay until she received her School Certificate, which could qualify her to enter college. My school, on the other hand, was a preparatory school, one that would prepare me for what is called in Great Britain a "public school." (This is the strange terminology of the British school system: public schools are far from public; in fact, they are private and very exclusive. The most famous are Eton and Harrow.)

Papa took me and my sister Ruth in April 1935 to Eastbourne and made sure that we entered the schools smoothly. We journeyed via a luxury train called "the Rheingold" from Mainz to Hoek van Holland, where we took an overnight ship, cabin and all, to arrive early the next morning in Harwich, on the English Coast. There we boarded an equally luxurious train, going directly to the dining car, where we were served a copious English breakfast. On arrival in London, we went directly to the Waldorf Hotel and then visited our cousin Walter, the head of the H. Sichel & Sons Ltd. in London, who would look after us for the next several years. After a night in London and dinner at Simpson's, famous for its roast beef and Yorkshire pudding, we journeyed to Eastbourne on the Sussex Coast.

Eastbourne is a pretty residential town that now has close to eighty-five thousand people, a large part of whom are retirees. When I was sent there in 1935, it was considerably smaller, and its main occupation was education. At that time it had a large number of boarding schools, both primary (preparatory) and secondary (public) as well as colleges. There must have been, at the time, at least fifty schools taking advantage of the good climate and the pastoral surroundings. The high chalky cliffs, called the downs, facing the English Channel afforded plenty of opportunities for the Sunday outings of the students. We would see long lines of students from other schools being escorted on Sundays on their constitutional outings. All this changed with the war, since Eastbourne was on the English Channel and was considered a possible target of a German invasion. When the war started, all schools were evacuated, and a lot of them never opened up again. One that did was Moira House, where my sister Ruth was a student.

The school I entered after the Easter holiday of 1935 in Eastbourne was called St. Cyprian's. I was twelve years old and did not speak one word of English. I was surrounded by boys as young as seven or eight and as old as thirteen or fourteen. There were about one hundred boys all told, and I was assigned to a grade, where I had no trouble following the curriculum. We all lived and were taught in the school building, surrounded by ample grounds. We were also forced to jump into a nonheated swimming pool before breakfast all year round, in the buff. This was meant to harden us against colds and other diseases and was supposed to develop our character.

This was the first time in my life that I paraded stark naked with other students, and it took me some time to get used to it. It was also interesting that most, if not all, of the students were circumcised—and this in a school that had very few Jews. Since the boys came from upper-class families, this was not surprising; their parents knew the advantages of circumcision as a healthy precaution against sexually transmitted diseases.

Somehow, within three months I had acquired sufficient English to be able to follow the teachers, though the three months exposed me to many taunts from my fellow students. Because I was bigger and stronger than most of them, it did not become a problem. In addition the wife of the headmaster, Mrs. Cicela Wilkes, known to all the boys as Mum, protected me. The headmaster was Mr. Lewis Vaughan Wilkes, and his deputy was his son-in-law Bill Tomlinson, but the overall boss was the formidable Mrs. Wilkes, who taught English, knew all the boys, and ran the school by dint of her personality. You either liked her, as I did, or hated her as George Orwell did. One of the pleasures as a student was to serve her and her guests at her regular Sunday-night dinner parties, a privilege reserved for her favorites. It improved our diet and was extremely amusing, though George Orwell, a scholarship boy who went there about twenty years before me, found it degrading. I can only say that English boarding schools are not for the faint of heart.

There was a strict routine in our lives. After our jump into the pool each morning, we assembled for breakfast, an ample meal with porridge, eggs, toast, marmalade, and the blackest tea I have ever tasted, to which we added milk and oodles of sugar. After breakfast we read one chapter of the Old and one chapter of the New Testament, and on Sundays we learned either a chapter or a Psalm by heart. We then went to our classes, which lasted until lunch, which was the main meal of the day. I remember that we ate an enormous amount of rabbit, all shot by Bill Tomlinson, the deputy headmaster.

After lunch we usually played games—soccer in the winter, cricket in the summer—and at times played against other schools in the area. There was also target shooting and a group that played tennis, but I do not remember playing rugby. We were probably too young for this rather more aggressive game. After our games we would have tea, a rather large meal, where we often were served tiny shrimps that had been boiled and were served in enormous quantities with toast and butter and cake. I also remember that we often ate hard-boiled eggs, which were stamped "CHINA," and we all assumed that they came from China. (Although we never found out why, this memory remains with me!) When a boy had a birthday, the parents often sent a birthday cake large enough for the entire student body to enjoy. I once asked my mother to send enough frankfurters for the whole school to enjoy, which she did; they were appreciatively consumed by all and enhanced my standing. What little time remained between tea and our bedtime, we used for homework, often getting a glass of milk and a biscuit before going to bed. Owing to our proximity to the English Channel and the lack of heat in our bedrooms, I suffered terribly from the cold rooms and wet sheets on our beds and snuck my wool socks over my feet every night to keep them warm.

Though I had good relations with most of the boys, I do not remember making any really close friends. Though I was happy, I realized that I was different. But this did not bother me. Mrs. Wilkes's friendship sustained me during the eighteen months I was there. She ensured that I made progress with my English and that I did not feel too lonely and homesick, and she helped my father with his selection of a public school. This was not easy, and without the reputation of Mr. and Mrs. Wilkes, it would have been impossible. The endorsement of a boy could make or break his acceptance at a better school.

There were two schools that Mr. and Mrs. Wilkes recommended: a Quaker school and a rather recent new public school, Stowe. My father rejected the Quaker school, though he had high regard for the Quakers, because it was hardly the right school for a boy who would later be a wine merchant. Therefore, he chose Stowe, located in Buckinghamshire, less than one hundred miles northwest of London.

In due course the headmaster of Stowe, J. F. Roxburgh, asked me to come and present myself, so that he could look me over. Up to that time Stowe had never had a German student. The student body had few foreigners—the odd American and such students as Rainier, Prince of Monaco. There were few Jewish students, and those were mostly from the British upper class, often with titled fathers. (After being accepted at Stowe, we students had to attend chapel services on Sunday morning and afternoon, and it never occurred to me to have myself excused on the basis of my religion. I attended with the other boys and sang lustily the hymns but, as mentioned before, neither kneeled nor said the creed or the Lord's Prayer. I was not the only boy who took part selectively.)

I journeyed to Buckingham with Cousin Walter, who ran the Sichel company in London, well scrubbed and instructed on how to behave. I believe that by that time, I had passed whatever entry exam I had to pass to qualify for Stowe, but this interview was to determine whether I would "fit in." J. F., as I learned to call him once I was a student, was a remarkable man—well dressed, perhaps even a dandy, with a melodious voice, a captivating personality, and an ability to talk to anyone. He quickly established what he thought of me and told me that I would do, under two provisos: First, I should let my hair grow from the ridiculous short brush of a hairdo I had and part it on one side, so that I looked less German. The other proviso was the pronunciation of my name: instead of pronouncing my name "Seashell," I should call myself Sitchell, to prevent my classmates from making fun of my name. I adopted this name henceforth and carried it from 1937 until I changed it back to Sichel when I joined the family business in 1960. As small as these changes were, I am sure they made my life considerably easier in my years at Stowe and thereafter.

Stowe House, the main school building, was once the home of a succession of Dukes of Buckingham. Originally begun by Sir Richard Temple in the seventeenth century, the principal structure was enlarged a hundred years later into a great neoclassical countryseat. With its landscaped gardens designed by the renowned Capability Brown, Stowe House continues to amaze visitors to this day. Various famous architects left their imprint and made it one of the most important houses and estates of England. The owners and their relatives dominated much of eighteenth- and early-nineteenth-century politics, and the Temple family provided four prime ministers in about fifty years. A lavish lifestyle brought ultimate ruin to the family in the middle of the nineteenth century, and the estate was sold and resold until it was saved by the foundation of Stowe School in 1923; its celebrated gardens and woodlands are managed now by the National Trust.

The first headmaster was the same one I met that day when I visited to be "looked over." Mr. Roxburgh had helped to found the school and was determined that this would be the first of the new public schools to bring education and fair treatment into the twentieth century. He was resolute that every pupil leaving Stowe would "know beauty when he sees it all his life." When I went to Stowe, there were about six hundred–plus male students, most of them boarders, with very few day students. Today the school is coeducational and has well over eight hundred students.

I still visit Stowe. The present headmaster, Dr. Anthony Wallersteiner, is as remarkable, in his own way, as J. F. was. Dr. Wallersteiner has the personality and the vision necessary for a great school. I have been involved in helping Stowe, particularly to help preserve the extraordinary buildings and bring them back to their former glory. We have created a Friends of Stowe Foundation in the United States, and my long years on the board of trustees of the World Monuments Fund were also helpful in bringing attention and help to a great historical building that is Stowe. Every visit brings back my happy days there.

Stowe made an enormous difference in my life. When I first journeyed there with Walter Sichel and saw the buildings and the park, I was bowled over. I had never seen such an imposing and beautiful place before. The palace was the principal building, where we ate and had our daily assembly, and we had our classes in some of the rooms, though there were other classrooms in an attached building. The boys were domiciled in so-called houses, around eighty to a house, where they slept and studied and spent their time when not in class or active in sports or one of the extracurricular activities.

CHAPTER ELEVEN

Stowe—A Separate World

Stowe was a world all its own, quite different from St. Cyprian's. Before I started there, my parents were sent a long list of things I should acquire before arriving at Stowe. This list also recommended that most of my clothing be bought at Harrods, the luxury department store in London. That is how I acquired a Harrods account at the tender age of fourteen. The school uniform was a gray flannel suit for daily wear and a dark blue suit for Sundays—an outfit consisting of gray flannel pants and blue blazers and white flannel shirts and so on. There were the usual school ties, though I do not remember whether each house had its own. It was a community that was self-sufficient and self-governing.

At Stowe, I was assigned to Cobham House, where the supervising master was D. I. Brown, who could not have been much more than thirty, but who immediately had the trust and cooperation of all the boys. The school was a self-contained community. Each house—and there were eight during my time—had a master and a matron. The job of the former was to administer the house and make sure that the boys lived in harmony, did their homework, and took advantage of the extracurricular activities. The matron of our house, a Miss Slater, looked after our physical well-being, made sure that our clothes were laundered and repaired, and ensured that we were ministered to when we had a cold or other complaints of ill health. Miss Slater became in the true sense of the word a replacement for the mothers we missed, and she contributed mightily to our feeling of security.

I felt from the first "at home" at Stowe. I made friends immediately and threw myself into all or most of the extracurricular activities, which were an important part of life there. After all, the Duke of Wellington had reportedly said that "the battle of Waterloo was won on the playing fields of Eton," implying that the officers had learned to work together by playing together at various sports in their public school. I played rugby and cricket, tennis, squash, and fives, a type of handball. I sailed and fished pike in the lakes and became an avid golfer on the Stowe golf course. But the two sports in which I excelled from the beginning of my time there were swimming and water polo. I made the swimming team and water polo team in my first year and enjoyed competing against other public schools. No doubt, my having swum in the rapid currents of the Rhine had made me a strong swimmer. There is some aura that attaches to you when you make a school team, particularly early on, and your ability to be accepted and make friends is enhanced thereby.

However, the most remarkable part of my time at Stowe was the education. Whereas I had previously learned what I had to with diligence but little enthusiasm, and often by rote, Stowe instilled in me a curiosity to acquire knowledge. We had a considerable choice of subjects, within a menu that included required courses and alternate choices. The teaching approach was one of engaging us and, to the extent possible, mining our creativity. Most of the masters (teachers) were young and enthusiastic, though there were older teachers also, particularly in the arts. To this day I have a love and appreciation of music that I acquired at Stowe. I am able to identify many works of music by their composers, and often the specific works, a skill that goes back to the amazing music-appreciation courses I took there.

The variety of what was offered and the way it was offered all originated with J. F., who dominated with a light touch and plenty of theatrical talent the multifaceted life of this dynamic institution. He knew every student by name and probably the student's entire family background and taught one class a week in every grade. When I left Stowe, I started a correspondence with J. F., which I continued until well into World War II, and he would reply to the letters I sent from Algiers or wherever I was. J. F. apprised me of the tragic death of all my friends early in the war, of the news of my masters (teachers) going to war, and of the death of my beloved matron, Miss Slater, at Cobham. J. F. was headmaster until 1949 and died shortly thereafter. He remains one of the great men I had the privilege to know, and like so many of his students, I felt that I had a special relationship to him. I am sure all his students had that impression.

When I left England in July 1939, I had no idea that this would be the last formal schooling, outside of some commercial courses, I would ever have. But I was quite independent by that time, largely because I had traveled internationally since the age of twelve by myself; this was an era when travel was much more complicated than to-day by air. I had also lived away from my parents for five years. More importantly, however, my years in Stowe had taught me a degree of self-reliance I never would have achieved had I stayed in Germany. This self-reliance stood me in good stead during the next year and a half, when war and flight tested my mettle. For some reason my sister Ruth lacked the self-confidence that was to be so import-ant for the next phase of our lives. Indeed, this would be a problem for the rest of her life.

CHAPTER TWELVE

What It Means to Be a Refugee

Part of my youth was spent trying to emigrate to escape persecution, and part was spent trying to survive as a refugee. These are not necessarily the same thing. Emigration may be the long-term solution to evading persecution and war, whereas being a refugee is, in every case, a short-term solution to a very pressing problem.

My first experience with what it means to be a refugee was early on during the Nazi regime. Shortly after the Nazi takeover, they announced a campaign to boycott all Jewish-owned shops. This was in 1933, when the nature and full scope of the Nazi takeover was still unknown. My mother—who had warned my father and his associates about the reemergence of the Middle Ages in Europe (pogroms, wholesale slaughter of Jews, enforced exile, etc.) and the coming murder of the Jews—was afraid that this was going to be the first deadly pogrom of the new age. She persuaded my father to send my sister and me to Saarbrücken, to an aunt and uncle, to sit out the then recently announced Nazi boycott. Saarbrücken was in the Saar, a French-administered area, whose fate was to be decided later in a plebiscite. The boycott turned out to be unsuccessful, and we returned home after a couple of weeks.

Nothing much happened; it was too early in the New Order. In spite of Nazi SA (paramilitary) men in uniform posted in front of stores and large streamers warning Germans not to buy from Jews, the population largely ignored this, since they bought where the prices were the best, having little money to spend.

Many of our friends and relatives thought that the Nazis would learn from the experience and not repeat such an exercise. My mother, however, was convinced that the Nazi Party would learn from this and improve on their strategy. It was from that time on that she urged my father and his partners to prepare their emigration from Germany. Since the business was going well, and we, as a family, had no difficulty with the new regime, my father and his partners took little note, convinced that the Nazi government was but of a short duration and would ultimately fall, like so many governments before it.

This, however, was not the case. The Nazis consolidated their power and soon remilitarized the left bank of the Rhine, which had been specifically prohibited in the Versailles treaty. Then, on June 30, 1934, the Nazis consolidated their power by assassinating Ernst Roehm (who was head of the SA, the paramilitary organization of the Nazi Party and a Hitler rival) and with him a good portion of the SA paramilitary leadership. They had been the only remaining threat within the Nazi Party to

Hitler's preeminence and his dream of total dominance of Germany's political system. This paramilitary force had become a second power in the state, usurping civil authority, and Hitler was not willing to have either a permanent revolution or two separate authorities running the country.

After the Roehm assassination in 1934, my family finally saw the light and doubted that there was a future for Jews in Germany. They sent my sister and me to school in England and applied for exit permits for the whole family after the Nuremberg Laws, which deprived Jews of their civil rights, were passed in 1935. This application was necessary since emigration did not only require a visa to a country willing to accept the émigré; the German state required the émigré to get permission to leave Germany and imposed a high tax, in addition limiting the amount of money and property the émigré was able to take out. It must have taken a good six months for this application to be made on behalf of the whole family, since it also involved the ultimate liquidation of the business and the transfer of trademarks and other intellectual property. Wisely, in the 1920s the partners had created a holding company in Holland, which owned the business in Germany. It turned out that the Nazis never knew this.

The family notified the authorities of their intention to leave Germany, which they couched originally in a request to be permitted to establish a second residence outside of Germany. This required negotiations to establish how much property and money they could transfer from Germany to a second residence in a foreign land.

There were negotiations with the German state on and off during 1936 and 1937 on valuing the family's wine business and assets and on details of the *Reichsfluchtsteuer*, the special tax payable to be able to leave the country, which was called the "tax for escaping the Reich." All these negotiations were friendly, but none of them resulted in a final decision and approval. So in late 1937, Cousin Franz, who lived in Berlin, paid an official in the interior ministry to have a look at our file. This file had the following notation: "The Sichels are economically valuable Jews. They should be well treated, but never permitted to leave Germany." (At this time, Germany was in great need of foreign currency, and the Sichel company brought many millions of marks' worth of foreign currency into the Reich.)

From that moment on, all the Sichel partners were convinced that they must leave Germany, at any cost. This was far from simple. Though they all had passports, these were useless without the exit visas necessary for each foreign trip. Two of the partners, Charles and Franz, had permanent exit visas, their jobs requiring frequent trips to the Sichel companies in England and Bordeaux. That left the senior partner, Hermann, and his wife, as well as my parents. Hermann was dispatched to America to make some necessary changes in a difficult new market, where Charles had oversold to the US importer at the time, W. A. Taylor, whose owners wanted to return a large portion of their merchandise. Since Hermann was over seventy and suffered from heart disease, it was fairly easy to get the authorities to authorize a passport for his wife to accompany him. They went to the United States and then ultimately, instead of returning to Germany, went to London, as part of the family plan to leave Germany.

Only my father and mother remained. My father, at that stage, was running the head office in Mainz, and there was really no ostensible reason for him and my mother to leave the Reich. For a while the family planned to have my mother and father swim across the Mosel to Luxembourg; alas, my mother was not good enough a swimmer to make it across the river. So that idea was abandoned. The plan that ultimately did get them out involved my sister in England being delivered to a hospital, presumably suffering from meningitis.

Here exactly is how Mama and Papa's escape was pulled off successfully: Cousin Walter in London had been in touch with the headmistress of Moira House, Gertrude Ingham, who with Edith Tizzard and Mona Swann formed a wonderful team running a school that to this day exists and enjoys a high reputation. He had explained to them our need to flee from Germany and worked out with them a most sophisticated plan: Miss Ingham called my mother and advised her that Ruth had suddenly come down with meningitis, and it was questionable whether she would survive. She counseled my mother and father to come quickly, while she was still alive. (The plan had been well rehearsed to gain maximum authenticity for German authorities.) So my mother and father ran in tears to the Mainz police headquarters—read: the Nazis—and were given an exit permit for two weeks to visit their dying daughter. By this ruse, everyone in our immediate family was out of Germany. Once everyone had left Germany, the partners notified the appropriate German authorities that they had left Germany for good and were liquidating their business.

The Nazi authorities sent a man to London to try to get the family to come back to Germany but to no avail, and in due course the four partners were accused of having illegally transferred money out of Germany and were sentenced to millions of marks of fines and five years of hard labor in absentia. The monetary fine was used to seize all the property of the partners; this sentence became a nightmare when we were caught in France after the German victory.

In due course my parents settled in Bordeaux, where my father took over the management of the family wine business. Since Hermann, with his son Walter and cousin Charles, were in England running an important import company, and Franz had decided to go to the United States, to avoid getting embroiled in World War II, it was left to my father to take over the management of the Bordeaux company. He often complained that Franz, without a family, had forced him, with a wife and two children, to face an uncertain future. They settled into a small and cheerful apartment near the Barrière du Médoc, not far from the big boulevard that encircles the city. It was there where my sister and I lived when we joined our parents during the summer holidays of 1939, intending to return to England after the holidays.

My parents had made some friends in Bordeaux, some of whom were in the business and others of whom were refugees, like us, who had found a new home. Among the *a husband & wife, both doctors,*

new friends were a doctor and his wife, also a doctor, Otto and Annemarie Hirsch: two quite extraordinary people. Otto was born in the Saar and had opted for France when the Saar reverted to Germany in 1935 and was therefore a French citizen. He was ultimately called up as a doctor during the war. (The Saar province, a region rich in coal that bordered on France, was put under League of Nations trusteeship in 1919 and eventually decided its national fate by a plebiscite. The population voted to be once more German, and the French offered any citizen who so desired residence in France and eventual citizenship.)

Otto was recommended to us as a doctor, and indeed he became our doctor and lifetime friend. He had studied medicine at various universities in Germany, where he had met his wife Annemarie, who was also a medical student and who later took her degree in Bordeaux. He must have graduated shortly before or after the Nazi takeover in Germany. He moved to Bordeaux and quickly established a practice and became the preferred doctor of the small group of German émigrés in Bordeaux, as well as a respected physician generally, who was particularly interested in helping the less privileged. He must have been six foot five or six foot six, and he was extremely handsome and charming and highly competent. Though he practiced as a general practitioner, his field of specialty was neurology. He and his wife were superb musicians and charming people who became lifelong friends, and that friendship has extended to their oldest son Michel and his children.

Our 1939 vacation was spent partially at Royat, in the Puy de Dome of Auvergne, an old Roman spa where Papa took the waters, and we enjoyed the chocolates of the local Madame de Sevigny chocolate factory, played tennis, and took long walks in the beautiful hills. This ideal holiday was suddenly terminated when France and England served an ultimatum on Germany, after Germany had invaded Poland. We rushed back to Bordeaux, just in time to hear the declaration of war. Our peaceful existence ended: we had to report to the police as enemy aliens and use political connections to not be interned by the French. Our first thought was to return to England, and fortunately, our English visas were renewed, but the French government refused to give us exit permits. So we were forced to try to build a life in France in uncertain times and with a questionable future.

The first seven months of World War II saw little action on the Western Front. The French and German armies faced each other, but no attempt was made to break through the Maginot line, a collection of heavily protected concrete bunkers and fortresses thought by the French military establishment to be a foolproof deterrent to the Germans ever invading France again, like they did in 1914. This "phony war" was called by the French the *Drôle de Guerre*, the funny or strange war. Those months were also for us a sort of *Drôle de Guerre*, one full of darkening portents.

Both Ruth and I were at loose ends, on one hand hoping to still be able to eventually return to England, but on the other hand also wishing to figure out what to do with our lives in the meantime. My problem was quickly solved by my taking an apprentice position in the Sichel wine business, which would teach me the wine business and also teach me skills necessary in commerce. I also took French lessons, studying Rabelais, with little success.

But what could Ruth do? She also was given French lessons—I guess both of us were not as fluent as we ultimately became. But all this left a big void in her life, and she had practically no friends outside of the family, since she had never lived in Bordeaux. She continued to be charming and well behaved and pleasing, but these were outside characteristics that hid an inner void.

We suddenly noticed that Ruth had started to refuse her food, and little by little, she became thinner and thinner and had visions, some of which were religious. No doubt, the exposure to the Church of England had had an influence. By the beginning of 1940, this had become a major problem. At first Papa tried to convince her to eat, and we had terrible scenes at meals of Papa getting down on his knees to implore her to eat. That went on for a little while, until Mama rightly decided that it was a medical problem and called in Dr. Hirsch. The doctor tried to solve the problem with various medications, but to no avail, and finally decided to put her in the hospital in Bordeaux. At that time anorexia nervosa had not been identified, nor was any treatment known for a yet little known condition—not that this has improved markedly since. The hospital tried various treatments coupled with intravenous feeding and finally gave her shock treatments, which cured her.

Uncle Franz had become a French citizen through his excellent political relations in France, just about the time he decided to leave France in the beginning of September 1939. His connections, however, proved useful for keeping my father and me out of internment camp, which we had been ordered to report to as enemy aliens shortly after the declaration of war on September 1. It was a nervous time. This exemption had to be renewed periodically, and we did not know how long these connections would work. They involved complicated communications between Paris and Bordeaux.

In the meantime, I started working for Sichel & Fils Frères, learning every facet of the wine business. I went each morning with my father to the office and was assigned tasks such as topping barrels in the cellar, fining wine in barrels, and assisting in the tasting room during the almost daily tastings, as well as acquainting myself with the correspondence with customers. Twice a week, I attended a commercial school, where I learned to type and learned shorthand, bookkeeping, and commercial correspondence. I enjoyed my work and enjoyed drinking wine, to the extent that my father once reminded me that the purpose of being a wine merchant was not to drink wine, but to sell it!

France and England were at war with Germany, but there were no signs of it in our daily life, except for the publicity that could be seen on practically every street corner announcing that France would win, boasting of the country's vast resources. "We will win because we are the stronger," proclaimed large posters, which then gave statistics of various products, comparing the German and Allied production. There were a goodly number of people circulating in uniform, but otherwise there were no signs of war. Our business was still shipping French wine to Great Britain and America and other Western markets— maybe a little less but still sufficient for us not to worry. There was, however, the depressing uncertainty of our ability to avoid being interned. This was made no easier by stories from friends in Paris who had been interned under difficult conditions and seemingly had no prospects of getting out and earning a living.

It is hard to recreate the atmosphere in our house. Papa felt it was his responsibility to continue running the business, and he never questioned the ability of the French to repulse a German invasion. Mama, on the other hand, was convinced that once the war started in earnest, France would collapse, and we would have to run for our lives. Papa considered Mama's fears disloyal, since France had given us shelter, work permits, and an opportunity to build a new life. I also believe that Papa just could not visualize once more pulling up stakes and starting anew. He was almost sixty at the time, suffering from high blood pressure, and feeling increasingly insecure and frustrated. These conversations, which took place almost daily and usually at the dinner table, were highly emotional. Papa did not realize the weakness of his arguments, seeing that we could be interned at any time. The fact that Mama argued without raising her voice, marshaling her facts and reminding Papa of his previous reluctance to leave Germany, made for a tense and depressing atmosphere.

My parents greatly worried about Ruth. Fortunately, at that moment we were asked by a good friend to take in her daughter, Anne Meyer. Anne had been my sister Ruth's friend and neighbor in Mainz; her parents were close friends of our parents. Her father had committed suicide subsequent to Kristallnacht, when she was in school in Switzerland. She subsequently had moved to Paris to stay with relatives, who farmed her out to relatives in the country after the outbreak of the war. Unfortunately, the farm she ended up in and worked for was very poor and not heated. She came down with the most awful chilblains, a condition of severe cold affecting one's extremities, including feet and hands. My parents were glad to offer her shelter, hoping at the same time that she would contribute to a more cheerful atmosphere. Her chilblains were quickly cured, and she became in a very short time a valuable member of the family, and she has remained as such ever since, ultimately marrying Otto Sichel, my second cousin.

With the arrival of Anne, our apartment became too small to house everyone, and we immediately looked for larger quarters, convinced that we would end up sheltering more people. We found a lovely villa in the suburbs of Bordeaux, not far from where we lived, with more room and a little garden. This enabled Anne to move in with us. We must have moved there around the beginning of 1940.

Around May 10, 1940, the Germans started their war in earnest and marched into Belgium and Holland to end the *Drôle de Guerre*. All hell broke loose. Suddenly, there was talk of the Germans having infiltrated a fifth column into France, and all German nationals—and we were still German nationals, albeit with a large J for Jew in our passports—were ordered to report to assembly points to be interned. This command applied to both men and women over the age of seventeen. The order must have been for a little later in the month of May because by the time Mama, Papa, Anne, and I reported to the assembly point, the first French refugees from Paris and the North had started arriving in Bordeaux. The first to arrive was a cousin of Mama, Gustel Restiaux, daughter of a prominent attorney in Mannheim, who had married a Frenchman and worked in one of the Rothschild enterprises. She arrived just before many others. Since we departed about the same time to report to an internment camp, she took over our household, acted as host to the refugees we sheltered, made sure they had enough to eat and drink, and supervised the chief clerk in my father's business. She continued to do this after we fled from the Germans and liquidated our household, before she ultimately returned to Paris, which was occupied then by the Germans.

Mama and Anne were sent to Gurs, an internment camp that had been established in the 1930s near Oloron Ste. Marie, a town in the Pyrenees, while Papa and I were transported to a camp along the Dordogne in Libourne, some fifty kilometers from Bordeaux. At the same time Ruth was hospitalized, and Otto and Annemarie Hirsch assured us that they would take care of her. Obviously, our world totally collapsed, with our not knowing when we would see each other again, let alone what the future would hold.

Obviously, our lawyer sent written requests to the authorities to get us released, but since every day brought news of the fast-advancing German armies, we held little hope of regaining our freedom.

We suddenly moved from being émigrés to being refugees and enemy aliens, a marked difference in this world. The camp in Libourne was temporary, unlike Gurs, which had served for many years to house refugees from the Spanish Civil War and would ultimately house German-Jewish internees sent there by the Germans. The Libourne camp was in a converted warehouse, in an area demarcated with barbed wire, where we internees slept, ate, and passed our days, largely doing nothing, except to repeat rumors we heard. The French Civil Guard was charged with running the camp, which contained as many Jewish refugees as it did loyal Germans, whose aggressiveness increased with the news of each new German victory. It was not a pleasant environment, but the officer who ran the camp prevented fights from breaking out between the two groups of very different internees.

Paris fell on June 14, 1940, and the French government was evacuated to Bordeaux. The armistice would be signed on June 22, to go into effect on June 25. Meanwhile, around the nineteenth or twentieth of the month, we witnessed columns of refugees passing by the camp, so some of my fellow internees and I took it upon ourselves to tell the French commander that some of us would have a bleak future should we still be in the camp when the Germans overran it. The French commander saw our logic and gave us the necessary documents to enable us to leave the camp and find safety where we could.

Papa and I were fortunate enough to find a truck that

took us to Bordeaux, where we reached our house, which was full of refugees, mostly friends and some relatives who had fled from Paris and the North. Gustel was in charge. There were mattresses everywhere, and somehow she had organized the feeding of all of them. I still remember my admiration of her ability to create order amid chaos.

Papa knew that we could not tarry but had to move on. He was a convicted felon, having been sentenced by the Germans in absentia to five years of hard labor for leaving Germany without an exit visa. He would end up in prison if caught by the Germans. We spent the night in the house and went the next day to the train station to try to board a train to Biarritz and the Spanish border. Alas, that was not possible. All the trains were full to capacity, with people hanging on the outside. Fortunately, Papa had drawn funds prior to leaving for Libourne, so his nephew Friedrich Mayer-Alberti, the son of his sister Margret, organized a taxi to take Friedrich, his wife and child, and us to Bayonne, a city close to the Spanish border.

We five, along with the most essential luggage, started from Bordeaux early the next morning, driving along an endless column of refugees traveling in cars, buses, trucks, and horse-drawn carriages, walking on foot, and pushing carts, interspersed with a column or two of Polish soldiers in uniform who marched in formation. Every conceivable possession was lashed to the vehicles: mattresses, chickens and other birds in cages, pots and pans, and whatever was precious for the people fleeing. From time to time German airplanes took a swipe at this column, and we stopped and dove into the ditches along the road to avoid being strafed.

CHAPTER THIRTEEN

A Miraculaous Reunion
with Mama

Papa, cousin Friedrich Alberti and his wife and toddler son, and I arrived in Bayonne late in the day and, wonders upon wonders, found a hotel that gave us a room. We had no need to go to the Spanish border; it was closed to anyone who did not have a Spanish visa and certainly to anyone who was a German refugee. The word spread quickly. In the meantime the German-French armistice had been signed on June 22, and the occupation of the land along the Atlantic was to go into effect on the twenty-fifth, and here we were in Bayonne on the twenty-fourth. Once more, just as he had during our flight from Bordeaux, Friedrich did the impossible and organized a car to take us out of the zone of occupation to Pau and hopefully Oloron Ste. Marie, south of Pau in the French Pyrenees, the town closest to Gurs, where Mama was interned.

June 25 was a stormy day, and our taxi driver told us that that was good, since we were to pass the new frontier between occupied and nonoccupied France around noon, and no respecting gendarme would be at his post around lunchtime. He turned out to be right, and we made the trip to Oloron Ste. Marie without difficulties and in record time. As we drove into Oloron along the main road, we saw Mama and Anne, who had just been released from Gurs.

Somehow the authorities were well organized to settle refugees. There was a government office charged with assigning refugees to shelters, and we were assigned quarters in a broken-down chateau in Escout, about three miles (five kilometers) north of Oloron. It became our home for the next six months or so. Escout was a village of a few hundred souls, all hardworking farmers who had livestock and who mainly grew corn. The area became extremely muddy after rain, and the farmers wore *sabots*, wooden clogs, which they left outside their houses, changing into felt slippers inside. We soon adopted the same footwear and were warm and happy for it. It was a poor village, with a good mayor and a friendly population.

We were soon joined by my sister Ruth, who after release from the hospital found shelter with Dr. Hirsch and his wife and was duly smuggled by their maid to join us. At that time the border between occupied and nonoccupied France was still easy enough to cross, particularly with French identity papers, which we all had.

The chateau had seen better days. It was set in a magnificent park with a long alley of trees leading to its main entrance. It had fallen into disrepair; many of its rooms, which had wooden beds with straw mattresses, were without windowpanes. But thankfully, the broken-down chateau did have a kitchen with a working woodstove and the most elementary sanitary facilities. It was shelter, and we could improve on what we found.

There were twenty or so refugees lodged in the chateau. Our group, the Germans, consisted of Mama, Papa, Anne, and me and soon Ruth, who had been cured by the shock treatment, had survived the German occupation of Bordeaux, and after our arrival in Escout, had soon been smuggled across the border by the Hirsches. Besides our family, the refugees included a cultivated, middle-aged musicologist named Hans Cahen Brach and a former colonel of the Spanish Republican Army named Baumann, with his wife and son. Baumann had been interned when he arrived from Spain but had been released with everyone else after the German-French armistice. He would ultimately become chief of police in Saarbrücken after the war. The other ten or twelve refugees were Polish-Jewish diamond merchants or polishers from Antwerp. They had a low opinion of German Jews, and it took us some time to establish a workable relationship with them.

Friedrich and his family left us at that stage, since he had French papers as a result of his birth and family residence in the Saar, along with a license to practice law. He established himself in a nearby town and started to help refugees with their endless problems of finding a safe haven in another country. He soon established a viable practice and became an expert in all the legal details of emigration and immigration.

The most immediate problem was finding a way to

communicate with the outside world without endangering Papa, who might be claimed at any time by the Germans as a convicted felon. The armistice agreement stipulated in Article 19.2 that the Vichy government was to surrender all German refugees identified by the Nazi government. That this never happened in Papa's case was extraordinary. It was probably due to the Germans going after political enemies at this early stage of the war. This was also before records were computerized, and it was a great deal more difficult to identify individuals. The Germans had encountered enormous difficulties in their initial anti-Jewish campaigns to establish lists of Jews in Germany.

Knowing the dangers, we took precautions. We arranged to get all of our mail under Anne's name, Mayer, at the post office in Oloron, a mere five kilometers from Escout. Papa was able to arrange a monthly check from a friend in Cognac, André Renaud, then the owner of Rémy Martin cognac, who had been a business partner in Germany. So we had no pressing financial problems. Our problem was getting out of France before the Germans caught us. We were convinced that the war would be long—that sooner or later the Germans would occupy all of France, and we would never be safe on a long-term basis in unoccupied France.

We settled into a routine, with Baumann and me doing all the cooking for our "German group" and arranging what food supply we could, with the help of the others. Baumann and I had arranged to work for a farmer, sawing up felled trees with a two-man saw. This employment extended later into helping with the slaughter of pigs and the preparation of the different meats and sausages, a major source of income for the farmers. The famous Bayonne hams were, after all, produced in this area. We were paid in produce. When we first arrived, it was summer, and the fields were full of corn, fruit aplenty, and the best figs I have ever eaten, which we put up as jam for the coming winter. There were recipes aplenty for how to do this without using scarce sugar.

We took turns picking up the mail in Oloron, either bicycling or walking the five kilometers. We were careful doing this, ever afraid that someone was looking for Papa. There must still have been communications with England because I picked up a telegram announcing the death of Hermann, who had retired with his wife Marie to live with their son Walter in England. Shortly thereafter, we also received the happy news of his grandson's birth. Slowly, contacts were reestablished with Mama's three sisters in the States and with Franz in New York.

Once more, Papa spent a great deal of time corresponding with as many contacts as possible, trying to get news of what had happened to different members of the family and to see how and to where we could get a visa to escape from France. We made new acquaintances among all German and Austrian refugees who were circulating in that part of southwest France—by historians' estimates, there were close to ten thousand such refugees at that time—and seeking, as we did, to get out of Europe. We quickly learned how difficult the task would be. Most countries had closed their doors. Shanghai was one option; volunteering for the Foreign Legion, another.

I wanted to volunteer for the Foreign Legion but was prevented from doing so by my parents. The Foreign Legion accepted any recruit without any questions asked.

My parents still thought that we should be able to get an American visa, and for that purpose we all went to Marseille to register, but alas, we were told that it would be many years before our number came up. So we considered Brazil and various other South American countries. We were greatly helped in all our efforts by a civil servant in Oloron's *sous-préfecture*, the local administration, who was extremely helpful. He was instrumental in getting Papa an Ecuadorian passport, just in case the Germans were to march in overnight. The Ecuadorian honorary consul, who sold passports to make a living, explained to Papa that he could go anywhere with that passport, except to Ecuador!

We were, on the one hand, German refugees trying to get visas to leave France and settle elsewhere. On the other hand, we had to survive until that moment came. Survival meant many things, including keeping busy, which given the difficulty of finding enough food, meant that some of us spent almost all our time foraging for food. I forget whether we had ration cards, but I assume that we did, though they provided only a little meat, butter, and sugar.

We had our old identity cards from Bordeaux, identifying us as legal residents of France, and Papa had an identity card provided by the mayor identifying him as a French citizen, just in case the Germans marched in. Since we were not the only ones who lived this uncertain existence, exposed to the danger of being identified by the

Germans as either criminals or politically tainted, we were forever worried. It was the early days in Vichy France, and fortunately, it took the government a long time to get organized. Once Vichy took stricter control over its part of France, which never happened during our time, things would be different.

The Vichy government passed a law on September 3, 1940, authorizing the internment of undesirable foreigners without trial. It also passed a statute in October 1940 authorizing the internment of all foreign Jews, which obviously was not fully enforced and implemented at the time. At that time in Vichy France, General Pétain still stated that he was not interested in handing Jews over to the Germans. All this changed for the worse shortly after we left France.

Anne and I spent some time reconnoitering the French-Spanish border by bicycle, to see if we could all slip into Spain and make our way through Spain to Portugal and to the larger world. The border was lightly patrolled, and it would have been quite simple to slip over it. But that was not the problem, as we found out from other enterprising refugees: they reported that the controls in Spain were very tight, and anyone found without adequate identification would be put in prison. The Spanish prisons were reportedly harsh, and the prisoners were being starved. So we gave up that option.

Nevertheless, Baumann gave all of us Spanish lessons, just in case we ever needed to speak that language. We established a great sense of camaraderie. There were hardly ever any controversies, and we all helped each other. We celebrated birthdays and holidays, and our spirits were not broken, in spite of our situation. Keeping us fed took some doing, and with the odd jobs we were able to get, we were busy most of the time. The fact that the local people, who were poor, were friendly and helpful also contributed to our high morale.

The summer turned into fall, the rains came, the streets turned into mud, and suddenly, things looked less bright. We could heat the rooms in the castle only with wood fires in the individual fireplaces, which—with the bad repair of the castle—made the heating inadequate, though wood was plentiful. And then in the end of October, we heard that thousands of German Jews had arrived in Gurs, and suddenly, we realized that we were not safe at all.

The story of the shipment of the Jews of Baden, between 6,500 and 7,500 individuals, was one of the strangest incidents of the entire grim history of the deportation of the Jews. After the German victory over the French, the *gauleiter* (governor) of Baden was given the added responsibility for Alsace. He decided to get rid of all the Jews left in Baden by shipping them to Gurs. It is the only case where Jews were shipped west instead of east. This was before the Wannsee Conference, in January 1942, which decided the elimination of the Jews and the administrative methods of the "Final Solution." At that time, there was still a plan—in which Eichmann, who was in charge of the "Final Solution," otherwise known as the Holocaust, was involved—to settle all Jews in Madagascar. It is possible that the shipment to Gurs was to be the first stage of a resettlement to Madagascar.

In any case, the Germans just dumped these poor people on the French and washed their hands of them. It was up to the French authorities to handle the lamentable situation. The Germans were no longer involved once the transports had dumped their human freight. The Gurs internment camp had been previously administered by the military during the Spanish Civil War and had largely been emptied after that war's end on April 1, 1939; in the aftermath, the French camp commander had burned all the records to prevent former inmates from having difficulties with the Spanish authorities. A lot of them were Communists, former Spanish Republicans. Then Gurs had been used to intern German women, including German-Jewish refugees, after the outbreak of the war in September 1939, with an additional influx of Jews in May 1940, after the start of the German offensive. All of the German inmates had been released after the German-French armistice. At that stage, the Vichy government had transferred the administration of the camp to the civil authorities.

The camp, constructed for the many refugees who had flooded into France near the end of the Spanish Civil War, had largely served as a holding area until these refugees either returned home or found new homes elsewhere. It was on a plain, with 382 ill-constructed cabins, little sanitation, and no running water or plumbing. The camp was muddy when it rained and generally miserable. It was in no way a punitive camp; there were no watchtowers, and its barbed-wire fences were but two meters high. There was no sadism, no cruelty. It was more of a holding area for people who had lost their home but were still hoping to find a new one.

The Jews from Baden who ended up in the Gurs camp were largely old women, as well as some old men and children. Shortly after they arrived, our cousin Gustel, who had been so helpful during our Bordeaux flight, wrote us that her mother was among the detainees and that she had obtained a residence permit for her from the Paris authorities and wanted us to intercede on her behalf to have her released and sent to Paris. I duly got on my bicycle, cycled to Gurs, presented the residence permit, and obtained the release of old Fanny Jesselsohn, who informed me that a mutual cousin of ours was also there. I had last seen cousin Friedrich Loeb on one of my return trips to England, when we had met in the Brussels railway station and had lunch between trains. He had been living in Brussels and had ended up as a refugee fleeing, with his girlfriend, from the Germans. I looked him up and asked him if I could get him and his girlfriend a residence permit to enable him also to be released. He refused. He was a musicologist who had never worked, receiving a monthly check from his father while he lived in Brussels. His father had died, followed by his mother shortly thereafter, and with the German foreign currency restrictions, he no longer received his monthly check. Though only in his fifties, he was sick and tired of running and had no resources, and in spite of my urging him to accept my offer and my assurance that we would somehow be able to take care of him, he refused. This was before the Final Solution, and I had no idea that he would end up in Auschwitz to be killed, but nevertheless, I still blame myself for being unable to convince him.

The Gurs internment camp was a terrible sight. It had rained before I came, and the narrow paths between the huts were muddy and slippery. The inmates had strung wires along the paths to support themselves when they moved around. The open-pit latrines stank, and the inmates were a very sad sight. Strangely enough, there were local farmers who circulated in the camp and sold food to the inmates. This was in the truest sense a resettlement camp, and before the Germans took over, two thousand inmates were able to emigrate, and seven hundred were able to escape and disappear among the local population, though others died when typhus and dysentery ultimately broke out. On June 18, 1942, the Germans took control of the camp, and the remaining 5,500 Jewish detainees were re-transported east to their death.

Our living conditions deteriorated after the onset of winter, and my parents decided to look for other quarters. We moved to Nay, a small and pleasant little town twenty kilometers from Pau, the regional capital. We found a pleasant furnished flat and even found the time to visit Lourdes, not far from Nay. My father, ever the tourist, had us read up on Bernadette and the many wonderful miraculous healings she had supposedly performed.

The news of the war's progress, however, made us ever more anxious to find a way out of Europe, and finally, in February 1941, my mother's oldest sister Melly in New York wrote us that she had been successful in getting us all—and that included Anne—a special emigration visa to the States and that it was being sent to the American consul in Marseille to be handed to us. We duly went to Marseille and received our visas and then made our application to obtain our French exit visa. We were conscious that this exposed us to the danger of the Germans getting wind of our existence, which could well result in Papa's arrest and transport to Germany.

If we were anxious before, we became doubly anxious now. Our anxiety increased with the intercession of cousin Friedrich, the same nephew of Papa who had been so instrumental in our getting taxis during our flight. Being a lawyer, and licensed to practice in France, he now specialized in getting refugees visas to emigrate, as well as exit permits from France. He had established some type of relationship with the appropriate government offices in Vichy and traveled regularly to Vichy for his clients, who were all around us.

Papa consulted him on the question of our exit permit, which we had applied for through the prefecture in Pau. It must have been about three or four weeks after we made our application when Friedrich appeared one night around eleven o'clock at our front door to inform us that our exit permit had been turned down, but he had found an official willing to give us our exit permit for a payment of fifty thousand French francs. We were all asleep when Friedrich arrived, and after Papa talked to him, he woke us all up, told us the story, and asked us whether he should give Friedrich the money, which would completely deplete us of all funds.

By that time I had taken a big dislike to Friedrich. He

had repeatedly given us the wrong information on emigration and other matters and had tried to get whatever
money he could from Papa. I did not believe him and
furthermore thought that he had heard that we were going
to get our exit visa and wanted to cash in on this. It was inconceivable to me that he would be able to pay off a Vichy
government official to do his bidding. This, to my mind,
was much too dangerous. So we sent Friedrich packing.
He left with the direst warnings about what would happen
to us.

Lo and behold, the next morning brought an official letter from the government in Vichy approving our
exit visa. The joy, as well as the disappointment of what
Friedrich had done to us, made that day a very strange one.

It was now left to us to get a booking on a ship from
Lisbon to New York, a requirement for our transit visas for
Spain and Portugal. Our relatives arranged for a booking,
and we obtained the necessary visas without difficulties.
We packed whatever bags we had, small enough for each
of us to carry our own, and made arrangements to go by
train from Pau to Madrid and from Madrid to Lisbon.
We gave up our apartment; said good-bye to our friends,
promising to try to get them visas once in New York; and
left on a sunny March day. For all the visas except the
American one, which was on a separate document, we
had reverted to our old German passports with the large
J stamped on the first page. In addition, the names Israel
for men and Sarah for women had been added, just in
case people did not see the large J. There was still the fear
that Nazi officials would catch Papa either when we were

exiting France or during the transit in Spain, but seeing that the French had given him an exit permit, we assumed that he had somehow fallen through the cracks.

We arrived duly on the Spanish frontier, passed the French controls, and then faced the Spanish entry controls. The border official said to us, pointing to Mama, Papa, Ruth, and Anne, "You can come in and transit through Spain and go to Portugal." And then, pointing to me, he said, "You can come in, but we will not let you leave Spain. We have an agreement with the Germans not to allow any German of military age go to any neutral country." Here we had worried about Papa, and it turned out that I was the joker.

A terrible emotional scene developed on the spot. Mama said, "We will all go back to France if Peter cannot come with us." There were tears and consternation, and I somehow became quiet and determined and told them all that they should go on, and I would manage to follow soon. It must have been the confidence in my voice and the fact that I was in no way emotional that made them quickly accept my solution. To this day I cannot understand what gave me the *sang-froid*.

I went back to Oloron to ask the good lady in the *sous-préfecture* what I should do next. She told me that she could provide me with a stateless travel document, which would serve as a passport, and could arrange the transfer of my transit visas through Spain and Portugal. So I left a few days later once more to try the Spanish border, and this time I passed without any difficulty. In due course I also arrived at the Portuguese border, where I was body-searched by the Spanish border official and ended up giving him a little gold pillbox and my Montblanc fountain pen. I arrived at the railway station in Lisbon, got into a taxi, and gave the chauffeur the name of the hotel where my parents were staying. As we entered the main boulevard of the city, I saw my parents, Ruth, and Anne walking in the street. I stopped the taxi and joined them to their great surprise and joy. They took me to a café to buy me that hot chocolate with whipped cream that I had dreamed about all these years and had talked about to the family all the time. Alas, it made me sick. I was no longer used to rich food.

Papa spent the next few weeks showing us the cultural monuments of Lisbon and its environs and relating to us the rich Portuguese history. We all left around April 1, 1941, on the SS *Siboney*, an American export steamer, and arrived ten days later in New York Harbor on a brilliantly sunny day. The ship was met by two of my mother's sisters, but we could not land because the consulate in Marseille had listed my mother's year of birth as 1996 instead of 1896. Since families were never separated, we were taken to Ellis Island. We appeared in an immigration court hearing the next morning and were admitted shortly thereafter as permanent residents of the United States.

We spent the first six or so weeks in the comfortable house of Sophie in Westport, Connecticut. She was Mama's second oldest sister, seven years older. Sophie's husband Eugene had a great deal of charm, loved gardening, and did not mind all these Loeb sisters and their progeny being forever in his house. They took us in, in the truest sense of the word, celebrated our flight from Europe, and made us feel not only at home but also wanted.

Eugene gave me my first job in America, when I was almost nineteen: I was to pick up a dog at Grand Central Station and deliver him to Westport. It was the first dollar I made in my new country. I had met Eugene a number of times as a boy in Mainz, when he came to visit us on his way to or from visiting his mother in Zurich. He would come for lunch, probably between trains, and invariably gave Ruth and me each ten dollars. He was truly our uncle from America, as we had read about so many times in books in Germany. He never said much and was a little embarrassed. He sat invariably in the same big chair in our living room, wondering what to say.

Those first few months in America were magical. After six weeks at Sophie's, we moved into a sublet for the summer on Lexington and Eightieth, not far from where my wife and I live now in Manhattan. We ultimately settled in an apartment in Kew Gardens, Queens, not far from the Kew Gardens subway station. Papa joined the small import company that Cousin Franz had established when he came from France in 1939, which now also had his brother Charles working in it as the star salesman.

Once we had settled in Kew Gardens, I was fortunate enough to find employment at J. Einstein and Company, a shoe supply company whose offices were at 1 Park Avenue. I was first an office boy but quickly rose to stock clerk, taking evening classes in accounting, typing, and short-hand, the latter of which I never really learned either in New York or in Bordeaux. I remember the subway and buses costing five cents, except the Fifth Avenue bus, which cost ten cents; the cream-cheese sandwich and milk I had at the Chock Full o' Nuts was priced at thirty-five cents, and at the Italian restaurant near my office, I could get a three-course meal for sixty-five cents.

After what we all had been through, our family was happy to work and happy to be together without fear and uncertainty, though we were still worried about Europe and were actively trying to help friends and relatives get an American visa or a visa to just about anywhere. Papa was back on his heavy diet of letter writing and accomplished a lot, getting visas to the few places left that would give them.

The happiest of all of us, however, was Mama. She finally had accomplished the near impossible and gotten every one of us out of Europe. She was with her family in the truest sense of the word and reunited with her three wonderful sisters. They could not get enough of each other. She would come back to Kew Gardens laden with packages, announcing that they were all purchased in incredible sales. It took her some time to realize that New York had constant sales!

Ruth worked for a while as a sales lady in a department store and then went to Adelphi College to get a bachelor's degree. I do not know if she ever got it. She was still a little disoriented but more or less adjusted to the happy new environment. We were really all happy in a way we had not been for years. All the worries of the past had suddenly disappeared, and we were confident that we could build a new life in America. The fact that many of our friends and relatives from Europe were also in New York, as well as a number of Sichel cousins and Loeb relatives outside of the three sisters, helped get us settled very quickly.

But we soon found out that all was not as well as we thought. There was discrimination against Jews, both socially and otherwise. Not everyone shared our hope that America would join the war and help defeat the Nazis. I worked for an Irishman, a kind and friendly man, who prayed for the victory of Germany over England. He was not the only one. A local movie theater played *Victory in the West*, the Nazi propaganda film depicting the German defeat of the French and British in 1940, on Eighty-Sixth Street in Yorktown. The German "Bund," a Nazi-infiltrated German organization, was also busy spreading propaganda, warning America to stay out of the war. Charles Lindbergh appeared in mass meetings in New York repeating the same line. All this had a strong anti-Semitic element to it.

We were not as worried as we had been in France and Germany, but we were worried nevertheless, realizing that America was far from committed to entering the fray. We also knew that without America the outcome of the war was in doubt. We realized, a little more maturely, that there was no assured security and safety anywhere: certainly not as long as America did not join the fight against Nazi Germany.

This made us anxious, but we did not worry about our

safety. These matters did not take away our joy over having successfully fled Europe and over building our future. Though shocked by the Japanese surprise attack on Pearl Harbor on December 7, 1941, this resolved our last worry. We now knew that Nazi Germany would be defeated, no matter how long it might take. I, for one, was happy that at last I could volunteer to join the fight against the Nazis.

PART 2

My Intelligence Career

CHAPTER FOURTEEN

Espionage 101:
Confidential Funds

I volunteered for the US Army the week after Pearl Harbor. This time my parents agreed that the time had come for me to join the war against the Nazis. It took eight months for the army to call me up. It is possible that they checked my security, since I had arrived in the United States only a few months before Pearl Harbor. I was assigned to the US Army's medical corps and shipped to Camp Robinson in Little Rock, Arkansas, for my basic training. I remember little of my basic training, except that I was excused from most disagreeable duties, since I was assigned to look after two soldiers who spoke only Canadian French and were illiterate. I ended up, like Cyrano de Bergerac, writing and reading their love letters, and in exchange they shined my boots, made my bed, polished my buttons, and did my kitchen duty.

After basic training I was assigned to a general hospital in Brigham City, Utah, and quickly became a staff sergeant and one of three noncommissioned officers to run the admissions office. It was there that I first encountered the wonder drug penicillin. A soldier was brought in from Alaska who had mastoiditis, an infection I'd had as a child, which at that time could be handled only by an operation. The patient came in with a fever of 105. He was given penicillin, at that time suspended in beeswax, and twenty-four hours later, he had no fever and was healed.

Sometime in early 1943, I took the Army Specialized Training Program (ASTP) exams and soon thereafter was assigned to study at the University of Wisconsin in Madison, but for reasons unknown to me, I was actually transferred to the University of Utah in Salt Lake City, where I waited for my transfer orders to Wisconsin. (ASTP was an army program that selected candidates who had an IQ of 120 and above to study, at government expense, for positions the army would ultimately need, such as doctors, engineers, civil administrators, and linguists.) Soon after my arrival in Salt Lake City, I was asked to the commandant's office and introduced to two gentlemen in civilian clothes. They seemed to have knowledge of my prior residence in the Pyrenees in Vichy France and questioned me about the region and my familiarity with the particular area where we had lived. They also were interested in how well I spoke French. After an introductory conversation, which could not have taken more than half an hour, they asked me whether I would be willing to be dropped behind the enemy lines on an intelligence mission. I replied, "I am a soldier, and whatever I am commanded to do, I have to do."

They told me that this was different. They wanted only volunteers, who knew of the dangers they would face. They did not specify what was involved, but it was clear that the assignment would entail working in occupied France fighting the Germans. I told them that I had joined the army to defeat Hitler, not to get a free university education, and that I was willing to volunteer. They told me that I was not to tell anyone of our conversation and that they would arrange for my transfer orders to Washington. Soon after that, I received travel orders, tickets for a sleeper train to travel from Salt Lake City to Washington, DC, and an envelope of instructions regarding where to report after my arrival. As I later realized, this was my official transfer to the Office of Strategic Services (OSS), the new US intelligence agency.

I arrived in Washington after close of business, called the telephone number I had been given, and was told to report the next morning at 0800 at a certain address in Foggy Bottom, the nickname of the neighborhood surrounding the State Department. To my question as to where I should spend the night, they told me to go to the YMCA, which happened to be new, clean, and comfortable. I duly reported the next morning, waited most of the day in a garage, and was finally shipped off with an odd assortment of Koreans, Serbs, and other Central Europeans to Area B, which I believe is now known as Camp David, today the presidential retreat located in nearby Maryland.

We were assigned rooms in a temporary building, and for the next three weeks, a number of other people and I were fed and housed, but not given any training, indoctrination, or indication of why we were there. I spent my evenings playing poker with people who were much better at it than I. At Camp David, I made one friend, Maurits Edersheim, called Mauk, a Dutch banker whose family had owned the largest private bank in Holland.

After about three weeks, Mauk and I were shipped back to Washington and informed that the mission for which we had been recruited had been canceled, and we were to be reassigned within OSS. In the meantime, we were given a housing allowance, and Mauk and I rented an apartment and waited for our assignments. Mauk, who became a close, lifelong friend, ended up doing Dutch research and analysis for OSS. I was put to use as a confidential courier between the different buildings of OSS. After doing this for a month or so, I went to the personnel office and asked to be sent overseas to a proper job or to be returned to the army and my previous assignment, to study at the University of Wisconsin. Within a couple of days, I was assigned as a "confidential funds" clerk to the OSS mission in Algiers, Algeria.

In September 1943, I was sent to Newport News with transfer orders to Algiers, and soon thereafter I departed on a troop transport to Bizerte, Tunisia. It was a slow convoy of about seventy ships in a crossing that took almost three weeks. I was trained during the voyage to man a Beaufort antiaircraft gun, and I shot at German torpedo planes shortly after we passed through the Straits of Gibraltar. We lost three or four ships that day. After our arrival in Bizerte, we were put in forty-and-eight railway cars (forty men or eight horses) and within two days reached Algiers.

At that time, Algiers was the headquarters of the Mediterranean theater of operations, and the OSS detachment was billeted and worked out of two villas, called Magnole and Sinetti, on the hills overlooking Algiers: each beautiful villa was set in gardens full of citrus trees. Initially, I was assigned to a tent in the garden of one of the villas and assigned as clerk to Major David Crockett, who was in charge of confidential funds. The confidential funds were the funds used to finance both agents and underground forces in occupied Europe. There were two functions: acquiring the currencies used in the countries where we had agents and disbursing those currencies, as well as gold coins, of which we seemed to have an inexhaustible supply.

David Crockett was a Boston Brahmin, son of a Boston doctor who had taught at the Harvard Medical School. He was one of the brightest, most charming, and most original persons I have ever met, and he became a lifetime friend. He knew many of the officers, who all came from the same background: Ivy League schools and good New England or New York families. These gentlemen were lawyers, advertising executives, or just wealthy. It was no accident that OSS was referred to as "Oh So Social." This did not prevent the men from being highly intelligent and committed individuals who were dedicated to their mission. The task of the OSS Algiers mission can be subdivided into the following missions:

*SI (Secret Intelligence): SI gathered intelligence through agents in occupied Europe, largely communicating with them by clandestine radio. Some of these agents were dropped by parachute; others infiltrated by sea. They usually had a number of safe, secure addresses of people who could receive and shelter them, as well as assist them in their mission.

*SO/SOE (Special Operations, which was American, and Special Operations Executive, which was British; members of the latter were also called Baker Street irregulars, after the address of their headquarters in London): SO/SOE largely supported resistance groups across occupied Europe, providing material and organizational support, the latter by parachuting radio operators and Allied officers and equipment into resistance groups. The Allied officers acted as coordinators of the resistance groups and communicated with Algiers by clandestine radio. By and large the cooperation of the British and the Americans worked well, and I have never heard of any major problem in coordinating operations.

*X-2: The members of X-2, an acronym whose origins I never discovered, were concerned with counterespionage; their job was to monitor the security of our operations and recognize when one of our agents or resistance groups was being played by the enemy. They were also entrusted with the radio-intercept reports, developed from decoded enemy-coded messages. An important part of their mission was also to "play back" enemy agents who had been caught and feed misinformation to the enemy. A typical "play back" involved an enemy agent who was discovered and who then, under the control of our counterespionage service, fed a mixture of true and deceptive information back to his original handlers. If such play-back agents did not cooperate, they could well face execution.

The Algiers headquarters, when I arrived, was concerned with part of occupied Europe, mainly Italy and France, but it also served as a base for a very important mission into Hungary and may well have been concerned with other areas when I was there. Notably, there was always a high degree of compartmentalization, information being limited to what we "needed to know." Sometimes, however, particularly when there was an exciting accomplishment, information spread a little further than the "need to know" category. (The aforementioned Hungarian mission was the dispatch of an officer into Hungary to act as communications link between Admiral Horthy, the Hungarian dictator, and Allied headquarters. An OSS officer was parachuted at a prearranged time to a prearranged drop zone, arrested by the Hungarians, and jailed. He brought his own radio equipment and code pads and acted as communications link at a time when Horthy was trying to arrange a separate peace with the Allies.)

Shortly after the Allied Armies took Rome in June 1944, part of the Algiers headquarters was moved to the massive Caserta Palace, just north of Naples (today, this royal edifice, with more than 1,200 rooms, is a United Nations World Heritage site). The OSS had three distinct headquarters in the European theater: London, Algiers, and Cairo. Some of the operational supervision shifted as more and more of Europe was liberated. Whereas our unit was initially under the command of Caserta when I landed in France on August 16, 1944, within a few months our OSS detachment with the Seventh Army became responsible to OSS Paris and indirectly to OSS London. William J. Casey—who later became director of the CIA under President Reagan—was chief of secret intelligence in London and therefore our ultimate boss in the OSS. He visited our unit once, as did General William "Wild Bill" Donovan.

The OSS group in Algiers was lively and intelligent, pun intended. There was little distinction of rank. Everyone who had some specific duty in the mission was treated more or less equally: there were commissioned and noncommissioned officers of the army, marine corps, and navy, as well as civilian men and women, a colorful collection of charming and interesting people working hard in their specialties and in their area. My job, initially, was to provide the financial wherewithal for our missions into occupied Europe, whereas David spent most of his time acquiring currencies of the occupied territories in such places as Beirut, Tangiers, and Lisbon. He also obtained good supplies of Havana cigars and Scotch whiskey. I fitted easily into this mix of people. I was slowly introduced into the so-called acquisition of enemy currency business. Sometime during that first winter of 1942/43, David decided that I should be an officer, so I was given a direct commission as second lieutenant.

We spent quite a bit of our free time in the city of Algiers or at the Club des Pins, a beach club that was also used as a training area. Algiers was a lively place, with good restaurants, an opera house, and shops that sold many local handicrafts. It is a beautiful city, a dramatic huge amphitheater, a bowl around a natural bay, which makes it an ideal harbor. The Casbah, the native Arab quarters, was a warren of white stucco houses climbing the hill, divided by narrow streets. It was there that I learned to drive, my sergeant showing immense patience to teach me as I lurched, learning to change gears and go forward and in reverse in my beloved Willys Jeep.

We were running short of French francs and were stymied by the French authorities, who wanted to sell us French francs at the official exchange rate, which to the best of my recollection was fifty francs to the dollar. But David had learned that the Germans, when they fled Cap Bon in Tunisia, had left many cartons of new French francs, which then had been distributed to various Tunisians. We had no knowledge of who had received them but had fairly reliable information indicating that they were somewhere among the population. The possession of French francs was illegal for Tunisians. So we decided to try to find these francs and buy as many as we could at a reasonable price. This was right up the alley for the creative mind of David Crockett.

The American vice consul in Tunis, L. Pittman Springs, was sent on holiday to Lisbon, and I was sent, in civilian clothes, to replace him during his absence. I arrived with a field safe full of louis d'or gold coins ("louis d'or" was the collective name given to twenty-franc gold coins, regardless of mint date, largely dating from before

World War I; it was an international currency and is still accepted to this day in many countries). I took over Mr. Springs's residence in the Casbah, as well as his servants, car, and driver. Most importantly, I was given a contact by the name of Max, a Maltese Jew who ran a very popular bar called Chez Max on one of the main streets of Tunis. (Max was a character straight from *Casablanca*; he could have been played to perfection by Peter Lorre!)

Max and I came up with the following plan: We would let it be known, by word of mouth, that someone was interested in buying French francs for gold. That person was going to be at the main synagogue at a specific time, ready for business. At the time specified I was in the synagogue with my little chamois bags of gold coins, waiting for the sellers to appear. The first one to appear brought an orange crate and claimed that there were fifty thousand francs in the crate. I asked him to show me his merchandise. He lifted the lid, and the crate was empty. He thought this was a trap to catch people who had illegally kept French francs. All the other people who showed up were similarly there to check out the situation, not to deliver money.

Max and I realized that we would never accomplish our mission in this way. So on Max's suggestion, I set out with my car and driver to visit various villages where Max had established that there were French francs and where he had access to key people in the community. He guaranteed my bona fides, and within a week or two, I collected fifty million francs. I also bought a cellar of cognac and scotch, which made our lives more pleasant in Algiers that winter. We had been forced to drink Fundador, a Spanish brandy that we called "Franco's revenge," a brandy that at that time had not been aged enough in wood to soften its taste. I trucked my loot, both money and liquor, back to Algiers, where we mixed and aged the bills to break up the serial numbers and make the bills look somewhat used. It was not easy.

During all this time we were preparing for an August 1944 landing in southern France. I tried to convince David that I should be given the chance to parachute into southern France before the invasion, as part of the advance team, to help coordinate the underground prior to and during the invasion. After all, I had volunteered for just such a mission when I joined OSS. Instead David assigned me to be the confidential fund officer with the team that would go into southern France with the Seventh Army. I was duly shipped with my field safe and a competent finance clerk to Naples, to be available to join the OSS Seventh Army team for the invasion.

Prior to the invasion, I spent a month or so in Naples. I visited the OSS headquarters in Caserta and tried to keep out of trouble. In due course my Jeep and trailer with the field safe and its gold and money were loaded on a Navy communications ship, and I was given a cabin for our trip from Naples to the French Coast. The luxury of that cabin, as well as the food and service during the trip, with Philippine mess boys serving us at any time, day or night, was a welcome break. We arrived off the coast of France, near St. Tropez, on August 16.

The invasion had taken place a day before we arrived, so we were taken ashore by landing crafts unopposed by the enemy. It had turned out to be the easiest invasion of the entire war. The Germans had been taken completely by surprise. The US Seventh Army quickly moved up the Rhône valley, the US Air Force having completely destroyed the German Eleventh Panzer Division. Our OSS detachment moved along with the Seventh Army's march north, changing our location as often as the headquarters of the Seventh Army did. We ended in Saverne in Alsace in November 1944 and stayed there for a few months, until about February or March of 1945. The war, which up to that point had moved swiftly in our favor, changed to a more intense confrontation with the German armies, with little progress being made in an extremely harsh winter.

CHAPTER FIFTEEN

Infiltration behind Enemy Lines

From catching up with our French agents and resistance groups to debriefing and resettling them, we were suddenly faced with the necessity of finding people we could infiltrate through the German lines or parachute behind their lines, to bring us useful intelligence. Our unit was pretty well fluent in French, but suddenly, OSS realized that it required fluent German speakers. Finally, I was needed.

We worked and were billeted in a nunnery in Saverne, and we had safe houses in Strasbourg. Our operational headquarters, far from the lines, was in Lyon, and we had a training and dispatch center in a chateau near Dijon, in Burgundy. I left the finance job largely to my excellent clerk and spent most of my time visiting POW camps to recruit German prisoners of war to spy for us. I was one of a team of three; the other two were marine officers who had fought in the Pacific and had recently been assigned to our unit in France. They were Peter Viertel, who subsequently became a famous screenwriter and whose family, after leaving Austria, was prominent in Hollywood, and Karl Muecke, a native New Yorker whose parents had taught him German as a child. Karl ultimately became a federal judge in Arizona after the war. Both men were fluent in German, bright, and enterprising. We recruited POWs and trained them for their various assignments.

There were a number of other people in our forward team, including George Howe, a Washington architect who provided the necessary documentation for the agents, a job that became easier as we captured German Army clerks and a whole Wehrmacht military company and regimental headquarters, with their blank identity cards and other documents as well as the necessary rubber stamps to authenticate them. George Howe became an expert in German documentation: his documents always passed muster, and no agent was ever caught for having false documents.

Our security officer was Lou Eastman, a New Yorker whose family owned Dromedary Dates and who would become a lifetime friend. Our reports officer and expert on German order of battle was Jeff Carre, a professor of French who had taught at Bowdoin and would teach at Amherst after the war. He had fallen in love with a French girl in Algiers, whom he ultimately married in Dijon almost at the end of the war. In total, our group comprised most interesting and lively intelligence officers, as well as a collection of communications specialists with their equipment in special vehicles, where they busily communicated with both our headquarters and our agents. In all, there must have been about fifteen in our group working close enough to the front lines to be able to infiltrate agents and also close enough to Seventh Army headquarters to be able to provide up-to-date intelligence to their G-2 (this was the name for the intelligence staff of the US Army). At this time, our chief contact in the Seventh Army was Colonel William Quinn, the head of G-2, who could not have been more supportive of our behind-the-lines intelligence work.

We ran two types of missions behind enemy lines. The first type was "tourist missions," which usually involved a captured German soldier whom we debriefed and then trained to work for the OSS. We furnished these agents with false papers (and new identities, when needed), permitting them to go on home leave, where their routes would enable them to identify troop dispositions or specific targets. These agents were often infiltrated through the German lines, though some were dropped by parachute. An example of this type of mission was the location of a heavy artillery piece, called a Big Bertha, that had been lobbing shells from time to time into Saverne, the location of the Seventh Army headquarters. One of our German agents found this artillery piece mounted on a railway car only twelve miles from Saverne, with a tunnel nearby, where Big Bertha could be hidden when not in use. The US Air Force bombed the tunnel, and the shells stopped coming. Another mission was to find the airport used by German jet fighters. The US Air Force could not find the field where they were based. An agent of ours found that they were parked under trees along the Autobahn between

Augsburg and Munich and were using the Autobahn as a runway. They did not do that much longer after we provided this information to the air force.

The second type of mission was more complicated: it involved dropping agents into specific localities where they were to establish themselves and report on a regular basis, either by Morse code over the radio or by voice (this method was called "Joan and Eleanor," a high-frequency, two-way voice radio system that communicated with a plane that would fly over a designated area at specific times). This usually involved a team of at least two, an agent to collect the intelligence and a radio operator, who often was a veteran of our French networks before the invasion. We were not limited to agents documented as German soldiers or even to Germans; by that time of the war, there were many nationalities involved in the German war effort, and false documentation could be easily provided for them.

Henry Hyde, who was our chief and whose headquarters was in a mansion in Lyon, ran the whole effort. He was a New York lawyer, educated in France and England and bilingual in French and English, with a good knowledge of German. He was dynamic, creative, and inspiring to work for, and he became a lifelong friend. The total effort required a multitude of experts, including a person to brief the agent on his documentation and cover story and make sure that he had adopted it like a second skin and an expert on order of battle, who could brief the agent on his targets and how to report what he saw. There was a great sense of urgency. The army needed the information to know what to expect in their increasingly difficult progress as the war approached closer to Germany.

The air force, from a small airport in Dijon, flew our agents to their drop zone. They also provided the planes to enable us to have our officers communicate regularly with our agents who used "Joan and Eleanor." In addition, all of us, at one time or another, got involved in working with the army to infiltrate agents through German lines. This was usually done by having the agent go to ground in our lines, having our line fall slightly back if the Germans attacked (which was customary since they tested our defenses regularly), and then having the Germans advance enough so that our agent would be behind their lines. Subsequently, the Americans would advance again to reestablish the old pattern. This did not always work as simply as it sounds. On one occasion a fellow officer stepped on a shoe mine and lost his leg. On another, John Hemingway, a son of Ernest the writer, did not leave quickly enough after putting his agent into a hiding place and was surprised by a German patrol and captured, though the agent made it safely through the lines. This caused us a great deal of anxiety: we did not know whether Hemingway had been carrying a small book of instructions, which would have revealed to the Germans some details of missions he was involved in. He was wounded during his capture but fortunately threw away his little book, which was never found. He was liberated a few weeks later from a German POW camp. He quickly recovered from his wounds.

There was great camaraderie among our team and a feeling that we were doing something useful. Like all wars, there were periods of long, hard work followed by periods of inactivity during which we played bridge or chess. We had assured ourselves of a good cook, and I used the family connections to buy wine in Burgundy, so we were not wanting. We also shot the occasional wild boar in the Vosges Mountains, which provided variety to our diet.

I would say that these missions were limited to the period between about October or November 1944 and when we finally moved into Germany in February or March of 1945. After that we moved too quickly to run more than short-term tourist operations, through more and more fluid lines.

I became acquainted with a number of German agents I had recruited and followed their careers. There were various motivations for their having volunteered, when they could have refused and spent a comparatively short time in the comfort and safety of a POW camp. Though none of our agents were believers in the Nazi Party or especially enamored of Hitler, most of them were patriotic Germans who wanted to end the war, end the killing, and end the destruction of their fatherland. Some of the young ones were rabidly anti-Nazi and were motivated more by this than by anything else. The older ones, often conscripted in the latter days of the war, and some who were in so-called *Strafkommandos*, units that were composed of conscientious objectors or people who had offended the authorities by what they said or did, were sometimes motivated not only by a wish to end the war but also by the possible benefits they would reap from their work for the Americans.

In the first category we had some of the finest young

men I have ever met: men willing to die for their ideals. In the second category were people who were promised by Henry Hyde that their work for us would result in their getting a Ford dealership in Cologne, as did happen in one case. Regardless of their varied motivations, of all the recruits—and I was involved with more than thirty agents—not one turned out to be a bad egg. We lost three who were killed and one when he lost his nerves shortly after he parachuted into a village near Heidelberg and started shooting when faced with a document control in a restaurant. Another agent, with his radio operator, was caught by triangulation, the art of locating a radio signal by detection equipment. One other team landed on an SS barracks during an open-air film performance. The two agents were captured, and the Germans played them back to feed us false information. Having been well trained, they used their emergency signals to indicate that they were under German control, and we played them to keep them alive. We even supplied them with an air-drop to prove their bone fides to their German control. Ultimately, their German masters made a deal with them; as we got closer and closer, the captors used them to get better treatment after they in turn were captured.

One young man, the twenty-three-year-old son of a Berlin physician, stood out as special. He had been drafted and was serving in the medical corps as a noncommissioned officer. Though young, he was politically sophisticated and determined to do his bit against Hitler. He was given more extensive training than most, and he parachuted with a radio operator into the Mannheim area.

It was that mission that was discovered by the Germans through triangulation, and as best as we could establish, he drowned trying to escape by swimming across the Rhine. We had all been so impressed by the young man that George Howe wrote a novel in the late 1940s about this mission, titled *Call It Treason*. Antonin Litvak made a film from the book called *Decision before Dawn*. When we discovered that the young man had a brother ten years younger, George, with the help of Allen Dulles, arranged for that younger brother to be sent to Princeton on a full scholarship. That younger brother ended up as a top diplomat of the German republic, serving as ambassador in several key posts. He remains a close friend of mine to this day.

We moved into Germany and changed our location frequently as the German Army crumbled, and we were outside Munich when the Nazis finally surrendered. I had been recruited in Paris in December 1944 by Dick Helms, who later became the director of the Central Intelligence Agency, and Frank Wisner, who was for many years the CIA's deputy director for plans (the head of secret intelligence in the CIA, who so tragically committed suicide), to be part of the postwar OSS team in occupied Germany. When the war ended, there was a rush on the part of my colleagues to go home, particularly among those who had served long enough to be able to leave the army. It was for that reason that Helms and Wisner wanted to be certain that they had an adequate team of professionals who could staff the OSS German station.

I ended up being the last wartime chief of the OSS

Seventh Army Detachment and spent a month or so set-tling the agents who had served us so well. It came down to seeing that they had a place to stay, a job if possible, and enough food and money until they could establish them-selves. We never had any complaints, and it was obvious that the Germans who had volunteered to work for us did not think that we owed them anything. These, at most thirty Germans (and there may not have been even that many, since we also employed Alsatians and in one case a White Russian, a refugee from Czarist Russia, fleeing from the Communist regime) are probably the reason I never hated the Germans as a people or a country. I knew that there were Germans who shared our ideals and were willing to fight and die for them. I also felt that the mis-ery brought about by the destruction of the cities and the suffering of the people was a punishment, which to some extent was recognized by the Germans as such.

I ended up in Heidelberg as head of a small OSS unit still attached to the Seventh Army, but this time with the mission of finding high-ranking party, army, and other officials who might have gone underground, as well as scientists and technicians working on sophisticated weap-ons-related projects.

Amazingly, Heidelberg was untouched by the war; I was working out of a pretty apartment on the right bank of the Neckar and did not take life too seriously, often driving to Paris for the weekend. My bosses sat in Wiesbaden-Biebrich, in the Henkell *Sekt* (sparkling wine) factory, where I went at least once a week to deliver my reports and receive instructions. I was taking life pretty easily, expecting to live a pleasant and relaxed life in Heidelberg, a city untouched by the war in a pretty rural setting, while serving whatever time was necessary until my release from the army. Little did I know that this was not to happen.

CHAPTER SIXTEEN

Occupied Berlin—A Ghastly Sight

I was suddenly transferred on October 1, 1945, to Berlin. I arrived with my belongings at Tempelhof Airport on a military transport plane, where I was met by Dick Helms, at the time chief of the overt OSS office in Berlin. He explained to me, as we were driving from Tempelhof to Zehlendorf West, on the city's outskirts, where the headquarters of a small clandestine unit was located, that I had been appointed the chief of an undercover OSS unit, called the Peter Unit. All the city teams of the OSS in Germany after the war were assigned male first names, and it was a pure coincidence that I would head the so-called Peter Unit. My predecessor in that job, a major, had gotten heavily involved in the black market, as had a number of other officers, and it would be my job to clean out the offenders and reestablish a working base. Zehlendorf West was in the western outskirts of the city, in a section of private homes with gardens that had been little touched during the wartime bombing campaigns.

I shall never forget the first sight of Berlin. There were whole sections of the city completely leveled to the ground and battalions of women, in working clothes and head scarves, clearing the streets, building mountains from bricks and concrete that they collected from the ruins. They were called *Trümmerfrauen*, literally women of wreckage. Some wore high-heeled shoes because that was probably all they had. They had invariably a scarf shielding their head from the dust, and they worked in chains, passing bricks and lumps of concrete from one to the other. It was a sunny day, and it was not cold, but the sight of the city—the mountains of debris and the forlorn, sad, and impoverished look of the population—was ghastly.

As I got to know the city during the next months, I came to appreciate the total misery that the destruction had visited on the population. The destruction was due not only to the aerial bombardment by the Americans and British but also to the street-by-street fighting that had occurred when the Russians captured the city. Six hundred thousand apartments were destroyed; the city's population shrank from 4.3 million inhabitants to 2.8 million. Several hundred thousand civilians had lost their lives due to bombardment and street fighting, and endless more German soldiers died during the last four weeks of the war, during the battle for Berlin. There has always been a question of why the Russians decided to take the city fighting to capture every street, when they could have starved the city without much loss to Russian lives.

Whole areas of the city were totally destroyed; some houses were cut open, with a portion of the house destroyed and a part still suitable for shelter. Apartments that were formerly supplied with central heating could no longer be heated because the fuel was not available. The apartments that were still viable were shared by many families, with one room often accommodating a whole family. Stoves were installed in each room, the stove pipes finding their exit through the nearest window. Food was scarce in spite of rations, rations that did not provide the necessary number of calories. Fortunately, Berlin was surrounded by farms, and there was a lively exchange of goods for food. Money meant nothing. Cigarettes, coffee, and chocolates—as well as, to a lesser degree, warm clothing—were the new currency. The first winter, 1945/46, was not harsh. The subsequent one, however, 1946/47, was brutal, and many Berliners died of cold and starvation. We helped where we could, but the problem was greater than we.

You can never forget the devastation and misery that war brings once you have seen it. In addition to the physical misery, there was the complete destruction of a society that, but a short time ago, had provided food and shelter, employment, and social contact. All these things were gone. People were left to their own devices, trying to survive the best they could, using whatever they had to exchange for what would enable them to live another day, be it food or fuel or shelter. The city tried to provide the essentials, but the job was greater than the resources, and those who were active in helping were too few and lacked also the resources and experience to deal with a total humanitarian disaster. It was the cities that had put Hitler in power. It was mainly the cities that had been destroyed, and they truly paid for what had happened.

No one I ever spoke to in the first few years of the occupation blamed us for the aerial bombardments, which had resulted in the near total destruction of most major cities. They knew what misery they had visited on their neighbors and did not complain about their punishment. Only in recent years has the destruction of cities been a subject of some discussion. To make things worse, the US Air Force conducted a study after the war and established that the destruction had had little effect on war production or the morale of the population. Of course, Berlin was different: only a part of the destruction was caused by our aerial bombardment; the far greater part was caused by the street-to-street fighting that ultimately resulted in the capture of the city by the Soviets.

On that day of my arrival, Dick Helms and I were driven through the center of the city to the suburbs of Zehlendorf and Zehlendorf West, the center of the American presence, where the former Luftwaffe headquarters served as the American headquarters, and large areas of villas with gardens seemed to be little touched by the war. The Peter Unit was housed in a large, modern, extremely well appointed villa with a large garden. It was the property of the number-two official in the German Central Bank, who had been arrested and deported by the Russians. His wife and two small children, however, had been permitted to stay in the servants' quarters in the basement, and the OSS had taken over the rest of the villa and its staff, which included a butler. There must have been close to ten bedrooms, a large living room with a grand piano, and an equally large dining room, which faced the garden. I arrived just in time for lunch, and Dick Helms introduced me to my staff, which consisted of officers both male and female and a number of civilians.

As I sat down, my second in command, a Captain Bookbinder, looked at my watch and asked me if he could sell it for me; it would easily fetch $1,000, he said. Though cigarettes and coffee were the main barter goods that decided the new economy, watches and cameras had their own intrinsic value, being the most priced acquisition of the Russian occupiers. It was an appropriate introduction, and over the next couple of weeks, I cleaned house.

My officers were largely OSS personnel who had worked in Switzerland or with OSS detachments in France or England. It was a rather remarkable group of people: Fred Statler, who had worked with Allen Dulles in Bern during the war, largely in a support function, and had become a case officer handling agents in Berlin; Andrée Rittner, a good reports officer, Swiss by birth and devoted to her work; and Calhoun Ancrum, a polyglot son of a marine colonel, who had spent the last year of the war in a Mosquito (a very fast wooden plane used for talking to agents by "Joan and Eleanor" voice radio transmissions), risking his life every day. Ancrum would ultimately marry a niece of the last emperor of Russia and finish his life as an Episcopal minister. In addition, there was Henry Heuser, an economist who would end up as a high official in the World Bank some years later, and Captain—later Major—Phyllis Sills, our administration officer, who kept things going smoothly. And last but not least was Sig Hoexter, who had been a socialist professor of mathematics at Frankfurt University and had escaped to the United States after getting involved in fights with the Nazis. He turned out to be a most valuable scientific intelligence officer. And then there were the others who had little to recommend them and were soon sent home.

I little remember what our targets were in those first weeks in Berlin. We were not the only OSS presence. Allen Dulles and Dick Helms had an overt OSS office, working with General Lucius D. Clay's headquarters and with American ambassador Robert "Bob" Murphy, Clay's political advisor, who had been involved in the North African landing and was an old German hand.

I do recall that these first days in the former German capital involved looking after some of the wartime contacts of Allen Dulles, the so-called crown jewels—senior German officials, ostensibly Nazis, who were in fact feeding classified military, economic, and diplomatic intelligence to the Allies. I was also asked to look after some of the survivors of the July 1944 attempt on Hitler's life, and this included some of the plotter's widows.

My other mission was to try to get information on the whereabouts of German war criminals and scientists. The work was a combination of a charitable foundation for survivors, a criminal investigation on undesirables, and a search operation for people who needed protection from the Russians. Often the wartime contacts of Allen Dulles were useful for some of these tasks.

The Berlin situation was very fluid during my first three years there (between my arrival in October 1945 and June 1948). We moved freely in the four occupation zones (the city was then divided into American, British, French, and Russian sectors) and socialized with everyone, including the Soviets. This was the spring of hope after the war, a spring that did not last long. It was at times hard to distinguish who was who, hard to know what the future would hold. We established contacts with the local German authorities, met our British counterparts, and found our way in a Berlin that slowly was organized once more into a well-run city.

In early December 1945, Allen Dulles and Dick Helms went back to the States, and the two OSS units were merged, renamed the Berlin Operations Base (BOB for short), and put under the command of the German station headquarters in the Henkell sparkling wine factory in Wiesbaden. I was appointed temporary head until the new OSS chief, Dana Durand, arrived from the United States.

Then suddenly, we realized that the Soviets were preparing East Germany, and possibly Berlin, for a Communist takeover. Up to this point, General Clay had still hoped to work with the Soviets and the other powers for a unified Germany under Allied supervision. General Clay, the US supreme commander, had come to Germany with every intention to work with the British, French, and Russians in the High Commission to establish a viable democratic society in Germany and to hand the administration of the country over to the Germans in due course, when they were ready to assume that responsibility. It soon became obvious, however, that the Russians did not subscribe to that plan. Their intent was to initially turn East Germany and East Berlin into a Soviet-controlled territory, ruled by a totally subservient German Socialist United Party (read: Communist party). It took some time for General Clay to accept that truth after he had been so committed to a different scenario.

Through some of the leading politicians, both Socialist and Christian Democrat, contacts we had picked up largely through Allen Dulles's group of wartime crown jewels, we learned that the Soviets were forcing the Socialists to merge with the Communists in what soon would be christened East Germany. The new party was called the Sozialistische Einheitspartei Deutschland (Socialist United Party of Germany, or SED). The Russians had permitted the creation of political parties very quickly: on June 12, 1945, the Communist Party was registered, closely followed on June 17 by the Socialists, on June 25 by the Christian Democratic Union, and finally on July 14 by the Liberal Party. All of these parties were controlled by the Soviets.

I first heard of the plan to merge the Communist and Socialist Parties just before Christmas of 1945, from our Socialist sources. The official negotiations, under strong pressure from the Communist Party, supported by the Russians, started on February 26, 1946, and the final merger took place on April 21. During that period I received detailed reports on all these political shenanigans, including details of the arrests of those who opposed the merger. The Soviet attempt to force such a merger in Berlin totally failed, however. What became obvious was that the Soviets intended to use the political process to take over and control Berlin, beyond their own zone, and, if possible, extend this to the rest of Germany. They had no intention of making the wartime four-power mechanism work.

I spent the days before Christmas 1945 and well into the new year reporting all of this to Washington in great detail. We had informants in the German Socialist Party and some in the bourgeois parties, often people who had been part of Allen Dulles's network in Germany or people involved in the plot against Hitler.

After the end of World War II, OSS was split up. The foreign intelligence, or FI, function of collecting intelligence, largely by clandestine means, was transferred to the US Army, where I had continued to serve. Research and analysis was moved to the State Department. The unconventional warfare functions were dissolved. What had been the OSS then went through a number of name changes during 1945 and early 1947—being first called the Strategic Service Unit (SSU) and then the Central Intelligence Group (CIG). President Truman, recognizing the need for a postwar, centralized intelligence organization, signed the National Security Act on July 26, 1947, which created the CIA, an independent agency serving all elements of the US government. It had four basic components: the Directorate of Intelligence, the National Clandestine Services, the Directorate of Science and Technology, and the Directorate of Support.

When I went to Washington on home leave in spring 1946, to go on inactive service from the army and accept a job with the Central Intelligence Group, Colonel William Quinn was the director of CIG. I had last seen Colonel Quinn when he was head of G-2 of the Seventh Army, when I had almost daily contact with him to brief him on the German order of battle (details of the disposition of German troops and equipment trying to prevent us from moving forward into Germany). When I saw that our troops were about to capture Mainz, I had asked him to allow me to enter Mainz with the first army detachments to secure any family property that still might be there. He had agreed to that but insisted that two other officers accompany me to make sure that I did not do anything foolish.

In Washington, I was debriefed and shuttled around to different sections of the agency and government to give my take on what the Soviets were up to in Germany. At the same time I insisted that we be given a clear mission, since we were still operating on a more or less police-type mission, to find high-ranking Nazis and the like. The war had been over for almost a year by that time, and the situation called for more up-to-date intelligence targets.

There was still a strong feeling that maybe we could work with the Soviets, but I certainly tried to disabuse the government officials with whom I met of this notion, based on my firsthand information on how the Soviets had their own game plan, which was to control their own zone and their part of Berlin, by political parties under their control. They hoped to extend that control over all of Germany, using the parties they controlled in their zone.

So the euphoria over creating a unified democratic Germany with the four powers working together was obviously a chimera. We started to work on a new mission statement. This was made easier since in this interim stage (before the establishment of the CIA) we were under the command of the army. General Edwin Sibert, the head of G-2 of the army in Germany, was anxious to have us collect order-of-battle information on the Soviet forces, and so we ended up with a clear mission to cover East Germany to gather military, economic, political, and scientific intelligence. Our initial intelligence uncovered the senseless dismantling of industrial plants for shipment to the Soviet Union. In most cases the equipment deteriorated so extensively that it could never be used again. We watched and reported the Sovietization of East Germany and East Berlin. We also reported on the shipment of engineers, scientists, and other highly qualified East Germans to the Soviet Union. Last but not least, we were involved in denying the Soviets as many scientists and specialists as we could identify and save.

Max Loeb, 1861-1911, father of mother.

Hermann Sichel 1791-1862 and
Margarete Wolff Sichel 1805-1863
great grand parents.

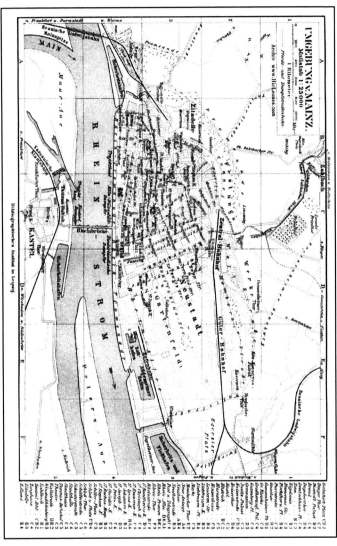

Map of Mainz on Rhine

Ferdinand Sichel 1839-1916 grandfather

28 Kaiserstrasse. Mainz

Three Loeb sisters: l. to r. Sophie,
Franziska (mother) Melly 1906.

Eugen and Franziska Sichel (parents) Paris 1931.

The author around age 9

ST. CYPRIAN'S,

EASTBOURNE.

Dear Mr. Sichel,

Peter has another very good report
and has now reached a most satisfactory
standard in his subjects.

I do like to see the keeness with
which he undertakes anything he sets out
to do, whether it be in school or on the
cricket or tennis field.

He is rather unsteady in his
shooting at present.

His general conduct has been
excellent in every way.

Yrs sincerely

W. V. Tomlinson

Letter from St. Cyprian's headmaster to father re author.

*Water Polo team Stowe School , England
1938, author extreme right.*

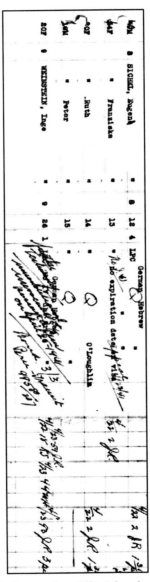

*Record of arrival at Ellis Island of author
and family 4/21/41, National Archives*

Author as private in US Army, 1942

Wiesbaden 1945 with Leslie Prial

6. Job description.

Lt. Sichel is the liaison Officer of the SI Branch with the 7th Army. In this capacity he is fully responsible for the relations between the Army and OSS/SI and for obtaining the Army's assent and cooperation to the many special requirements of secret intelligence work. The excellence of these relations, which have proved of the utmost value to SI operations, are wholly due to the initiative, sound judgement and tact displayed by Lt. Sichel. In addition to these responsible liaison duties, Lt. Sichel has developed and successfully directs the activities of a number of important intelligence agents. The qualities of imagination, reliability and energy so abundantly demonstrated by Lt. Sichel have rapidly caused him to be regarded by his superiors as one of the most effective and resourceful intelligence officers in the SI Branch, and unquestionably qualify him for the rank of Captain.

7. Remarks   Throughout his tour of duty with SI Germany, Lt. Sichel has shown himself a quiet but highly efficient and capable officer who is able to achieve results with a minimum of direction. His willingness to assume responsibility, together with his thorough knowledge of the highly specialized demands of secret intelligence work continue to achieve a superior performance.

(signature)

Branch Chief

*Frank Wisner's recommendation that author
be promoted to Captain. National Archives*

Peter team in 13 Flensburger Strasse, Berlin Zehlendorf-West. Butler Franz serving author, Mr. & Mrs. Look and other team members.

Hugh Cunningham, Chief CIA Berlin and author, Foehrenweg, Dahlem, the CIA headquarters in Berlin, 1947

Author's junk in Hong Kong 1957

General "Wild Bill" Donovan, courtesy Veterans of OSS

CENTRAL INTELLIGENCE AGENCY

WASHINGTON 25, D. C.

OFFICE OF THE DIRECTOR

8 February 1960

Mr. Peter Sichel
342 Madison Avenue
New York, New York

Dear Peter:

I felt really sad when we said goodbye the other day. I only hope that the separation is a temporary one.

You have done an outstanding job over the past 15 and more years, and have become a real professional in your work. We shall miss you sorely.

I am sure that there will be opportunities when we can get together over the future.

Sincerely,

Allen W. Dulles
Director

*Letter Allen Dulles to author on his
resigning from CIA, 2/8/60*

Richard Helms, director CIA, 1966-1973, courtesy
Georgetown University (Richard Helms Papers: Part
1, Box 24 Folder 31, Georgetown University Library,
Special Collections Research Center, Washington, D.C.)

From Left to Right: Cynthia Helms, Richard Helms, Geoffrey Jones (President Veterans of OSS), Stella and Peter Sichel, Hugh Cunningham CIA, Veterans of OSS dinner Washington 1967 or '68.

The author with his cousin Peter Allan Sichel of Bordeaux launching "My Cousin's Claret"

*The author with Philippine de Rothschild,
owner of Chateau Mouton Rothschild
and other properties. 06.14.1964*

*Diana Sichel of Chateau Angludet, Margaux,
and her five sons, all in the wine business.*

The author with Gloria Steinem during a promotion for MS Magazine, New York in the 70s. Courtesy Impact Photos Inc.

Alexandre de Lur Saluces, at Chateau d'Yquem with the author in the 1970.

Author with his wife Stella

CHAPTER SEVENTEEN

Investigating Soviet Nuclear Capabilities

One of the CIG's earliest targets was the Soviet atomic bomb project. We were able to find out that a group of top German atomic scientists had been taken to the Soviet Union shortly after the end of the war. From our wartime intelligence, we knew that there were considerable uranium deposits in East Germany, and we assumed that the Soviets knew this as well. Our sources told us that the Soviets had created a company called Wismut to mine and process uranium. Through sources in the IG Farben Plant in Bitterfelt, we also learned that the Soviets were producing distilled calcium there, which is used in the production of uranium-235. Other penetrations and sources provided information on the extensive exploitation of other German industrial facilities to supply the Soviet atomic weapons program, such as the Teva plant in Neustadt that produced wire mesh for the production of uranium-235. We were instrumental in persuading key craftsmen in that plant to leave the factory and be resettled in West Germany. The Soviets established a series of Soviet joint-stock companies, administered by the Directorate of Soviet Property in Germany, not only to produce equipment for the Soviet bomb project but also to enable them to order needed equipment from West Germany. We were able to deny some of the equipment to the Soviets and stop the acquisition of essential supplies from the West by identifying the suppliers and causing them to discontinue supplying the East Germans with the equipment, often helping them find other, more reliable customers for their business.

The Soviets, as well as the Western powers, showed an early interest in German scientists and technicians, and both sides were anxious to deny these experts to the other side and to employ them for their own projects. Early on, the Soviets hired scientists and technicians for their atomic projects and other weapons and missile projects. Their methods were very sophisticated. They realized that no scientist was worth having unless that scientist could be persuaded to fully cooperate. So they used both the inducement of a life without economic worries, where housing and food would be provided, and the challenge of scientific discovery to recruit top scientists for their various projects. Most of the people they hired were devoted scientists and technicians who wanted to continue their research; most of them had been apolitical. They were sent to mostly pleasant parts of Russia, where their families could follow, and most of them ultimately returned to Germany to retire, after they were no longer needed by the Russians.

It is hard to describe what it was like to be part of the occupying forces in Berlin in the first three years after the end of the war. Though the center of the city was largely destroyed, large parts of the suburbs, particularly in the west, were largely untouched. It was there that the wealthiest and most influential part of the population had lived. Like all conquering armies, we requisitioned houses, giving the owners twenty-four hours to get out or in some cases asking the owners to continue to live there in the servants' quarters and become our domestic servants. Since there were hardly any men left, with most having been killed or taken prisoner, this solution usually was accepted since it provided the owners with not only shelter but also and even more importantly food and fuel. In a lot of cases, where the owners were no longer young, we also saw no objections to the husbands staying with their wives and helping to run the house.

In most cases the former owners and the American "occupiers" lived in harmony with each other. A couple of months after the Peter Unit was integrated into the main OSS detachment in December 1945, and I had become the acting chief, I moved from the house in Zehlendorf West to a smaller and very comfortable house on the Podbielsky Allee in Dahlem, which was closer to our headquarters in Foehrenweg, which was also in Dahlem. The house belonged to a mining engineer who no longer could work in that industry at that stage, and so he and his wife remained in the house and helped run it. They were both extremely nice people who saw nothing wrong in serving as domestic caretakers in their own house, which also gave them an opportunity to make sure that their house would be taken care of.

When I planted an extensive vegetable garden during the Soviet blockade of Berlin from June 1948 until May 1949, I also discovered that my housekeeper was an excellent and devoted gardener. We established a friendly relationship, and when the couple ultimately moved to West Germany, where there was a job for the mining engineer, they provided me with a professional housekeeper, Fräulein Tucholsky, who looked after my needs until I left Berlin. We worked together in harmony, and I have never seen a woman as competent in the house and as discreet in her bearing. She would work for other members of the CIA after I left, moving with them wherever their careers took them.

The requisitioned houses were largely for officers and civilians, of which there were increasingly more as time went by, since the Allied Control Council and military government ran the city and the country. The military took over a number of barracks that had not been destroyed, principally the old German Luftwaffe (air force) headquarters in Zehlendorf, which was on what later was named Clay Allee, after the US military governor of Germany, who had made his headquarters there.

Parallel to this was a Berlin where almost three million people subsisted the best they could, with a housing inventory that had been 75 percent destroyed and a food and fuel supply that had completely collapsed, where each day meant a feverish search to provide the necessities of life. Money meant little; as mentioned previously, West

Germany's postwar economy became one of barter. All possessions had a value, some more than others, and the people usually bartered them for food and fuel, either with members of the occupying powers or with other Germans, such as farmers from the backcountry. (Unlike West Germany, which had always depended on the eastern part of the country or on imports for a large part of its food supply, East Germany had always been self-sufficient.) Obviously, some items had greater value than others, and these were usually bartered in the Tiergarten, a large park in the center of town, near the famous Brandenburg Gate. Barter often went through two stages: a German would sell his flatware for cartons of cigarettes and then use these cigarettes as currency to buy his food and fuel. Cigarettes were the ideal barter good; they had a value by the pack, and the pack had twenty cigarettes, so the value could be broken down into smaller units. Other consumer goods unavailable on the German market, such as coffee, chocolate, sugar, and tea, had an intrinsic value, but they could not be used as easily as a unit for barter.

This was the official "black market," where Allied soldiers and officers bartered with Germans for their necessities of life, but where a not inconsiderable number of Allied officers and soldiers also were trying to become rich. The Russian soldier bartered to obtain objects he had never dreamed of owning, such as watches and cameras, the most desirable merchandise. The Germans bartered to survive. Again, the main currency was cigarettes. Hundreds of thousand of cartons of cigarettes changed hands, and the cost of any barter item was quoted in packs or cartons of cigarettes. A pack of cigarettes cost members of the armed services fifty cents in 1945. They were rationed but could be ordered by mail, usually for $1.50 a carton. In Germany, the dollar value of a carton of cigarettes was $150. (I supplied cartons of cigarettes to the family business in Mainz to enable them to rebuild a small office building. The other barter currency the family business in Mainz used was wine.) The army store, where we bought everything, was the post exchange, PX for short. Other barter items were coffee, sugar, chocolate, and nylon stockings. The latter helped to obtain sexual favors. We were not supposed to "fraternize" with the Germans, and certainly not with the German fräuleins, but this was hardly enforceable.

Berlin is a city with lots of parks and lakes, as well as a river and various canals, which made it possible to ship goods by water to the Atlantic ports. The city itself is rather ugly, though well laid out. What makes it attractive is the large number of parks and lakes. Being in the northern latitude, it has long summer days and short days in winter. Long days make it possible to do much with little sleep and lots of energy, so we worked long hours in the summer and played long hours as well. We often did not get to bed until three or so in the morning, when we saw the first light of day. I had a sailboat on the Wannsee, the largest of the lakes, where my colleagues and I sailed either late in the afternoon or over weekends and found what relaxation we could.

There was a little of a Wild West atmosphere in Berlin in 1945 and '46 and into '47. On one hand, an enormous joie de vivre and creative energy was released with the end of the war and the end of the Russian occupation of Berlin. The Russians had unleashed their troops to pillage and rape, followed by a well-coordinated policy to carry east everything worth "liberating," including qualified scientific and technical personnel. The worst part of this occupation was the uncertainty of what might happen and when. The population had survived the initial Russian occupation and was still traumatized by it. The Soviets were forced to leave the greater part of the city when, by prior agreement, American, British, and French occupation forces took over sections of the city. The arrival of these Western occupiers was greeted as a liberation by the Berlin population. There was no more pillaging, rape, or midnight arrests, and slowly the rule of law was introduced in the western sectors.

In spite of the dire shortage of food and the lack of shelter and fuel, a rich cultural life blossomed almost immediately. All the arts flourished. Many world-class painters had survived the war and lived in Berlin. Opera and theater, often presenting the most recent plays, sprang up from nowhere. As political parties and local government started to appear, so did political cabaret. A mixture of professional people, artists, and businessmen made for a varied and exciting social mix. I became part of this mix, spending many free evening hours not only getting to know the movers and shakers of this postwar world but also often gaining the background we needed for our intelligence work. Bars and restaurants sprang up in the center of the western sectors, mainly on and around the

Kurfuerstendamm, where we met friends for drinks or dinner or after dinner and drank wine or beer until late at night or early the next morning. Making friends with some of the survivors who were close to my family also helped to make me part of a lively social set. The one advantage to being the head of a so-called friendly intelligence service is the "light cover" it affords you. A person in my position would only rarely be in contact with an intelligence agent. Though I never acknowledged what my job was, it nevertheless was assumed that everyone knew. This often led to valuable contacts resulting from social contacts. After all, we were all anxious to ensure the Russians would not come back, either as an occupying army or in the guise of a Communist government.

I found a number of survivors who were either related or close to my family and became close friends with them. One of these was Rudolf Goldschmidt, whose father, a prominent banker, had been a classmate of my father in the gymnasium in Mainz. After graduating from law school in Germany, Rudolf had attended Oxford for a year and spent part of his youth playing tennis and table tennis, in both of which he was a world-class competitor. He had become the representative of Metro-Goldwyn-Mayer films in Germany in the early 1930s and was highly successful representing them. Being half Jewish, he continued working almost up to the beginning of the war and then disappeared from the scene, convinced that sooner or later the Nazis would eliminate him since he had been a prominent fixture in the art scene and an outspoken opponent of the Nazis. He had a French girlfriend, whose father was an aeronautic engineer, working for Messerschmitt. She hid him from 1940 to the end of the war in her apartment in Berlin. When I asked him what he did during that time, he told me that he watched the fish in an aquarium and read books. At the end of the war, he became the czar of movie distribution in the American occupation zone of Germany. He had a wide net of contacts, through both his movie industry connections and his tennis background, a game that was almost completely limited at that time to the elite in Germany. He became a close friend and an invaluable source of information on people—who they were and how they had behaved during the Nazi dictatorship.

I also made friends with a lot of Germans who had been involved in various resistance groups. Perhaps the most impressive was Harald Poelchau, a Protestant minister who was the chaplain in the prison where the plotters against Hitler were imprisoned prior to their execution. He was a remarkable human being, and his humanity and insight into those horrible years enabled me to understand to some degree the inhumanity of the Nazis and the courage of those who plotted against them. I also realized that the Germans were totally unsuitable for revolutions. Their respect of authority and regulation prevented them from thinking outside the box. It was inconceivable to me that some were not willing to plot against Hitler because they had sworn allegiance to him as the commander in chief of the army. Others could not agree to his assassination because of Christian scruples.

I became close to an evangelical organization that was involved in helping the needy in those first postwar

years. It was called the Evangeliches Hilfswerk, literally Evangelical Aid Organization, with headquarters in
Stuttgart. It was supported by a Lutheran organization
in St. Louis, Missouri, that provided both money and
supplies. The head of the Hilfswerk was a Protestant
minister by the name of Eugen Gerstenmayer, who had
been involved in the Kreisauer Kreis conspiracy against
Hitler. Some members of this conspiracy were involved
in the attempt on Hitler's life in July 1944. The Gestapo
arrested him with a Bible in one hand and a pistol in the
other. He was badly beaten up by the Nazis, and during
his trial for conspiracy, he pretended to be a backcountry idiot. He ultimately was saved, shortly before his
execution, by American troops overrunning his prison.
His was an amazing family; he had a brother who was a
doctor in Berlin and a sister who worked in his foundation, and all were solid Swabians. He ultimately became
the speaker of the Bundestag, the postwar German parliament. I remember an evening when we both were in
the apartment of Marion Yorck von Wartenburg, whose
husband had been executed after the July 1944 attempt
on Hitler's life. Marion suddenly remembered that at a
meeting of the Kreisauer Kreis, shortly before the unsuccessful plot, they had hidden the document outlining
how Germany should be governed after Hitler in the
false ceiling of her living room. She climbed up a chair,
and there were the papers. It was incredible, but that was
typical for Berlin in the late 1940s, when all kinds of Nazi
information and relics and documents were surfacing in
an unbelievable flood.

Right up until the Soviet blockade, there was free access to all the sectors of Berlin and free access to East
Germany, though train service was still haphazard, and
all food and fuel were in short supply. People suffered
hugely, particularly in the harsh winter of 1946/47. Our
team was trying not only to find our way in this confusing
world but also to determine what was worth collecting
as intelligence and what was not. Suddenly, intelligence
became a major industry.

I initially had fifteen or so people in the Peter Unit,
including intelligence officers, communications clerks,
report officers, and support personnel. The CIA detachment ultimately must have numbered some fifty to sixty
people—and after I left in May 1952, considerably more.
There were about fifteen to twenty case officers (the intelligence officers whose job was to run agents, who gathered
information of interest to us), a half dozen reports officers, three or so communications specialists, and various
other support personnel. We were in the old headquarters
of Field Marshall Keitel, the former chief of staff of the
German Army. It was a self-standing building built by
Albert Speer on Foehrenweg, in a nice garden in Dahlem,
close to the American headquarters of General Clay. It was
surrounded by a high fence and had been built to make
unauthorized entry extremely difficult. It was a little bit of
a fortress, ideal for our purpose. We had a large car pool
of mainly requisitioned cars. Throughout the war, from
the landing in southern France to our first years in Berlin,
our motor transport was either Jeeps or requisitioned cars.
Our Berlin car pool had everything from Jeeps to prewar

Buicks, Mercedes, and BMWs to Volkswagens and, as cars became available both in Germany and in the United States, more modern models.

The Berlin Operations Base was divided into two distinct branches: an intelligence-gathering branch called FI (for "foreign intelligence") and an X-2 branch. The latter was charged with counterespionage activities. X-2 also checked the security of all FI agents, either clearing their security or refusing to clear them. X-2 was the only branch of the OSS entrusted with signal intelligence. It also handled most of the liaison with friendly services, including the Berlin police.

The chief of X-2, for most of my time in Berlin, was Henry Heckscher, who was half Jewish and a former German like me. He had studied law and, not being able to practice it in Germany, had immigrated to the United States in the 1930s. Henry had been a top interrogator during the war and had interrogated Hitler's sister. He and his deputy in X-2, Tom Polgar, an enormously intelligent former Hungarian who would have a remarkable career in the CIA, were able to establish close relations with the Berlin police president Johannes Stumm and the *Ostbüro* of the Socialist Party of Germany. They were also instrumental in establishing good relations with the CIC, the Counter Intelligence Corps of the US Army, to the profit of both the CIC and the CIA.

My officers and support personnel were partially transferees from OSS, though most of them were new recruits—young college graduates who either had served only a little time in the war or were on their first job. They were all bright, well motivated, and anxious to do their bit in what they perceived as a "cold war" to deny the Soviets new territory. Life was really simple at that time: we were the good guys, rebuilding Europe and West Germany into successful democracies, and then there were the Soviets, anxious to extend their empire. Having witnessed the crude kidnappings in Berlin and the east, we had no doubt that we were defending the Western world.

We were young, full of energy, and convinced that we were involved in the most important job in the world. We played as hard as we worked. When I look back, I am amazed that so many of us survived. We drank heavily, partied intensely, and enjoyed life to the fullest. It is a wonder that none of us ever got involved in a traffic accident because at that time, we drank and drove—and at high speed, through the almost empty boulevards and streets of Berlin. This was before combining alcohol and driving, or for that matter, smoking, was considered a no-no. Some of us had acquired German girlfriends, and some of us, including me, ended up marrying them. It was a great time because the world was simple: the good guys and the bad guys. It was a great time because we were young and enjoyed life to the fullest. It was a great time because we did produce intelligence that turned out to be useful and was highly appreciated. Much of our intelligence work was not sophisticated or high-level, but of a type that enabled us to fathom realistically the Soviet intentions. This was, at the time, extremely important. A wrong assessment might well have led to another war.

CHAPTER EIGHTEEN

The Nitty-Gritty of Espionage

In running intelligence agents, there is a certain tradecraft to follow, those tried-and-true practices borne of experience that any professional intelligence service follows and follows religiously. When I was in Berlin, we had a multitude of agents because the main targets were Soviet order of battle—that is, identifying Soviet troop dispositions—and Soviet logistics, so that we could assess to what extent the Soviets were preparing for an offensive against the West. This required a large number of essentially low-level observation agents, some permanently located in key places in the Soviet zone, while others were sent on "tourist missions" to cover areas we could not cover with resident agents. The work also required couriers who could pick up reports from residents and bring them safely to Berlin.

Each agent, and this included the couriers because they were basically agents, had to receive security clearance from Washington. This was all before we had computers, and everything had to be done more or less by hand, via the laborious effort of checking index cards on each individual (or other piece of information) that might or might not lead to some negative record. The local checking included checking the files of the Berlin Documentation Center, a depository of the files of all the members of the Nazi Party, the SA, and the SS and other valuable background on Germans, as well as records from the German Archives. These files were used to check not only our agents, but all Germans who were considered for civil service jobs and other responsible positions in renascent Germany. They were also the main records consulted by the denazification courts, which either cleared former civil servants or limited their possible reentry into the German civil service. We also had a trusted police official who could check the Berlin police records, if need be, to find out whether our prospective agent had a criminal record. And names were checked in Washington, to see if a name had figured anywhere else. No doubt, that included records from decoded Soviet communications intercepted by the Armed Forces Security Agency (AFSA). AFSA was the forerunner of the National Security Agency, which was later established by President Truman in 1952.

On principle we could not employ an agent until all these details had been checked, nor could we train him in his specific tradecraft or the knowledge he needed to "observe" correctly such things as antennas, bumper markings on trucks, shoulder patches on soldiers' uniforms, the type of tank or cannon he might see, and a multitude of other details. All this was set against a background of political tension, where our "customers," the army and other branches of the government, were anxious for up-to-date information to assess Soviet intentions.

It is no wonder that this anxiety to get information led the army to branch out into the intelligence collection game on its own. They did not share our security preoccupations with checking potential agents. This led to their employing fabricators of intelligence, of which there were many, both former German officers and in one case a very imaginative White Russian who at one time or another supplied a number of Western intelligence services. These fabricators pretended to control whole networks of agents, a veritable industry of deceptive information (and a huge waste of money). Ultimately, after the army had been led up the garden path too many times, we established a system with the CIC of the army to limit their exposure to fraud and penetration as much as possible. It took a long time to convince them that this intelligence game had certain rules of security and that failing to follow them could lead not only to unreliable (i.e., false) information but also to deception and endangerment of some of the people they employed.

In the early days in Berlin, we had to learn our lesson as well. We initially started by using former German Army officers who ran chains of agents, largely former soldiers or officers they knew and trusted, who were located in different parts of the Soviet zone. We soon learned that they did not follow our security instructions, including that the head of a chain should never venture out of the western sector of Berlin and that the officers should never acquaint an agent with the name of another agent, even if he was an old buddy from the war. Our former German officers were overconfident. These newly hired agents underestimated the high degree of professionalism of the Soviets and ultimately the East German security services. As a result, these relative amateurs of ours were subject in one case to a simple provocation that led to their arrest in the Soviet sector of Berlin. We had hired and trained a highly competent former Wehrmacht officer, who was set up in West Berlin to recruit subagents for observation missions in East Germany. We had instructed that he was never to go to the Soviet sector of Berlin or East Germany. We had warned him that his capture would endanger all the subagents he had recruited and run so successfully. The Soviets captured one of his subagents and used him to induce our agents to go to East Berlin, by the ruse that a Soviet officer wanted to supply information but would not agree without first meeting the Western intelligence contact. Without checking with us, this agent went to East Berlin and ended up being tried for espionage and sentenced to many years of hard labor in Russia. We ended up appreciating the discipline and tradecraft talents of the other side and the strictures they imposed on our collection efforts.

To support all these agents, we needed a network of safe houses—that is, apartments or houses in Berlin where we could safely meet the agents and couriers to brief and debrief them and also give them the training they needed. This was another complex problem in a city that was short of apartments and houses and where most people shared their apartments and houses with others. It often meant recruiting additional personnel to run these safe houses so that there would be no suspicion that could lead to security problems.

Since there was a large supply of elderly *Bürgers* who had not been bombed out but who had difficulty sustaining themselves, we had a fairly large pool of potential safe houses and people to run them. A lot of these people had suffered during the Soviet occupation and were well motivated to volunteer for this support function, which would also assure them of enough income to take away the worries of daily life. There were certain complications, of course, such as how to explain to their neighbors that they suddenly had a phone in a city where there was a long waiting list to obtain one and where people often needed a professional reason for having one. The very fact that most of the landlords we worked with were good, solid citizens but old and often sick made it possible, in a number of cases, to get telephones, in the interest of being able to get medical help in case of an emergency.

In addition there was a need at times to make sure our agents were not followed by Soviet agents, which required surveillance teams, for which we largely used our own personnel, both male and female. It took some doing to make a surveillance agent out of an American secretary, but who does not like to pretend to be a streetwalker on the dark streets of Berlin?

In the first couple of years, there was a big demand for car tires, and cars that were parked often had their tires stolen. Once, upon leaving a party at a German friend's house after midnight, I found my car on blocks with all

four tires missing. We ended up getting lug nuts no con-
ventional screwdriver could undo. We also installed car
alarms, which caused us to leave parties on the run to
prevent our cars or tires from being stolen.

On the other side of our intelligence-gathering world
was our penetration of East German ministries, East
German security services, and various Communist Party
agencies. We were also successful in acquiring an agent
in the central organ of the SED, the Socialist Unity Party
(essentially the Communist Party). After all, the party was
the state within the state. In many of the nonpolitical agencies, such as the police or postal service, we were helped by
the fact that Berlin had been one entity run by one central
service for each function before the occupation. Now that
Berlin was split, bureaucratic colleagues who had worked
together before and during the war found themselves on
opposite sides of the city. They nevertheless kept up their
contacts with their former colleagues.

The penetration of East German agencies, not to
mention the party headquarters, was an entirely different
thing. We depended there on so-called walk-ins. These
were largely individuals who wanted to leave the east and
were seeking safety in the west. They came as political
refugees to the refugee centers in the city, where they were
screened largely by the CIC, to make sure that they were
genuine and not planted there by the Soviets to penetrate
us. We had friendly relations with the CIC, who alerted
us to the more interesting refugees, whom we would then
interrogate and, if suitable, ask to go back to the jobs they
had just left and become informants.

This obviously depended on a quick turnaround. Since these individuals often left during a vacation, not knowing whether their refugee status would be accepted, it was possible for them to return before their bosses suspected anything. Obviously, it then took a long time to get them trained in situ to both protect their security and still enable them to furnish us with useful information. Most of these informers saw this as a way to earn themselves entry into better lives after serving time as intelligence agents. The best of them were able to immigrate to the United States.

I learned both from these in situ recruitments and from the rare Soviet officer who defected and was talked into going back to serve as a spy that they hated the system under which they lived and admired our way of life. This was the best motivation for espionage, which in most cases is political and only rarely involves money, though money often cements relationships. Espionage is much too dangerous to be solely committed for cash, though in rare cases it has been. Both the Soviets and we had our greatest successes by profiting from people who admired either their or our system of government. That the Soviets had the great advantage of a controlled Communist Party certainly helped them.

CHAPTER NINETEEN

The Berlin Blockade and the Korean War—A Serious Turn of Events

I served in the CIA Berlin base through two major crises. The first was the Soviet blockade from June 1948 to May 1949, and the second was the Korean War, which broke out on June 25, 1950, and was still going on when I left Berlin in May 1952. These were definitely times of crisis. We worked night and day to provide the intelligence needed to assess Russian intentions. Though we were but a part of the whole picture, the fact that we could prove that the Russians had not taken any steps to prepare for a march into Western Europe must have contributed considerably to the overall assessment of Russian intentions.

The Berlin Blockade was serious from the start. The Soviets wanted us to totally abandon Berlin and thereby enable them to integrate Berlin into East Germany. The initial reason the Russians gave for blockading Berlin was the currency reform in West Germany. After the war the Germans had continued to use the Reichsmark, and both the Western powers and the Soviets had the original plates from which the Reichsmarks were printed. The Soviets did not want to abandon this currency that they could totally control in their zone.

The end of the war saw a lack of consumer goods, and too much money chased too few goods. A lot of the money was printed by the occupying powers to pay for the expenses of the occupation, more being printed in the east than in the west. Germany experienced inflation of its currency, not the first time in its modern history. The Western Allies worried about the deteriorating economic situation in the western zones and instituted a currency reform, which stopped rampant inflation. The United States at the same time extended the Marshall Plan to Germany. The Soviets refused to go along with the currency reform, claiming that it would destabilize their zone. They also turned down the benefits of the Marshall Plan, considering it a capitalist plot.

When the blockade started, there were several options: to force access by using US troops and armor, to abandon the city through a negotiated timetable, or to attempt to supply the city with food and fuel. The army, for a while, tended toward abandonment, since the use of force might well have resulted in war. After strong recommendations from General Clay, supported by General Coady Wedemeyer, President Truman finally decided to use airplanes to supply the city, being assured that it was physically difficult but possible.

With the British and to a lesser extent the French, the US Air Force supplied the city for almost a year and thereby forced the Russians to lift the blockade. A plane landed and took off every three minutes from three Berlin airports and supplied all the food and fuel needed to sustain the population as well as transport manufactured goods to Western nations to help the economy of Berlin. I had a pass that enabled me to travel on these planes. This made it possible for me to temporarily look after our Frankfurt base while the base chief was on vacation in the States, while still mainly looking after the Berlin base. It was also possible to catch a plane at six o'clock to make a dinner engagement in Frankfurt and be back in Berlin shortly after midnight. The secret was not to take a plane hauling coal—because the whole plane was full of coal dust! We all planted victory gardens as well. I grew corn, carrots, tomatoes, and other vegetables in quantities large enough to supply a part of my detachment and my German friends.

Suddenly, we were no longer the occupiers, but part of a city fighting for its life. This represented an enormous turning point in the attitude of the population, an attitude that has survived to this day. When I was invited in 1998 by the city of Berlin for the fiftieth anniversary of the Berlin Airlift, the same feeling of solidarity still existed. It was the reason President John F. Kennedy was greeted so warmly when he visited Berlin, as was President Barack Obama more recently. Berlin's population to this day has an entirely different opinion of Americans than the rest of Germany.

The interesting corollary was the change in our, the occupiers', attitude to being in Berlin. When we arrived initially in 1945, we were suspicious of almost any German except the few who were known to us through their anti-Nazi activities. We then slowly formed friendships with others but still were suspicious of tales people told us of their lives under the Nazi dictatorship. If the tales told were true, there would have been not one Jew murdered by the Nazis. But slowly, our suspicions disappeared; you cannot work with people if you suspect their truthfulness all the time.

As the world around us changed, we became more and more partisan in the Berlin population's fight to prevent a second full occupation of their city. We joined the fight as full-fledged partners and felt that the fate of Berlin was our fate as well. We were totally committed to doing whatever we could to save the city. We were convinced that we were fighting in the front lines of the Cold War and were proud to be there.

I alluded previously to the difference in environment before today's electronic revolution. There also was a difference in interpersonal relationships in the postwar era; electronics had not yet reached the immediate, instantaneous, and pervasive communications stage, where information on what was happening is available on the Internet and on television almost as soon as it happens. The press was still more involved in in-depth reporting and analysis, and many a journalist was highly regarded by the public and the government.

Being head of a CIA station or base—and Berlin was

a base, though it was larger than most CIA stations—you are involved not only in running a complex collection operation but also in liaising with your counterparts in the armed services, the State Department, the friendly foreign services, and often the local security services. The State Department and American armed services are not only your customers, but you also depend on some of them for logistical support.

This role also may involve informing the other agencies of the government about some of the intelligence you collect, if you are given authority to do so; such authority will be limited to specific officials in the other agencies. The intelligence you can share might be only raw intelligence, not put into a larger framework, with intelligence on the same subject provided by other agencies or by other means. As you become established as someone knowledgeable, you get the opportunity to discuss your ideas with others who are close to decision makers. My senior staff and I all were invited to give opinions to high-ranking members of the State Department or interagency groups that were struggling with developing National Estimates. (National Estimates are reports written by the National Security Council outlining the policies and intentions of other countries.)

We were also much closer to the press than might be the case today. We had an outstanding press corps in Berlin with such people as Drew Middleton of the *New York Times*, Jim O'Donnell of *Newsweek*, and Margaret Higgins of the *New York Tribune*. They all became social friends and often checked their stories with us, since we could often confirm their information or add to it. Some of the senior executives of the CIA, particularly Allen Dulles and Frank Wisner, were close to the press and were personal friends of people such as Joe Alsop, at that time a highly regarded columnist. Dulles and other high-ranking CIA officers in turn asked us to share some of our knowledge with Joe Alsop, with "Cy" Sulzberger, a prominent foreign affairs reporter and commentator at the New York Times, and with others, when they visited Berlin. In due course, I developed friendships with such people, and I knew that they respected the fact that they could not divulge what they learned from us but could only use it as background to their news reports. In these tense days in Berlin, we developed very close relationships, which profited both them and us.

I was also asked to meet with high-level US diplomats such as George F. Kennan (whose brainchild was the so-called containment policy to combat the global threat of expanding Soviet influence) to discuss my ideas on current affairs. This, however, was different because it was within the government, and there was no problem sharing certain types of information. On the whole the relationship with the State Department was a mutually beneficial one.

The never-ending problem while I was in Germany, however, was the dichotomy between our intelligence collection and that of the army. In the last few years of my service in Germany, the CIA installed Lieutenant General Lucian K. Truscott as overall head of the CIA in Germany. He was not concerned with the collection or interpretation of intelligence but rather was focused on trying to keep the different services and government entities that in one way or another were gathering intelligence to their authorized fields and on coordinating their overall activities.

He also, obviously, was there to deal with the nascent German government and the myriad complicated entities of the CIA. One of these was the Gehlen Organization, a German intelligence agency, then under CIA supervision, that would ultimately become the CIA counterpart in Germany. General Truscott was a highly intelligent and effective goalkeeper. One of his tactics was to not permit any person to leave a meeting until a decision was made. Obviously, the pressure of the bladder often brought agreement, even on difficult subjects, such as who could do what.

The involvement of the CIA in Germany changed radically while I was there. Initially, during the period of 1945 to 1946, we were collecting information on high-ranking Nazi officials, as well as important scientists and technicians. We were also involved in denying the latter to the Soviets, often spiriting them out of Berlin to a safe haven in the West. We quickly changed these "targets" and spent most of our efforts from summer 1946 on collecting intelligence on the Soviet military, political, and economic activities in the east, both East Germany and East Berlin. As mentioned in a previous chapter, this involved information on the forced merger of the Communist and Socialist Parties into the Socialist Unity Party and the elimination of any prominent personalities in the bourgeois parties, who were largely forced to flee to the west. It also included details on the dismantling of factories in the east and their transfer to the Soviet Union. Again, this was a sad chapter since most of the dismantled machinery waited many months to be shipped east, often deteriorating during the wait, which made them useless.

The Soviet blockade of Berlin in June 1948 changed everything. We suddenly were faced with the possibility of the Soviets marching west to take the rest of Germany and perhaps even all of Western Europe. It may be hard to understand sixty years later, but at that time we were unsure about whether the third world war might not follow the Berlin Blockade. Our top priority from then on was to fathom Soviet intentions, by collecting information on Soviet troop disposition, logistics, and any information that would show whether the Soviets intended to march westward. This information was largely obtained through low-level observation agents, and we often used different agents to cover the same targets to make sure that the information was reliable. The interrogation of refugees and rare Soviet defectors added to this information, this being largely collected by the CIC of the army, with whom we maintained excellent relations.

We did have one valuable Soviet agent, a major in Dresden, who provided important information. Another agent in the East German Central Administration was equally useful. More importantly, we had a couple of agents in the East German Railway Administration. No army today can move without using the railroads to move equipment, troops, supplies, and all the logistical backups necessary for modern warfare.

There was a certain unreality to Berlin at that time. This was before the Berlin Wall was built in August 1960, to prevent the flight of the East German population. (In 1960, before the wall was built, about 2.5 million East Germans took flight to West Berlin, creating a serious lack of workers in the east.) Even during the blockade there were no restrictions on moving from the western part of the city to the eastern part, and many Berliners worked in one part of the city and lived in the other. The only thing that changed during the blockade was one of the urban train systems, which was limited to the east and did not serve the west. The other system worked for both parts of the divided city throughout the blockade, as did the train service to East Germany.

Even after the blockade was lifted in May 1949, when the Soviets realized that they had been unsuccessful in cutting off Berlin, we continued our collection priorities, not knowing whether another confrontation between the Soviets and the West would develop. It was just as well, since in June 1950 the North Koreans invaded South Korea, and we once more were not sure whether this was the beginning of a Soviet attempt to enlarge their empire and possibly march westward. Interestingly enough, although the Berlin Blockade at the time was a much greater threat to us all in Berlin, the Korean War was perceived, in many ways, to be more serious. It was also a brutal war, not a more or less political confrontation, which the Berlin Blockade really was. In Korea we saw aggression; in Berlin, a move on the chessboard. Whereas we had left wives and children in Berlin during the blockade, we evacuated them to West Germany during the Korean War. We considered it much more likely this time that the Russians might move west.

One factor that made us more wary during the Korean War was the fact that the Soviets had encouraged the North Koreans to move into South Korea. This meant to us that they were using North Korean soldiers to act for them. We reasoned that the Soviets might well also use East German soldiers or paramilitary units to do the same. Though we knew that they did not have the necessary East German military allies to be able to do that, we nevertheless were not sure whether East Germans might be used to spearhead a move west. (The Korean Armistice was signed on July 27, 1953. I was head of the German desk in the clandestine services of the CIA in Washington at that time.)

We had learned a goodly amount in tradecraft and security from the Berlin Blockade, and our collection efforts were better and more secure in the second big crisis. From an intelligence-gathering standpoint, the period after the Berlin Blockade was in many ways a more proactive one than the period before. For one thing the blockade had changed dramatically the attitudes not only of the population of Berlin but also of the officials with whom we dealt. This also applied to a segment of the political establishment in West Germany.

It was during this second crisis of the Korean War that I left Berlin. I had met a twenty-five-year-old art student who had crashed my New Year's Eve party as 1950 turned into 1951, and I fell madly in love with her and ultimately married her in May 1952. Cuy Höttler was high-spirited, blond, and sophisticated beyond her years. She was the daughter of a former head of IG Farben in China who had retired to Potsdam just prior to the war. She had grown up in China, and ultimately, when we ended up in Hong Kong, she remembered quite a bit of the Chinese she had learned as a young girl. Marrying a German required approval by the CIA and a mandatory transfer. The permission was quickly given, and a transfer to Washington followed shortly thereafter.

CHAPTER TWENTY

Washington, 1952–56

I left Berlin in May 1952 with my fiancée Cuy and drove to Zurich, where we were married a few days later. A dozen or so friends from Berlin and other parts of Germany attended the civil wedding in Küstnacht, a little town near Zurich, and our wedding dinner at the Grand Hotel Dolder in Zurich. We spent our honeymoon in Sicily and then drove to England to introduce my bride to my British cousins. From there, we boarded the *Queen Mary*, arriving in New York in early June.

We arrived in Washington a few days later, and after staying in a hotel for a few weeks, we bought a house with a pretty garden on Western Avenue, in the northwestern part of the city. There were four other colleagues from the CIA living in the same area, which turned out to be ideal once I started working. We formed a car pool, enabling our wives to use the family cars four days a week. It also made for pleasant commuting and a constant exchange of ideas.

I took up contact again with the three sisters of my mother, with Ruth, who married during my posting in

Washington, and with the various Sichel cousins in New York. We made frequent visits to New York, where my wife became a student of Hans Hoffmann, the famous painter, giving her reason to travel to New York more frequently than I. She also took lessons at the American University, besides running an efficient household and helping to entertain a large and varied Washington society.

I took over the German desk in the clandestine services, backstopping what I had been involved in for the last seven years. It is as well to explain here that as chief of base in Berlin, I spent a not inconsiderable amount of my time as the executive of a large base. A lot of my tasks had little to do with intelligence. Though operational supervision, reporting, and liaising were my main functions, financial budgeting, personnel management, and other supervisory functions took a great deal of my time. Though I had a chief administrative officer, a finance officer, and various other people charged with the minutiae involved in running a smooth operation, they still needed supervision and my involvement when questions had to be resolved.

In Washington, my functions had more to do with assuring the security of our operations, at that time done by laborious study of endless paper records, before the agency was computerized. I made sure that timely raw and semi-processed intelligence was processed as quickly as possible and obtained the attention of the appropriate desks. I was also charged with the administrative support, to make sure that people were regularly rotated, new personnel were sent to the field, and operations that involved other geographical areas were properly coordinated with the desks that had responsibility over them. Obviously, a lot of the tasks also involved the resolution of a number of crises, as well as the clearance of operations, some of which needed approval of the director.

This was still a period when the intelligence functions and the political action/paramilitary functions were segregated within CIA headquarters. The Office of Policy Coordination (OPC) was established in 1948. Its concern was political action and paramilitary operations. OPC was initially under State Department supervision until 1951, when it was transferred and became an integral part of the CIA. The gathering of intelligence by clandestine means (my area) and the proactive OPC function of political and paramilitary action were at that stage still in two ostensibly separate silos.

Frank Wisner, who had been the initial head of OPC at State, was appointed head of the Directorate of Plans, which today is called the National Clandestine Service (NCS), shortly after he and OPC were transferred to the CIA. He was in charge of both the action (OPC) and the OSO (intelligence function). Richard Helms became his deputy. It was recognized that Wisner would concern himself mostly with political action/paramilitary functions, the purpose of OPC, and Helms would work with secret intelligence. Obviously, both would at times be acting in either function, with Wisner the clear boss of what at the time was called the Deputy Directorate of Plans.

The two main offices of CIA at that time were OSO/OPC, now called the National Clandestine Service, and the Office of Intelligence, now called the Directorate of Intelligence. This latter office was charged with collecting all pertinent information, largely from overt sources, as well as receiving the information gathered clandestinely by OSO. It supplied reports of current interest to the president and to other departments of the government. It also periodically supplied national estimates both on other countries and on specific subjects, which might include such subjects as nuclear proliferation or the security of oil supply to the free world. In this function the Directorate of Intelligence worked with other departments of the government to arrive at a consensus, and failing that, the estimates would list divergent opinions by other government agencies.

In addition, there were offices that ultimately were called the Directorate of Science and Technology and the Directorate of Support. There was also a staff that dealt with public affairs, human resources, congressional affairs, and legal issues, as well as internal security. All these functions and some additional ones were not as highly organized as they are now. We were still in the infancy of the CIA.

As head of operations in Eastern Europe, I was concerned less with administration and more with supervision of operations of the different country desks of the Eastern European division. During this period I also got involved in coordinating operations with other areas and seeking help from some of the specialized staffs. In due course I got to know most of the senior people in the clandestine services and formed friendships with some of the better-known personalities, such as Jim Angleton and Bill Harvey, the latter of whom became my successor but one in Berlin. They both became controversial figures in the history of CIA, and I will discuss them in a separate chapter dealing with prominent CIA officials. I knew and worked with both of them during my time in CIA.

There was an element of "family" in working for the CIA at that time. A lot of us had worked by that time almost ten years in the secret intelligence business and had formed friendships with our colleagues. We not only worked but also socialized with each other. The officers who had joined after the war were made of the same cloth as the wartime officers. They had come from similar, mostly East Coast elite families and had been educated at Ivy League colleges. They were largely cosmopolitan and with few exceptions free of petty prejudices. They were also extremely hospitable. I was invited to dine at the homes of Frank Wisner, Dick Helms, and Allen Dulles, I swam in the backyard pool of Allen Dulles's sister Eleanor in Virginia, and I lunched with Jim Angleton and Bill Harvey frequently.

It was also a time when we all drank prodigiously. The likes of Angleton and Harvey would consume two drinks before lunch; Angleton would drink bourbon while Harvey downed dry martinis. They were not the only ones, and a whole number of senior officers would qualify today as alcoholics. This meant that most serious business was transacted in the morning; the afternoon would find Bill Harvey, for instance, snoring at his desk. We did not think this unusual at the time. We worked long hours, often came in during weekends when the job required it, and were all dedicated to our work.

The offices of the clandestine services were all in a long series of temporary buildings along the reflecting pools leading up to the Lincoln Memorial. These buildings had been constructed as temporary office buildings during World War I and were used from then on, until they were finally destroyed after the CIA moved to Langley in 1961. They were rickety but served their purpose. They were fairly well air-conditioned, and since the entire clandestine services was lodged there, it was easy to walk up and down the corridors to visit other area desks and services. There were assigned parking lots behind the buildings, and a treasured distinction of rank was a numbered parking space. The offices of the top executives of the CIA, as well as the offices of other directorates, were in other locations nearby, the director and his immediate staff being lodged in a former Navy hospital building up a hill from the temporary buildings and close to Foggy Bottom, where the Department of State buildings are located. A frequent CIA bus made it easy to move from one office to another.

CHAPTER TWENTY-ONE

Three Notable Incidents

There are three matters I either got involved in or dealt with during my time in Washington that are worth discussing. The first concerned a series of allegations made against me in 1955, which resulted in the Federal Bureau of Investigation (FBI) conducting a full security investigation of my family and me. The allegations included an accusation that OSS Berlin had withheld information on Soviet activities, that I had contact with questionable individuals, and that I had interests in foreign businesses. There was also an allegation that I lacked sympathy and loyalty to the US government and the intelligence objectives of the Central Intelligence Agency. The source of all these accusations was an American colonel who had been in charge of intelligence operations in East Germany for the army. Through our excellent relationship with the CIC of the army in Berlin, which channeled copies of army raw intelligence reports and source material to us for authentication and checking, I had been forced to warn the army that a considerably amount of their intelligence was fabricated, some by well-known intelligence mills. Intelligence mills were individuals who had created imaginary spy networks and fabricated information for sale to whoever was willing to pay. My refusal, as head of Berlin Operations Base, to authenticate the sources and intelligence became a major bone of contention between the colonel and CIA Germany. This motivated the colonel to accuse me of disloyalty and various other crimes.

In December 1955, I was duly notified and questioned by the security office of the CIA. The FBI and the CIA's security office investigated all of these allegations, and I was fully cleared in early 1956. Throughout the investigation I continued in my job and enjoyed the full support of my superiors. The very fact that the CIA let me continue while being investigated speaks to the conviction of my bosses that the accusations were not justified. (I have received, in the meantime, some of the records of this case from the National Archives and am amazed that a full-fledged investigation was based on such ridiculous allegations.) This occurred shortly after Senator Joseph McCarthy's witch hunts (1950–54), which had resulted in wild allegations against a number of top CIA officials, such as Bill Bundy. Allen Dulles rejected the Wisconsin senator's false accusations. Nevertheless, McCarthy's unsubstantiated charges and his numerous hearings into alleged Communist sympathizers ruined or shortened many careers of dedicated government servants, and much time and effort was needlessly expended in the need to follow up on all of these allegations to prove them either wrong or right.

I might add here that this was also a period during which the CIA tightened its security procedures. At each stage of change in name and status, we had to fill out personal history statements, which were checked by the FBI. Whereas during the war many of these statements might not have been thoroughly checked, the postwar statements were. Some rather senior officers were caught falsifying their statements, claiming educational degrees they had never received and other such embroideries about their lives, which might not have compromised their security but still were lies in which they were caught. Anyone so caught was immediately fired.

This was also the period where we all had to undergo lie detector tests. Not an inconsiderable number of homosexuals in the OSS and the successor organizations were filtered out, since they were regarded as a security risk. (Prior to World War I, the Russians had blackmailed a senior Austrian intelligence officer, who was homosexual, into spying for them, and we knew that the Communists were still using deviation from societally accepted norms to blackmail potential sources of information.)

I was quite active at the time in counseling certain colleagues to resign rather than be fired for failure to pass the lie detector test. I also counseled colleagues who, in my opinion, lacked the right personality for long-term CIA employment and career potential to resign and look for other work, lest they spend years in the CIA wasting their real potential. I remember having a long conversation with Frank Wisner on the subject. He thought that I was somewhat disloyal in counseling people to resign. I could not, however, tell him that most of the advice was directed at homosexual colleagues. Unfortunately, they were by and large extremely able, but McCarthy's oppressive political climate made their retention impossible.

I discussed with Dick Helms at the time how we might retain some of the people who were being let go for being homosexual or for other personal traits, since a lot of these officers were extremely able and dedicated to their work. It seemed to me that a confidential statement in their file would make blackmail impossible. Though Dick Helms was willing to overlook in some cases behavior such as excessive drinking or excessive womanizing, particularly when the officers concerned were specially qualified for their job, he felt that the climate did not permit that any exceptions be made for homosexuals. It would take many decades for the United States to come around to a more liberal view.

The second matter in which I was involved was considerably more serious. In early 1954, Otto John, the director of the Bundesamt für Verfassungsschutz, the West German government's interior security service patterned after Great Britain's MI-5 internal security service, came to Washington on an official visit. I was asked to look after him. In due course I shepherded him around the different offices; arranged a dinner attended by Allen Dulles, the director of the CIA, and various other interested officials; and entertained him at my house for dinner. Otto John had been in the legal department of Lufthansa, the German commercial airline. Through his brother, Hans John, who was in the legal department of the air ministry and was a close friend of Pastor Dietrich Bonheoffer, Otto had been involved in the plot against Hitler but had been able to flee to Lisbon after the failure of the July 1944 plot to kill Hitler.

He went from there to England and for the rest of the war worked for Soldatensender Calais, a British-run German-language radio station that beamed anti-Nazi propaganda to German troops. Strong British endorsement had resulted in his appointment as chief of what was considered the future German version of MI-5, though he had little qualification for the job. He strongly objected to the numerous former Nazi senior civil servants who had landed jobs in senior positions in the Adenauer government, and he spent considerable time warning anyone willing to listen against a resurgent nationalistic Germany. In addition, John drank excessively and bemoaned the fact that no one was making any effort to try to reunite the two Germanies, which would effectively neutralize, in his thinking, the Communist and fascist threats.

Allen Dulles, Dick Helms, and I were little impressed by him, though we felt a certain sympathy for his objection to the resurgence of former Nazi civil servants in the Bonn government. Since John was not concerned with the day-to-day workings of his office, our contact was limited to briefing him generally on security matters to assure a good relationship, on the working level, between his office and our liaison mission in Germany.

Early one morning around July 20, 1954, shortly after John returned to Germany, I received a telephone call from Dick Helms (at that time deputy director of DDP, in charge of all clandestine intelligence collection) telling me that Otto John had defected to the east. My wife had told Otto John that her parents lived in Potsdam, in the Russian zone, and had also divulged her maiden name. The CIA immediately resettled my parents-in-law and their other daughter with her husband and two small children to West Berlin. This turned out to be easy, since John never divulged either my name or the maiden name of my wife or the fact that my in-laws lived in Potsdam, in the East German People's Republic. An officer in the Berlin base called my mother-in-law asking her to meet him in West Berlin, claiming to have a present from my wife he wanted to give her. When she met him at the restaurant where they had made a rendezvous, he informed her of the possible security implications of John's defection and the American government's willingness to settle her entire family in West Berlin. My parents-in-law moved the next day to a hotel in West Berlin.

The John case occupied us for quite some time. He made accusations about the resurgence of Nazism in West Germany in a well-publicized press conference in East Berlin and claimed that his defection to East Germany was based on his anxiety to see the reunification of Germany. On March 10, 1952, Stalin had sent a note to the Western powers suggesting the unification of East and West Germany and the neutralization of a unified Germany. Though both the Western Allies and Germany turned down the proposal, it gained a certain amount of popularity with many Germans, who saw this as an opportunity to reunify the country and rid themselves of the occupying powers. It also was regarded as insurance against a resurgence of German nationalism. In 1955 a similar neutralization was accepted as the basis of a peace treaty with Austria, signed by all the Allied powers.

It turned out that John never gave any classified information to the Soviets and that the Soviets ultimately did not know what to do with him. (David Murphy, in his book *Battleground Berlin*, confirmed this, based on his conversations with Russian intelligence officers.) John ended up in East Berlin working for a while on German reunification, which of course no one but the occupying powers could have achieved. With the help of a Danish journalist, he went back to West Germany on December 12, 1955, and was immediately arrested and tried for high treason and sentenced to four years in prison, of which he served only a little over a year.

After John's release in 1958, he tried to get his conviction overturned but never succeeded since the judiciary in Germany at that time was staffed with many judges who had served in Nazi Germany. For a long time, the attitude of the judiciary and other former officials in the Nazi government, including diplomats, who were reemployed after the war, was that the plotters against Hitler had committed treason. It took a new generation of senior civil servants to recognize the value and human dignity of those who had plotted against Hitler and, more importantly, also of those who had worked for the Allies to hasten the fall of Hitler.

In Otto John's case, his strong anti-Nazi past and his strongly voiced objections to the rehiring of senior Nazi civil servants after the war should have been considered. Finally, President Weiszäcker of Germany arranged for a pension for John, who spent his last years in Austria, still trying to rehabilitate himself. He died in 1997.

The third significant matter I was slightly involved in was the most expensive operation the CIA had ever undertaken, up to that time, to gain intelligence: the famous Berlin tunnel. One of the constant targets of all intelligence services is the communications channels of unfriendly countries and their various intelligence services. We had established contacts early on in the East German postal service, contacts who were in charge of all overland communications channels, such as aboveground as well as underground cables. It turned out that all Soviet communications over landlines were channeled through Vienna or Berlin. To better exploit this fount of fresh, daily intelligence, our penetration of the East German postal service was soon taken over by specialists sent to Berlin from Washington, who operated outside of the Berlin base supervision.

When I returned to Washington, I was advised that the intelligence collected on the communications channels showed that the Soviets had switched most of their communications to underground cables and that most of these ran close to the western sector of Berlin. Bill Harvey, who was concerned with signal intelligence, was designated as the person to look into the possibility of tapping into these landlines. In due course he came up with an operations plan that involved the army building a warehouse near the East Berlin border and using that warehouse to tunnel under East Berlin to tap the cables the Soviets were using. This was all before the Berlin Wall went up, when there was free access between East and West Berlin.

A former FBI agent, Bill Harvey had been involved in some of the most successful anti-espionage cases against the Germans during the war. He was ideal for the project. He was a workaholic (and this was before his heavy drinking made him an alcoholic) and was extremely bright and very persuasive. He worked out the details of what would be involved and how it could be done. He then asked me to go with him to Allen Dulles to obtain his approval for the project. Approval was given, and I am sure Dulles felt that he had to obtain approval from the White House.

Shortly after receiving needed approvals, Harvey took over the Berlin base and was instrumental in bringing the project to fruition. It is a long story, including the fact that the Soviets knew about Harvey's tunneling-and-tapping scheme almost from the beginning. We had shared our plans with MI-6, the British secret intelligence service, which subsequently would be involved in the exploitation of the intelligence gathered. Meanwhile, the Soviets had recruited an MI-6 officer, George Blake, and he in turn informed the Soviets of Harvey's tunneling plans and our successful taps. Though the Russian intelligence service knew about our reading their traffic from the beginning, they did not want to endanger their double agent Blake and kept the knowledge of the compromised communications channel to themselves. Ultimately, Blake was identified when a Polish intelligence colonel who had defected to the west identified Blake as the treasonous British double agent. Once Blake was exposed, the Soviets "discovered" the tunnel and accused the Americans of spying on them.

The taps produced a wealth of clear text and encoded

information, of which the clear texts were translated by the CIA, which had to hire massively to keep up with the wealth of material, once more showing that the amount of information one can gather is useful only if enough linguists and analysts can be found to exploit the flood of information. This is a never-ending conundrum of intelligence. I remember Dick Helms pointing out another temporary building, which we did not identify as CIA, and telling me that it was filled with recent recruits, linguists who had been hired to exploit the take from the Berlin Tunnel Operation.

I spent almost four years working in Washington. I had arrived weighing 260 pounds and was told by the doctor who gave me my physical that I would have major problems unless I lost seventy pounds. He gave me a diet to follow, which I did. I returned to see him three months later, having shed seventy pounds. He was amazed: he had given the same advice to many others, but I was the first one who had taken him seriously. I must say that his argument for my losing weight was so persuasive that I took it to heart and have weighed myself every morning since.

My wife Cuy learned English, took painting lessons, and contributed to an active social life. We made many friends among our CIA colleagues and the German diplomatic community. It was a period where we all drank too much, smoked too much, worked hard, and lived intensely. We enjoyed Washington and its Maryland and Virginia suburbs, though we all suffered from the heat in summer.

CHAPTER TWENTY-TWO

Asia-Bound

In the spring of 1956, I was appointed chief of Station Tokyo, so I took some lessons in Japanese, attended lectures on Japanese history and culture, and read up on Japan. Alas, I was not to go to Japan: shortly before my posting, an army colonel was appointed military attaché to Japan, the same army colonel with whom I had experienced a number of controversies while in Berlin. Dick Helms decided that the colleague who originally was to go to Hong Kong would be sent to Japan, and I would be sent as chief of station to Hong Kong, at that time a British Crown colony. So we sold our house and packed up our belongings.

We took the *President Wilson*, a comfortable ship of the President line, from San Francisco to Hong Kong, stopping for a day in Honolulu, a day in Yokohoma, and a day in Manila in our eleven-day trip to Hong Kong. In Yokohoma, a CIA friend met us and took us to Tokyo to meet my colleague there. There were hardly any cars on the road. The road from Yokohama to Tokyo was full of potholes, and the cities of Yokohama and Tokyo were a sad sight, still being rebuilt from the heavy war damage. I have visited Japan many times since and can only compare the changes with those in Berlin, another completely destroyed city, which took long to be rebuilt to become a modern metropolis.

We arrived in Hong Kong on a muggy day in July 1956 and quickly settled down in a lovely apartment on Stubbs Road, halfway up the Victoria Peak. (At that time houses and apartments built on Victoria Peak, the mountain overlooking Hong Kong, were the most expensive and sought-after residences. The elevation gave them cooler weather and distance from the crowded city.) The building was called Raceview Mansion since it afforded a good view of the racecourse in Shatin. We had a lovely apartment with a sizable living/dining area, which proved large enough to give sit-down dinner parties for up to thirty, and a large terrace facing the harbor. The furniture we had brought from Washington, including a Steinway grand piano, easily fit into the apartment, and we added whatever else we needed, largely buying Ming furniture copies, excellently made by Charlotte Horstmann, who became a close friend. Charlotte was the daughter of a former Chinese ambassador to imperial Germany who had married a German and returned to China to become a successful banker. She, in turn, had married a German banker and then built up a successful antique business in Peking after her husband left her for another Eurasian woman. She fled after the Communist takeover in 1949 to Bangkok, where she worked for Jim Thompson, the man who created the Thai silk industry and who so mysteriously disappeared on a visit to Malaysia in 1967. Charlotte moved to Hong Kong shortly before we arrived, representing, among others, Jim Thompson's Thai silks. She was an amazing woman, building a factory to produce Chinese classical furniture, dealing in Chinese antiques, and employing a number of excellent Chinese tailors in addition to being the center of a social circle of Europeans and prominent Chinese.

We quickly settled into our apartment and hired an excellent and highly emotional Fukienese cook with his wife, who acted as *amah* and cleaned the house. Another *amah* did all the laundry, of which there was a lot in the hot, humid climate of Hong Kong. A Shanghainese driver completed the household staff. The driver had been a driver to high-ranking American military in China before the Communist takeover. He was a real gentleman, and we developed a close relationship to him, taking him with us when we spent weekends in a house of a friend in the New Territories. He turned out to be an excellent cook and was adept at killing poisonous snakes. Interestingly, we had people from three different Chinese cultures working for us: the cook and his wife, who were Fukinese; an amah who was Cantonese; and our driver, who was from Shanghai. They all cooked their own meals, refusing each other's food.

America has been involved extensively in China for more than 150 years, dating back roughly to the Opium War of 1842. A large American missionary presence had an enormous influence on the education of the Chinese elite and made for close American–Chinese ties. The great military commitment of America to freeing China from the Japanese and then the subsequent Communist take-over and flight of Chiang Kai-shek in 1949 to Taiwan with the Kuomingtang (KMT) government had far-reaching political consequences in the ideological confusion of the Cold War.

Though a highly competent and knowledgeable American diplomatic corps had reported on the corruption and failure of the KMT and the disciplined and popular appeal of the Communists under Mao Zedong, the "loss" of China to the Communists became a political weapon in the Red Scare politics in Congress of the late 1940s and early 1950s. The experts and diplomats, who had so faithfully reported on the inevitable victory of the Communists, were blamed for the Communist takeover in 1949.

It was a classic case of killing the messenger of bad news. When we needed these experts most, they either had been dismissed for Communist sympathies, which they did not have, or had retired prematurely because of their perceived sins. It would take decades for this wrong to be righted. At the time of my arrival in Hong Kong, only a few China hands remained in government service, and a corps of senior diplomats, steeped in both the language and the culture, often children of missionaries who had been raised in China, was replaced by a younger group of highly intelligent diplomats who would take years to acquire the knowledge, both cultural and linguistic, to once more be able to report on what, without any doubt, is one of the most complex societies in the world.

Hong Kong was the best and closest place to try to figure out what was happening in China. This was of great importance since the United States did not have diplomatic relations with China at that time. In addition to having a large diplomatic community, Hong Kong was the base for a large number of highly qualified journalists who covered not only China but also the whole Southeast Asian area. This was a time before the Internet, computers, or cell phones, when we depended heavily on journalists to inform us. We could well call it the golden age of journalism.

My three years in Hong Kong were during a momentous period of change in China. Hong Kong had a population of 2.2 million at that time; today it is home to about seven million people. In 1956 the world had a population of four billion people, half of whom lived in Asia, of whom half lived in China. China accounted, at that time, for one-fourth of the population of the world.

I arrived shortly before Chairman Mao launched the "Hundred Flowers Campaign." This campaign encouraged the Chinese population to critique the system and to suggest improvements. It was actually Mao's way to identify opposition, and it resulted in millions of Chinese being sent to the backcountry as laborers for reeducation. This was a major human tragedy and totally destroyed the better-educated classes. Mao wanted a permanent revolution to forestall corruption, which had always been widespread in China.

This campaign was followed in 1958 by "the Great Leap Forward," an attempt to industrialize China by creating communes that not only pooled their resources to grow food but also were supposed to start manufacturing farm machinery and produce iron in small commune furnaces. By 1958, 700 million people were organized in communes, the machinery fell to pieces, and the steel was frequently of low quality and could not be used. These efforts had taken the laborers away from the fields, so food and grain production were impacted, resulting ultimately in one of the greatest famines in history.

I quickly became acquainted with the closely knit community of Europeans in Hong Kong, both businessmen and diplomats. They in turn introduced me to a highly interesting group of Europeans and Chinese, who also became friends. They also introduced me to diplomats stationed in China, who frequently visited Hong Kong.

The other part of my job was to get acquainted with the intelligence establishment, which hopefully could provide some of the information we so urgently needed on what was happening in China.

The situation in Hong Kong was fraught with many difficulties. The Chinese Communist–Nationalist war was still being fought to no little degree in Hong Kong, and the British administration was trying to prevent it from getting out of hand. I was quickly introduced to the violence that this split in Chinese loyalty could suddenly unleash.

The Nationalists traditionally celebrated the October 10 Revolution, which had brought the downfall of the Qing Dynasty in 1911. This celebration, called Double Ten, was an occasion for the Chinese loyal to Chiang to parade and celebrate, very reminiscent of the political celebrations I had witnessed in Germany in the early 1930s. The celebration on October 10, 1956, turned into the worst public riots Hong Kong had ever experienced, resulting in the death of fifty-nine people and extensive damage to property. Chinese Communist-owned factories were sacked, some people were brutally beaten and killed, and finally, the colonial government had to call out the troops, who caused the largest number of deaths. I had a lunch party when the riots started, with Eric Kitchin as one of the guests. Having had experience with riots in India, he calmly informed me that these riots always burned out in forty-eight hours, regardless of what the authorities did. The riots, as predicted, did burn out after twenty-four hours. Maybe the colonial government should not have called out the troops.

It took me little time to settle down, get to know my staff, and get acquainted with whatever operations we were involved in. There were a number of similarities between Berlin and Hong Kong. Areas that were controlled by a Communist government surrounded both cities. We were not able to visit China since we had not recognized their government and therefore had no diplomatic relations. Though we initially were able to move freely in Berlin, to both East Berlin and East Germany, in Hong Kong we were restricted to our existence in a teeming city of 2.2 million. Though the New Territories, an area on the mainland opposite the main island that had been leased by the British for one hundred years, and various islands provided some variety to our lives, there still was a claustrophobic element to our existence. It soon became clear to me that to survive emotionally in such a city, I should, as I had in Berlin, buy a boat to relax from the rigors of the job and the ghetto atmosphere. With the help of an old China hand from America, Bob Drummond, I had a junk, the traditional Chinese sailing vessel used both for transport and for fishing, built to my specifications and installed a boat boy to look after the boat and help sail it.

I quickly got used to the frenetic social life, which had some of the intensity of the life I had experienced in Berlin. There were endless cocktail parties, followed either by dinner parties or by dinner in restaurants with friends or new acquaintances. Liquor flowed freely, and the more we drank, the more we seemed to want to drink. The fact that we lived a privileged life, in which we were served hand and foot and received a generous living allowance to be able to afford our lifestyle, made it all seem illusory. Nevertheless, we took to it easily and with great joy. We got to know most of the diplomats, many of whom had diplomatic relations with China and therefore were more up-to-date than we were and could potentially supply us with interesting information.

We had our favorite places where we lunched and dined, with the Foreign Correspondents Club and Jimmy's Kitchen, as well as a couple of Chinese dim sum places, being our favorites for lunch. These watering holes also usually brought us in contact with the people we wanted to see. Tillman Durdin of the *New York Times* and Jim Burke of *Time* magazine come to mind as our regular luncheon companions when they were in town. Other favorite restaurants were Gatti, the gourmet restaurant in the Peninsula Hotel, and for more relaxed dining or lunching, the Repulse Bay Hotel. We also lunched and dined in a number of superb Chinese restaurants, often following the chef from one restaurant to another. We all lived in a style we would never be able to afford again. Often, especially in the summer, we took a party on my junk, sailed to some bay from Aberdeen Harbor where I kept my boat, and enjoyed a sumptuous dinner prepared by my cook. We probably survived because we swam often and long.

I had a competent staff, including some old hands who had served in Korea, were real Cold War warriors, and had to be watched, lest they did things that would cause the British to declare them persona non grata. Though we all were there to fight a cold war against China, our responsibility in Hong Kong was to get intelligence, not to get involved in political or propaganda action. The British would throw us out quickly if we did, which they made clear from the beginning. My deputy was John Horton, an old Far East hand and a superb intelligence officer who was a real professional. A young language officer, Clair George, whom I had selected in Washington before I went out to Hong Kong, would rise ultimately in the agency to become head of the clandestine services. It was his first assignment overseas, and he took to the job as a duck to water, becoming a valuable member of the team. A lot of the information we gathered came from interrogation of refugees, from diplomats stationed in Beijing who came through Hong Kong, and from some prominent Chinese who had contacts on the mainland. None of this was espionage, but it supplied what little information we could gather. The only exception was an informant we had in the Bank of China who gave us valuable economic information and one high-level defector, who shall remain nameless.

We were also involved in supporting other stations to the degree we could. Hong Kong was the key to Southeast Asia, and I got involved in an operation that tried to collect some rather intimate information on President Sukarno of Indonesia, who was too close to the Chinese Communists for our government's liking. There was a rumor that Sukarno suffered from cancer, and the information I was able to get proved this to be false. A CIA-backed plot by high military officers against him during my time in Hong Kong failed miserably.

To President Eisenhower and John Foster Dulles, then US secretary of state and Allen Dulles's older brother, it appeared that the whole of Southeast Asia, including Laos and Cambodia, was in danger of being taken over by Communists. And from our strategic perch, we helped and supported the CIA stations in those countries to the extent we could, without endangering our own position in Hong Kong.

An old colleague of mine from Berlin, Henry Heckscher, was in Laos, and Campbell James, another old friend, replaced him when he left. Their mission was to prevent a Communist takeover of Laos. An enormous amount of money was spent to buy the elections of rightist candidates and to finance the Royal Laotian Army. This was the height of the so-called domino theory, which theorized that if one of the Southeast Asian countries became Communist-dominated, they would all fall in succession to Communist domination. President Eisenhower articulated this as the "falling domino" principle. In his view, the loss of Vietnam to Communist control would lead to similar Communist victories in neighboring countries in Southeast Asia and elsewhere.

Heckscher had been chief of X-2 in Berlin in the 1940s and '50s. He had been close to the German Socialists at that time, but slowly he had turned into a true imperialist. He was involved in the removal of Arbenz in Guatemala and got intimately involved in the military and political scene in Laos. The king wanted to keep Laos neutral, but Heckscher stirred the pot, trying to impose various strongmen, who turned out to be far from strong. It took years for the United States to accept that the king's wish to keep Laos neutral was the ideal solution. By that time, however, the king was in exile in Paris, having been removed by one of Heckscher's coups, and refused to see any Americans.

While Heckscher plotted military takeovers, his deputy and ultimate replacement, Campbell James, spent his time plying Laotians of importance with champagne, caviar, and Havana cigars, which I steadily supplied from Hong Kong. Campbell James in this way acquired a deep understanding of Laotian society and politics. Campbell, called "Zup" or "Zoop," a nickname given to him because of erroneous impressions that his money came from Campbell Soup, was an heir to a Standard Oil fortune who had been educated at Groton and Yale. He was a true character out of a Kipling story. Elegant and used to the good life, he also was imaginative and courageous.

I visited both Laos and Cambodia in January 1959 and took a three-day trip as guest of the king of Laos, in his personal DC-3 and his royal dugout canoe. I took pictures of people living in houses on stilts with my Polaroid Land Camera. These Laotians had never seen a camera, let alone received a photograph of themselves shortly after it was taken. It was an unsophisticated and rather happy society. There were probably no more than fifty miles of paved roads, if that much, at that time in all of Laos.

We had an endless stream of visitors, both from other CIA stations in the Far East and from Washington. They had to be briefed, entertained, and handled according to their status. During my time in Hong Kong, General Charles Cabell, who was at the time deputy director of the CIA, visited me. I gave a dinner party for him and his wife, who insisted on knowing the details of every dish served. When I told her that one dish consisted of what made a rooster a capon, she turned green and left the table.

The visitors were not only from the agency; they also included friends of high-ranking agency officials. For instance, I was asked by Allen Dulles to organize the visit of his friend Charles Wrightsman. Wrightsman had amassed an enormous fortune in oil and was the main shareholder of Standard Oil of Kansas. He and his wife were prominent socialites who had amassed a major fine art collection and had a mansion in Palm Beach, where Allen Dulles was a frequent visitor. I asked Allen to let me know on which flight Wrightsman would arrive in Hong Kong so that I could ease his way through customs. I was informed that he would arrive on his own plane from Moscow, quite unusual at that time. He duly arrived with his wife, a daughter from a previous marriage, and his son-in-law, who was Igor Cassini, also known as Cholly Knickerbocker, the columnist. I gave them, as I did for many, a dinner party where they mixed with high Hong Kong government officials and leading members of the European and Chinese business community.

Other visitors included Bill Bundy and Tracy Barnes, both of the CIA; they came at a time when Tracy Barnes was in charge of political action operations. In truth, Barnes had been responsible for some of the worst-run operations, and though an extremely charming and kind man, he was ill equipped for the many responsible jobs he held in the CIA. Bill Bundy, on the other hand, was a very thoughtful and highly intelligent man who, in his position as chief of staff of the Office of National Estimates, tried to make sense of the complex world we found ourselves in. He was the son-in-law of Dean Acheson, former US secretary of state, and would in due course become a key advisor to Kennedy and Johnson during the Vietnam War. It is a little-known fact that Bundy had been a top code breaker at Bletchley, the British code-breaking center, during World War II.

CIA director Allen Dulles decided in 1957 to visit a number of CIA stations in Asia and Southeast Asia. I had a good deal of trouble getting the appropriate authorities to agree to his visit to Hong Kong. The British were afraid that any press mention of Allen Dulles's visit would result in speculations about British–American cooperation in intelligence and political action operations into China, at a time when the Chinese were well aware of the CIA's parachuting of so-called freedom fighters into China. The delicate relationship between the Chinese government and the Hong Kong administration, which depended on Chinese cooperation for water and other trade and services to run Hong Kong, made the Hong Kong administration reluctant to provoke the Chinese government. I finally obtained their approval after I assured them that the visit would be a purely social one and would include a briefing by my counterparts and myself on the political and economic picture of the area. It would not involve any hanky-panky, for which Allen was famous; he was not called the great white case officer for nothing.

About ten days before Allen was supposed to arrive in Hong Kong, I received a cable from him advising me that his wife Clover had fallen ill in Karachi and asking if she could come to Hong Kong and stay with me until he arrived. I naturally agreed to this. Clover turned out to be a wonderful woman, down-to-earth and warm. When I told her that Charley Wrightsman had recently visited me, she discussed with me Allen's love of rich friends who could invite him to Palm Springs and other watering places. She did not mind that but did mind that they never accepted her invitations to dine at her house in Washington, and she felt that these people had befriended them only because of Allen's position.

She brought one of Allen's suits with her and asked me to arrange to have it copied in various materials. He would then have a fitting on arrival and be able to take the finished suits a day or two later when he left. I duly took the suits to my tailor and told him that they were for a friend who would arrive in a week and made an appointment for the tailor to come to my apartment to give my friend a fitting. Allen duly arrived, as did the tailor, who greeted Allen as Mr. Dulles—to his and my surprise. What both Allen and I had ignored were the interior labels of his custom-made suits, which gave his name and the date on which the suit was made. We were not all that sophisticated in our security, but no harm was done, and Allen visited Hong Kong without the press divulging his visit.

While we were trying to make sense of what was happening in China and trying to figure out whether the Chinese–Soviet disagreements were real or fictitious, our other CIA colleagues were involved in a most active campaign to destabilize China, alas with little success. They dropped seventy-five million leaflets into China. I have always wondered whether all the leaflets we dropped into Nazi Germany and occupied Europe during the war or into the satellite countries of Europe or into Communist China ever had any impact. I have the impression that someone set a policy, but no one ever really examined that policy. In the meantime the leaflets were designed and printed and dropped, by plane or balloon, without anyone having an idea of their usefulness. When I was in Algiers, Saul Steinberg, who would become a major cartoonist after the war, designed leaflets to make fun of Hitler and his army, which were dropped over occupied Europe.

I left Hong Kong in August 1959, having resigned from the CIA. My resignation took effect officially only after I returned to Washington and was processed for departure from the service. I took all the leave I had accumulated over all these years and flew to Europe to spend three months in Bordeaux and Mainz to get briefed on the wine business.

During my farewell lunch, CIA director Allen Dulles decorated me with the Distinguished Intelligence Medal (otherwise known as DIM) and told me that he was convinced that I would be back in the CIA within a few months. I told him that this was unlikely since I was anxious to live in the real world, having lived all these years in a world where I could not share my thoughts even with my then wife.

The reason for my resignation from the CIA was more complex than the one I gave to Allen Dulles. There were many factors, in fact, that made me decide to leave an intelligence career that had spanned almost seventeen years. I had joined OSS at the age of twenty, and except for working a little over a year in New York after my arrival in the United States in 1941, I had never really lived in a world where my work and position in society were known to everyone and where I felt that I fit openly into the world I lived in. I discussed this with Allen Dulles in that final interview and urged him to investigate a means whereby senior officers could transfer to other agencies of the government, particularly the Department of State, since otherwise they might burn out. The social isolation our profession imposed had put a lot of stress on senior officers, who had lived a large portion of their professional lives in the agency and its predecessors. This stress caused almost everyone to live intensely and drink heavily.

So when the agency had asked me to serve another tour in Hong Kong, I had declined, claiming that another tour would result in my becoming a total alcoholic. There were a lot of additional reasons, including that the agency had become more action-oriented than oriented toward "intelligence collection," which was my specialty; this trend alone contributed a great deal to my ultimate decision to leave the CIA.

Last but not least, at this time in my life, the fact that my wife had recently left me in Hong Kong also made it easier for me to reassess my life. My decision was also a lot easier because I had a family wine business I could join and not be worried about the future. All this contributed to my decision that it was time to leave the CIA and join the rest of the world.

CHAPTER TWENTY-THREE

An Informed Critique

I spent over sixteen years in OSS and its successor organizations: sixteen continuous years, in war and peace. I left in the middle of the Cold War, realizing that my ideas of what was necessary for the United States to prevail in that war did not coincide with the then-prevailing US government policy. I thought that we were too proactive and that many of our political action operations were unnecessary and counterproductive. Having become convinced over the years of the necessity of a strong intelligence-collection effort, I was disillusioned that the "action side" of the CIA did not heed the intelligence collected by the intelligence side.

Though I believed and still believe that the United States must have a strong intelligence capability, to be able to assess the strength, both political and economic, of its friends and potential enemies, I am of two minds about the extent and type of covert political action America increasingly gets involved in. I question it because I believe that it is often counterproductive: it fails to take into account local, cultural, and political realities. It tries to achieve political changes in societies that are structured differently from ours; it seems we have no appreciation of these complex factors, even after serial "regime change" debacles initiated by our government during the last fifty years. We need to learn that each and every society has to evolve over time, sometimes over generations, and on its own terms. In my view, diplomatic action would serve us better than covert political action, let alone paramilitary action.

Violent changes to the political makeup of some countries where we have clandestinely interfered were so foreign to the history and culture of their societies that the changes we imposed did not survive in the long run and resulted in a more dangerous outcome after our intervention. Such interference can also result in the destruction of a society that lived in relative harmony and suddenly finds its equilibrium destroyed, resulting in tragedy. Iran and Cambodia are ideal examples. Had we not been instrumental in replacing Mossadegh, a democratically elected prime minister of Iran, with the shah, Iran probably would have become in due course a socialist democracy, and not a Muslim theocracy. The toppling of Mossadegh was motivated by an interest in protecting British and American oil interests, and the wider geopolitical questions were not considered. We have suffered from the consequences ever since. Societies are delicate structures that have evolved over centuries, and interfering in them with the resources America sometimes has deployed can result in tragic outcomes. In many cases it would be better to leave them alone than to interfere.

We had two national policies, one after the other, that tried to address the challenge of Russia in the Cold War. One counseled containment; the other, confrontation and rollback. The policies were formed based on two contradictory interpretations of what motivated Russian behavior. The containment policy was based on the assumption that Russia's main "paranoia" was based on fear of encirclement by an unfriendly world. The second was based on the assumption that Russia had imperial ambitions and wanted to export its Marxist ideology and convert the world to Communism. After the iron curtain collapsed, and Russian archives temporarily became available, we learned that Stalin had shied away from anything that possibly would have started another war. He was conscious of the tens of millions who had perished during the war and was not about to start another war. On the other hand, having seen Russia invaded three times (including the Western support of the White Russians after World War I), he feared encirclement. His attempt to have Western democracies turn to a Communist ideological form of government was based more on his attempt to prevent encirclement than on an ideologically driven worldview.

The containment policy was based on the analysis of senior Department of State officer George Kennan and was adopted by President Truman. The confrontational policy was spelled out by Paul Nitze in the National Security Council (NSC) Report 68, of April 14, 1950; Nitze's report was titled "United States Objectives and Programs for National Security." Nitze replaced Kennan as chief of the State Department Policy Planning Staff in the Eisenhower administration. NSC 68 reflected more the philosophy of President Eisenhower. It was also more in line with the proactive and aggressive tradition of American foreign policy and the missionary zeal of the then secretary of state, John Foster Dulles, the son of a Presbyterian minister, who was active in running the Council of Churches and who regarded Communism and Stalin as evil.

The Truman administration issued in December 1947 the secret National Security Council Directive NSC4-A, which ultimately authorized the CIA to launch "covert-action operations." The directive was based on US concern about Soviet "psychological warfare" and was a direct answer to the Soviet challenge. There were some concerns by the State and Defense Departments about where the responsibility for covert action should reside, but ultimately it was lodged in the CIA, because it was only the CIA that had unvouchered funds, which enabled funding with a minimum risk of exposure. (Initially, this effort was to be guided in peacetime by the Department of State and in wartime by the Department of Defense. President Eisenhower in NSC 5412 of March 15, 1954, imposed an Operations Coordinating Board to ensure that covert operations were planned and conducted in a manner consistent with US foreign and military policies. This board had representatives from the Department of State, the Department of Defense, the CIA, and the president.)

When we worked in the 1940s and '50s, the world was relatively simple compared to today's twenty-first-century world of intelligence. The Soviet blockade of Berlin in 1947 posed a major foreign policy problem for Truman, but for us it represented the job of determining whether the Soviets intended to take West Germany by force, the same task we had when, a few years later, the Korean War represented another challenge to the free world. The CIA at that stage was mainly an agency to collect intelligence and to report and evaluate it. Only slowly did the agency become involved in political action to a greater and greater extent.

Since World War II, America has engaged not only in gathering intelligence by clandestine means but also in increasingly bold and brazen clandestine political and military actions with a hubris reminiscent of the "great game" the Russians and English played in the nineteenth and early twentieth centuries. The overthrow of Prime Minister Mohammad Mossadegh in Iran and the overthrow of President Jacobo Arbenz in Guatemala, as well as the Bay of Pigs disaster in Cuba, are good examples of when and where our American presidents found it expedient to dispose of those whom they and their national security advisors perceived as inimical rulers, to be replaced often by rulers and systems that were infinitely worse.

This could have been avoided if the clandestine efforts had been followed by a concerted effort by other agencies of the government to rebuild the societies we had so violently disturbed. Richard Bissell, the late former head of the clandestine services of the CIA, who lost his job after the Bay of Pigs disaster, addresses this in his *Reflections of a Cold Warrior*:

> The ball was not picked up in Guatemala. Nobody in the State Department or the

Agency for International Development recognized the urgent need to improve that society and no major program was undertaken to accomplish this purpose. In terms of an executive long-range policy, this is a glaring weakness. It was true especially in Guatemala because there we had destabilized a democratically elected government and therefore had a greater moral obligation than we did in most small Latin American countries to try to do something about the underlying situation.[1]

Bissell later reflects on his overall view of covert political operations:

Many, probably most, successes were successes only in the short run. Arbenz, for instance, was overthrown, but the long-term problems of Guatemala were not solved. Elections were won in several countries, but political parties and political systems were not permanently rejuvenated. Most covert-action operations (like military operations) are directed at short-term

---

[1] Richard M. Bissell Jr., with Jonathan E. Lewis and Frank T. Puldo, *Reflections of a Cold Warrior: From Yalta to the Bay of Pigs* (New Haven, CT: Yale University Press, 1996), 91.

objectives. Their success or failure must be judged by the degree to which these objectives are achieved. Their effectiveness must be measured by the degree to which achievement of the short-term objectives will contribute to the national interest. It can be argued that, although few uncompromised operations actually failed, the successful achievement of their short-term results made only a limited contribution to the national interest. Covert political action is therefore usually an expedient and its long term value, like that of all expedients, can be questioned.[2]

Since World War II, in my view, we have had a series of "imperial presidents" who have used the commander-in-chief authority to bypass the US Congress, legislation, and even national and international law. The rule seems to be that everything is legal if the president orders it and Congress votes the money.

A certain impatience to change things rather than watch them develop and change on their own accord is probably a typical American characteristic. It is often easier to act, especially with the belief that we are always right, than to wait and let problems solve themselves. This is the disease of empires. Although Vietnam, Afghanistan, and Iraq may be the most shocking examples, our other

---

[2] Ibid., 220.

involvements, intrusions, and failed or successful coups d'état have been equally destructive in the long run to the development of societies they violently disturbed. We seemingly have not learned anything from history; certainly, we did not learn from the all-too-evident postcolonial mistakes of the British and French, let alone the mistakes of the Russians and, after the 1917 revolution, of the Soviets. I am certainly not alone in the conviction and firsthand experience that foreign systems and ideas, such as market economies, representative democracies, and other signs of an evolving society, cannot be superimposed by violence and force; they must grow on soil that can support them, which usually means a society that is wealthy enough to be able to afford democracy.

There is a big question in my mind regarding to what extent the leadership of the CIA influenced US policy in the 1950s and '60s. At this time, there was a heady mix of extremely bright and "action-oriented" men in the State Department, the CIA, and the Fourth Estate (the news media). And many of them shared a similar, affluent social and educational background (boarding schools and Ivy League colleges), a strong commitment to public service to the country, and a missionary zeal to engage aggressively to prevent Soviet and Communist expansion of influence and control. These personalities were well described in Evan Thomas's *The Very Best Men*, which chronicles the intertwined lives and careers of Frank Wisner, Richard Bissell, Tracy Barnes, and Desmond Fitzgerald.[3] I served

---

[3] Evan Thomas, *The Very Best Men: Four Who Dared, The Early Years of the CIA* (New York: Simon and Schuster, 1996).

with all of these men during my career in the CIA and was a friend of most of them.

The CIA initially was the successor organization to the Office of Strategic Services, the US agency entrusted with the collection of foreign intelligence and paramilitary activities in World War II. When in 1947 the Central Intelligence Agency was created, its function was limited to the collection of foreign intelligence. It is not widely appreciated that at its creation, the CIA had no mission to engage in political or paramilitary action. The OSS personnel who ultimately became the core of CIA—of which I was one—were intelligence officers, more or less professional in the tradecraft of acquiring and reporting intelligence. A not inconsiderable number of officers who were involved in paramilitary action during World War II soon went back to their prewar professions, as did a number of the senior members of OSS who were involved in the intelligence side of the business. Obviously, one cannot make a fine distinction between the two clandestine functions, since some officers were involved in intelligence collection as well as political action and/or paramilitary operations.

The senior people who left OSS included Allen Dulles, Tracy Barnes, and Frank Wisner, who all ultimately came back after the CIA was entrusted with the mission of clandestine political and paramilitary action beginning in earnest in the 1950s. The senior people who had a seamless career from OSS through SSU and CIG included Dick Helms, James Jesus Angleton, and me. Then there were other senior officers who joined at a later date, such as

Dick Bissell and William Harvey. The latter came to the CIA from the FBI, where he had distinguished himself during the war in counterintelligence.

A considerable number of the senior officers, particularly those who had left and then came back, shared a similar background, including graduation from prestigious Eastern Seaboard boarding schools, with most having gone to Groton. All went to Ivy League universities, with Yale predominating, though Dulles went to Princeton, and some others to Harvard. They were close friends with men of similar backgrounds in the Department of State and other government agencies, as well as the news media. Among these were people such as Paul Nitze, Chip Bohlen, the Alsop brothers, and Phil and Kay Graham, the owners of the *Washington Post*. They socialized together; belonged to the same clubs, mainly the F Street Club, also known as the "Spy Club"; and shared a sense of mission in the Cold War. They were the "new elite" in a Washington that was considerably smaller than the machinery of government is today. They often dined together on Sundays, and in a Republican administration they were more progressive and tolerant than the political establishment.

Most of these senior officers, including Allen Dulles, Frank Wisner, Desmond Fitzgerald, and Tracy Barnes, considered their wartime career a highpoint in their lives and, to some extent, tried to recreate during the Cold War the excitement they had experienced in facing danger in the war. Though this was undoubtedly unconscious, it nevertheless motivated them to a degree where often their judgments could be questioned. An old colleague of mine in the CIA once questioned an order given him by Desmond Fitzgerald. He pointed out to Des that the Cold War hardly justified the extreme measures we had undertaken in wartime. Their predicament was very similar to the problem experienced by the pilots who had survived the Battle of Britain. They could not adjust to a more mundane daily life and had to seek challenges as close to their wartime experiences as possible. This might explain their large consumption of alcohol, their excessive partying, and their feeling that they were the only ones who stood in the way of Soviet domination of the world.

The last man to join this group was Richard Bissell, a man who had distinguished himself in the war by his brilliant organizational abilities in managing Allied shipping and who had then become equally adept at administering the Marshall Plan. He entered the CIA to solve one of the principal intelligence failures: to assess the strength of the Soviet missile program.

To that end, Bissell was responsible for creating the U-2 spy plane program and was a driving force behind the development of the necessary high-resolution camera to assure Eisenhower that there was no missile gap between the Soviet Union and the United States. Having been recognized as an extraordinary problem solver, he then ended up as the head of the clandestine services, without any prior experience in intelligence, let alone clandestine collection or action. We unfortunately live in a society where bright people are supposed to be able to handle any challenge. Having no experience in the tradecraft of the profession, he denigrated it and ignored the necessary professionalism and caution so essential in clandestine work. His ignorance led to arrogance and a failure to consult with the outstanding professional in the service, Richard Helms, who was his deputy for secret intelligence and who might have been able to prevent the Bay of Pigs operation, or at least limit its tragic failure, had he been consulted. Instead, Bissell went ahead without the necessary checks, and when the poorly planned operation failed, it cut short his own career, which would have ended, more than likely, in his appointment as head of CIA.

The CIA I knew was an extraordinarily "open society." Even before I became a senior officer—this designation being reserved for people who had "super grades" in the CIA, rather like generals or admirals in the services—we had the ability, at all times, to voice our opinions; I vividly recall that the interplay between the heads of divisions and the director and his deputies was open and honest. We all felt like part of an elite group who fought in the Cold War, had a sense of camaraderie, and due to our sharing secrets, socialized together to a degree, which was probably not all too healthy. We all, with some notable exceptions, also drank a good deal of alcohol, but that was widespread in our society at that time.

We who had been in OSS during the war and stayed on were close to the senior management in the CIA, who had shared our experiences. I knew Allen Dulles, Dick Helms, and Frank Wisner both socially and professionally. It is as well to discuss some of these former colleagues.

Allen Dulles

I have often been asked what I thought of Allen. He reminded me of a headmaster at an upper-class boarding school: usually wearing tweed and bow ties and smoking a pipe, he exuded friendliness and bonhomie. He showed no prejudices and was open to discussing operational problems openly, willing to listen to opinions with which he might not agree. He led by personality an agency with colorful and varied individuals that might have been better led by a more critical chief. This was a period in our history in which everyone was imbued with the mission of winning the Cold War, and Allen was as suitable for this position as if he had been picked by central casting. In due course the job called for a less colorful and personable director of central intelligence, but these were the formative years, where we had to learn from our mistakes.

I will quote once more from Bissell's *Reflections*:

> There is no doubt in my mind that Allen's strong stand against McCarthyism and his very able leadership were the key reasons the agency was able to attract so many capable people during the midfifties. Much of the challenge and sense of forward motion had gone out of the other parts of government, but he was able to keep those elements alive at the agency. The CIA was a place where individuals seeking intellectual discourse and personal challenge could still find a home. He

engendered a great deal of loyalty and respect, and I can't think of anybody in the
agency who didn't both like and admire
him, which is quite a tribute … In addition to having personal courage, he was
also a warmer and more outgoing person
[than his brother John Foster], and he was
more receptive to a wider spectrum of beliefs and backgrounds than his brother
was. As a result he was more inclined to
judge individuals by their competence
and personal qualities and less their actual or alleged political views.[4]

Richard Helms

The person I was closest to in the hierarchy of the CIA
was Dick Helms, who had initially recruited me for the
German station before the end of the war and whom I
replaced to some degree when he left Berlin in late 1945
to take over the East European desk of OSS and became
my "Washington boss." He moved up the chain of command quickly, and when I returned to Washington, he
was the deputy of Frank Wisner, being really in charge of
all OSO, the foreign intelligence branch, in the clandestine
services. Unlike his boss Frank Wisner, with whom he
worked well even if he often did not agree with some of
his operational decisions, he was an outstanding executive—well organized, able to handle an enormous amount

---

[4] Bissell, *Reflections of a Cold Warrior*, 79–80.

of problems and paper, and with a sharp mind that could make decisions, dictate clear instructions and reports, and understand instinctively the many problems that crossed his desk. He was urbane, having been educated partially at Le Rosey in Switzerland, an international school for the children of the world elites. He spoke French and German with a fair degree of fluency, had started his career in intelligence as an interrogator of captured German U-boat officers and men, and had then been recruited by OSS. Having been a wire service reporter before the war, he taught all of us what and how to report.

He was an outstanding tennis and golf player and a charming host and guest with a good sense of humor. Above all, he was a responsible intelligence officer, who never forgot the seriousness of the profession and the importance of saving the lives of those who were willing to spy for us. He shared with a number of us some reservations about the more aggressive parts of the action-oriented OPC. Whereas we (on the intelligence-collecting side) agreed with the support of radio stations and most front organizations to fight Soviet propaganda, we disapproved of most paramilitary and political action operations (undertaken by our political action/paramilitary operatives) because we felt that they were often counterproductive, insecure, and ill conceived.

But we were fighting an uphill battle against an administration and White House that wanted full engagement and the aforementioned policies of confrontation, as first articulated by Paul Nitze in 1950. Unfortunately, the "Cold War warriors" often did not take advantage of our experience to vet what they were doing. The Dick Helmses of this world do not make waves; his objections to specific operations were often ignored by both Wisner and Bissell, as well as Dulles. Bissell writes in his *Reflections* about the Bay of Pigs operation, "My deputy Richard Helms was not in favor of the operation, although he never expressed his opinion formally."[5]

Dick Helms showed courage, however, when he later became director of the CIA, by refusing to accommodate Nixon in the Watergate affair. He had a prestigious career after the CIA as ambassador to Iran, an appointment he received in part because he had gone to school in Switzerland with the shah. He was a close personal friend whom I saw periodically, including lunching with him in the new CIA building in Langley, Virginia.

Frank Wisner

The most complex senior official in the CIA, without any doubt, was Frank Wisner. Whereas all of us at the time were fully engaged and believed in our mission, Frank brought an additional degree of engagement, if not religious fervor, to his job. He had worked at the end of the war in Turkey and Romania and was involved in bringing out 1,700 airmen who had been shot down while bombing the oil fields in Romania during the war. He had then witnessed the Soviet takeover of Romania and helped the royal family escape. He had seen firsthand how the Soviets operated and how they took over a whole country. He

---

[5] Ibid., 177.

was to no small degree instrumental in the creation of OPC and was its first chief, before it was integrated into the CIA. Frank shared, with all the other senior officers, a great charm, a personal generosity, and a dynamic personality both in his job and in his social life. Although we were all appalled by the Soviet takeover of Eastern Europe and committed to preventing any extension of the Soviet Empire, Frank felt personally the pain of those who had to live under Soviet domination. This ultimately destroyed him, leading to his emotional deterioration and ultimate suicide. Frank may well have had bipolar disorder at a time when we knew little about that condition or how to treat it. Had it been known, he could have been treated, and a great tragedy could have been prevented. I knew Frank well and shared many professional decisions with him.

James Jesus Angleton

I would not do justice to a discussion of this team if I did not mention James Jesus Angleton. He was for a long time the counterespionage chief of the CIA and became a controversial figure. I knew him well, more socially than professionally. He was a brilliant man with considerable charm who handled, among other things, the relationship with the Israeli intelligence service. He had worked for OSS during the war and ended up in Rome, where he had spent part of his youth (his father owned the National Cash Register agency in Rome). He was involved after the war in helping to prevent a Communist takeover in Italy, before returning to Washington. Later in his career, he became a friend of Kim Philby and was devastated when Philby, a senior MI6 official who had been a liaison officer for MI6 in Washington, turned out to be a Soviet spy who had worked for the Soviets since before the war. Jim also got deeply involved in the case of a Soviet defector, whom he considered a plant. He became obsessed with finding a Soviet agent in the CIA and was instrumental in destroying the careers of two competent senior officers with his paranoia. Indeed, he was an extreme example of why a person should not serve too long in an intelligence agency, lest it destroy the person. Jim was admired as a brilliant head of counterespionage by some and considered totally mad by a number of his colleagues.

William Harvey

William Harvey, a highly intelligent and inventive operator, took over Berlin shortly after I left it. Unfortunately, he did not fit into the social web of senior officers, coming from a Midwestern background and service in the FBI, from which he had been fired for drunkenness. He was a brilliant chief of Berlin, but ultimately, alcohol destroyed him. He was smart enough to figure out that Kim Philby was a Soviet double agent, and he had the organizational ability to implement the Berlin Tunnel Operation, but when he was sent foolishly to Rome, he went to pieces. What made him suitable for the rough and tough environment of Berlin was exactly the wrong personality for the sophistication of a posting in Rome. In retrospect I am amazed that no one at the CIA at that time was conscious of the dangers of alcoholism, from which a number of the senior officers suffered. The CIA would have been fertile ground for Alcoholics Anonymous in the late 1950s.

William Casey

Though I had worked nominally under Bill Casey during the war, I knew him only slightly since I was in France working for the OSS detachment of the Seventh Army, and he was the nominal chief of foreign intelligence in London. He ultimately became the director of central intelligence in the Reagan administration, long after I had left the agency. I did know him, however, fairly well in the 1970s in New York, since he was a great friend of Henry Hyde, my immediate boss during the war. Bill Casey was another brilliant man, but he was consumed with paranoia about Communism and the Russians. This spelled trouble once he became the director, and on his watch there were certainly many operations that did more harm than good to the reputation of the CIA.

PART 3

*Being a Wine Merchant,
Wine Grower, and
Wine Personality*

CHAPTER TWENTY-FOUR

Back in the Wine Trade

Cuy, my first wife, was the daughter of a senior German businessman in China, whose own mother who, though German, had been brought up in England. Her father was quite old when she was born. She spent the first few years of her life in China and then moved to Germany in the late 1930s, when her father retired to a generous pension in Potsdam. Her parents did not participate in the Nazi craze; they lived an isolated private life and survived the Soviet takeover of East Germany with their house intact and a generous pension provided by one of the West German companies that survived the war. She was, in every way, part of the German postwar generation: a generation that tried to make up for the horrors and deprivations of war. She left her parents' house at the age of twenty-one, moved to West Berlin, and studied at the Art Academy (Hochschule für Bildende Künste), being a gifted painter and designer. She was part of the generation that spent long nights in bars and cafés, drinking and smoking and discussing the world. Getting a first-class education in painting, designing, and certain elements of commercial art, including dress design, she also designed scenery for plays and opera with considerable success. She combined a hunger for life, after the horrors of war, with a serious ambition to become a successful artist, be it as a painter or as a commercial artist.

I first made her acquaintance when she crashed my New Year's Eve party on December 31, 1950. As strange as it sounds, I had gained a reputation for throwing one of the better New Year's Eve parties in Berlin. My guest list included everyone I knew in Berlin: artists, lawyers, politicians, doctors, journalists, businessmen and women, and a very few members of the occupying forces, only my closest friends. There was also nary a member of my staff. I gave the party to get to know others and not for others to get to know my colleagues and me. There was the requisite amount of champagne, wine, and liquor and plenty of food. In that period of deprivation, champagne was an important element for a great party.

She crashed my party with a young escort, and many of my guests, particularly other artists, some of whom taught at the academy, knew her. She was beautiful, blond, and full of energy, and she quickly became the life of the party. It was a case of love at first sight. I was twenty-seven years of age and ready for a serious affair. Within a couple of months, we were lovers and inseparable. She spoke adequate English when we met and, in a very short time, learned to speak it well. She was popular among the people I knew and fit well into my social life, which was mainly among Germans.

I must have proposed to her within six months or so and applied to the CIA for permission to marry her. This was approved after a security check and resulted in my being transferred from Germany. We got married in Zurich. The day I married her, she said, "You should not marry me; I am not the marrying type: we should live together as long as we feel like it."

It turned out to be true. We went on our honeymoon to Sicily, which was as sunny as Berlin was gray when we left it. Our move to Washington was easy. We found a nice house in the district and made many friends, both among my colleagues and among the German diplomatic community. She fit in perfectly. She loved giving parties, was an excellent cook, and took her job as my wife seriously. Alas, she had a problem, or maybe we both had a problem. She had a lover three years after we married, a colleague of mine, which resulted in a big row between us. She decamped to a friend of mine in New York. We reconciled, and both thought the problem was solved. In due course we went to our posting in Hong Kong. In our third year there, she met a good-looking Englishman and had a far from private affair. That was the end: we decided to separate. It was toward the end of my assignment there. She decided to stay in Hong Kong, and I left the CIA and moved back to the States in 1959 to a new life in wine. We agreed that as long as we had no one else we wanted to marry, we would not get divorced. She got a job in the art department of an advertising firm in Hong Kong and continued to paint and sell her paintings.

I was devastated. At the age of thirty-seven, and after seven years of marriage, I could not visualize ever finding another wife or getting married again. Having lived with a highly entertaining and somewhat unpredictable, beautiful, popular woman, I felt extremely lonely, and only the challenge of a new profession kept me going. I was suffering from depression and decided that I had to do something about it. I found a Jungian therapist, enjoyed my sessions with him, and rather quickly got rid of my depression. He helped me to look at the world slightly differently; I stopped blaming others for what were plainly my shortcomings. This therapy helped me for the rest of my life.

In due course I met Stella, a Greek woman who had come to the States as a Fulbright scholar and then returned to Greece to marry and study law. She now had left her husband and returned to the States to work and be with her college friends. I met her at a cocktail party on Park Avenue. We became close friends because we shared a lot of common interests, such as music, theater, and literature. Not only that, but it turned out that our backgrounds came with a lot of the same customs, beliefs, and prejudices. The everyday culture of our lives was very similar, so that there were little if any points of annoyance. In due course we became lovers. I wrote Cuy that I wanted a divorce. Cuy took the next plane to New York and said that she wanted to come back as my wife.

It was complicated, but Stella persevered. It was a typical case of a woman who had made up her mind to marry a man and would let nothing stand in her way. It brought me to the realization that often women were the decision makers in marriages. This also made sense: they decided whom they wanted as father of their children. It was an eye-opener.

My marriage to Stella turned out to be everything a marriage should be. It has for more than fifty years provided warm and loving companionship, strong support both physical and mental, and sharing of burdens. Three loving, caring daughters and five grandchildren added to the feeling of belonging that only a family can provide. Stella became an integral part of the Sichel family, loved by all and loving to all in return. She has shown considerable diplomatic skills in often getting me to change my mind for my own good. We are lucky that we bonded without problems and that the bonds have lasted.

A little over two years into our marriage, my father-in-law died in Greece, and my mother-in-law came to visit us after our second daughter was born. She turned out to be an incredible person. Born on a large property near Smyrna, Turkey, in a Greek community, she had to move to Greece in the population exchange after World War I. She had lived through the brutal German occupation in World War II and had been able to feed her family and protect them. She was strong in mind and body, was generous to a fault, and had wisdom gained from living in a large family and on a large property as a child and from having survived the many challenges of being transplanted twice in her life. For me it was love at first sight, particularly since I had lost my mother at an early age. I suggested that she move in with us, which she did. She lived with us for over twenty years, initially going back to Athens to her apartment each summer. In old age, however, she stayed with us all year round or traveled with us to Greece in the summer. I dare say she was more important to and more loved by our children than we were. She certainly became the glue in our household, the ultimate proof that bringing up children in a three-generation environment gives all members a greater sense of belonging and security.

After Cuy, my first wife, and I divorced, we continued our friendship. Though she never lived in New York, I used to see her in San Francisco, where she was close to my cousins. She died, not yet sixty, in Hawaii and in her testament appointed me her executor, willing me all her paintings. It is as well to also mention here that she tried to get me to buy German expressionists, which were exceedingly cheap in Berlin after the war. Though I liked them, I could not figure out where to put them. Had I listened to her, I would be a very rich man today.

As mentioned in an earlier chapter, when I resigned from the CIA in 1959, I had a lot of accumulated leave. I arranged to take this accumulated leave to get myself updated in the Sichel German and French wine business. I flew from Hong Kong to Germany and spent two months in Mainz to find out what the Sichel German business was all about. I had grown up in the business, but though I had worked for a short time in Bordeaux in 1939 and 1940 as an apprentice, I had really no knowledge of the German part of the business. I had bought all my wines from the family business during my six years in Berlin and developed a taste for Rhine and Mosel wines.

I arrived in Mainz in early September 1959 and found a room in a hotel within five minutes' walking distance of the Sichel office. This was the newly rebuilt office building, in the same courtyard where the old office building had stood before American bombs destroyed it during the war. We had sold the bombed-out site to the local trade union, which had built an office building where the three family apartment houses had stood. They had given us a long-term lease for the courtyard, the office building, and the restored bottling plant as well as the old cellars. My cousin Walter, who had run the Sichel importing company in London since 1927, had survived the war by selling the large stock of wine the family had shipped to England prior to leaving Germany and by adding other products, such as a bottled scotch and soda, which he sold as Whiskoda.

He had also driven an ambulance at night during the Blitz and looked after many German-Jewish refugees who had made it to England and had difficulty finding jobs and shelter. He then traveled to Germany immediately after the war, was instrumental in getting the French occupation authorities to permit the export of wines, and organized, with the help of Artur Meier, the rebuilding of the old family business. (This was the same Artur Meier whom we found warming his feet in hot water in his mother's kitchen one cold winter evening in 1946, after having foraged for potatoes all day.) Artur had been a bright young man in the Mainz office in the mid-1930s but had left H. Sichel Söhne after the family left Germany, and the company was seized by the Nazis as retribution. He had resigned rather than work for the Nazis who had bought the company from the German state for less money than the value of the wines in the cellar. He had been conscripted and due to his fluency in French and English had been sent to Norway to intercept voice communications of British aircrews. He found his way home quickly after the end of the war, and after we hired him, he built up H. Sichel Söhne, having both the business training and the tasting experience. He assembled a staff of linguists who busily sent offers in the appropriate language and context to any potential wine importer in any country that imported wine and who were ready to fill the complex questionnaires and papers that were demanded by most importing countries. He hired a highly competent cellar crew and established excellent relations with wine growers and cooperatives, who were our sources for wine, which we largely blended. Fortunately, the Sichel importing companies in London and New York bought enough wine to keep the Mainz-based company afloat.

These first years were difficult: there was a shortage of everything and a high degree of bartering to get bottles, labels, corks, wooden cases, and all the additives needed to stabilize the wines. Then Artur had to reestablish relationships to brokers, wine growers, and cooperatives to enable him to buy the wines he needed. The business had been, before the war, increasingly in bottles and with an emphasis on export. Though there still was a large barrel business within Germany, this part of the business was less profitable and did nothing to spread the Sichel name. The local wine merchants who bought wine in barrels bottled and sold it under their own names.

Fortunately, the London and New York Sichel companies knew what they wanted and bought all their German wines from Sichel Mainz. By and large, they pre-tasted the wines before purchasing and helped the company blend to their specifications. They were also instrumental in building the price list for other markets and helped to secure the exclusive rights to prestigious estates. Charles Sichel, who ran H. Sichel Söhne Inc. in New York, an import and distribution company, and Walter, who ran H. Sichel & Sons Ltd., the London import company, were frequent visitors to Mainz. They quickly established relationships with the local authorities, the trade organizations, and the wine growers and brokers. Since no member of the family lived in Germany, Walter Sichel, my cousin, who charged himself with supervising the Mainz company, decided to concentrate on the export market, where we had a presence. There was a short attempt to import bulk white wine from Bordeaux, for which there was a large market in Germany after the war. It turned out to be far from profitable and a very difficult market.

It is as well to explain here the importance of blending in the wine business. A large number of wines that are sold are sold under geographical designations, and by law these designations delineate a certain area and impose restrictions as to grape varieties that can be planted and various other restrictions involved in the growing and making of wine. Wine merchants usually sell most of their wines under well-known geographic names, such as Liebfraumilch in Germany and Beaujolais, Pommard, Côtes du Rhône, and the like in France. These wines are blended from a multitude of bulk wines bought from growers and cooperatives, to a style and quality that each merchant considers its personal blend, very much like whiskey and cognac being a blend of various distillates of various ages and methods of aging. Blending is a great art; it involves not only taste, which often must predict the evolution of a blend in the bottle, but also price. The purpose is to field a wine that is recognized as good to excellent in its price category and that varies little from bottling to bottling and from year to year.

Upon joining the family company, I quickly learned the business side as well as the wine side of the business. I sat down with the people responsible for managing the relationships with specific markets, which I would be largely handling. This included initially the US market, as well as all markets in North and South America and the Caribbean. The man who handled these markets was a linguist who had held a senior position in the German code-breaking agency during the war. He was a researcher by nature and had accumulated background information on all the markets he supervised. It was obvious to me that his intelligence background was extremely useful.

On the wine side I put myself in the hands of Artur Meier, who introduced me to our main suppliers, which involved trips to the different wine-producing areas of the Rhine and Mosel. Since our mornings were usually spent in the office, with tasting sessions at eleven, just as in my father's generation, these trips usually took place in the afternoon. They involved tasting the wines of our suppliers in their cellars or offices and ended usually with beer and sausages and long conversations into the late afternoon or evening. The longer trips, to the Mosel particularly, usually involved our staying overnight rather than risking driving back after all the tasting and carousing. This was in fall. In later years I would take such trips in the winter, with icy conditions making the trips much more perilous.

I experienced the same embarrassing problems on some of these visits that I had experienced in Berlin after the war. People were anxious to tell me how well they had behaved during the Nazi period. I adopted the same policy I'd had in Berlin. The minute the subject came up, I made it plain that I did not want to hear about their behavior during the Nazi period. I pointed out that it involved their conscience, and if they had really behaved badly, they hopefully would have ended up in jail by now. This usually ended that conversation.

The tasting sessions, which by and large took place every working day between 11:00 a.m. and sometimes 1:30 p.m. or even later, were really the heart of the business. They broke down into segments: wines that were selected for purchase, wines that were blended, and wines that were tasted to see how they were developing either in cask (and later tank) or in bottle. All statistics and most records were kept on cards. The system we worked with went back generations: Long file drawers held cards recording total sales by wine, and other long file drawers recorded the blends that made up the different items being sold, their bottling, and their ultimate shipment. The records also included a short analysis of the wine, by alcohol, different acids, and most importantly, sulfur, a stabilizer, which was limited by law.

Our main business was selling regional wines, blended by us. Each new blend had to be as close to the former blend as possible. We wanted the consumer to buy the wine from year to year and experience the same taste as the last time he or she bought a bottle. We were able to achieve this fairly easily by blending wines from the same appellation, but often from different soils and even grape varieties. The wine also had to be within a certain price range, so that sometimes, blending decisions were also driven by consideration of price.

In spite of that, quality was never compromised, though we might have delayed our decision and asked our brokers to bring additional wines to taste. Artur was a superb taster, in spite of being a chain smoker and having to leave the tasting room from time to time to have a smoke. He also was a first-class bargainer, often calling a wine producer from the tasting room to lower the price of a wine that fit our requirements but proved to be too expensive. He was a man in his element and ultimately trained a whole generation of tasters. Above all he fully enjoyed what he was doing, was patient, and never hurried a decision.

My cousin Walter and I decided, shortly after Artur had become the managing director of our little company, to give him 10 percent of the shareholding of the company.

Since neither of us wanted to return to Germany to live, we wanted a manager who took an owner's interest. It was the smartest decision we ever made. When Artur Meier retired with a good pension and a payout of over a million marks in the late 1970s, he was a respected member of the industry who had given us, the Sichels, who marketed and sold the wines, the solid quality supply without which we never would have prospered. Unfortunately, Artur did not want to deal with computers and all the modern gadgets without which we never would have been able to grow the way we did. The world had changed; no longer could we keep stock sheets by hand and have a total oversight of the business.

I also used the two months in Mainz to get to know the main wine brokers who were so essential to our business. Each one specialized in a limited area of production, where he knew all the main growers and cooperatives and could supply us with hundreds of samples. In due course we would end up buying from the same growers and established strong personal ties to be able to influence their winemaking. I also got acquainted with the various associations in the German wine industry: the Export Association, the promotional boards, and the various growers' associations. I met with our suppliers for corks, glass, and the other various supplies we needed and depended on. The company was in the old location where it had been since the middle of the nineteenth century, including the extensive cellars, with lifts bringing the barrels and bottles to the courtyard. From there the wines went to the bottling plant and packing hall; trucks went in with barrels or tanks of wine and came out with cased goods or barrels.

In 1959 our Mainz company shipped 10,359 cases of twelve bottles of wine (a measure known as nine-liter case shipments in industry jargon—that is, twelve 750 milliliter bottles equals nine liters) to the United States and 14,761 nine-liter cases to the rest of the world. In addition the company shipped bulk wines to England, probably the equivalent to 20,000 nine-liter cases. There was a price advantage to bottling wines in England, though it reduced the profit of the German company.

I left Mainz after about five weeks, with a feeling that I had learned the basics of our business and had established some presence in the wine industry in Germany. I also had taken up social contact with a number of families in the Mainz region, which gave me some feel for the society where I was to spend a considerable amount of time during the next forty years. My next stop was Bordeaux, to learn the other half of our business. I had not been in Bordeaux since I had left it in a hurry in 1940.

When I arrived in Bordeaux, my cousin Walter met me to show me the ropes. My personal ties to this part of France were closer at that date than my ties to Germany. I was a mere twelve years old when I left Mainz, and my memories were of strife and persecution. Bordeaux, on the other hand, brought back memories of initial safety and new personal friendships, which survived the war and exist to this day. Though I had not visited Bordeaux since 1940, my personal ties were quickly reestablished, and I had a comfort level there, where I did not have to endlessly ask myself what a particular German had done or not done during the Nazi period.

Our Bordeaux presence, however, was even smaller than our German presence. The family had had a *négoce*, also called négociant éléveur (best translated as a trading house that aged and finished wines), since the latter part of the nineteenth century, called Sichel & Co., which had supplied mainly Bordeaux, Burgundy, and Rhône wines to the German, English, and American companies but which also had dabbled in sales to other countries, following the path of the German company. The original Bordeaux-based Sichel & Company was lost by the German partners when the Allies confiscated their ownership after World War I. Unfortunately, pride and some bad behavior prevented the reestablishment of the old partnership, so that the German company established another company under the name of Sichel & Fils Frères in 1929. That company had its cellars and offices in Rue Balguerie Stuttenberg, not very far from my British cousin's office of Sichel & Co. on the Quai de Bacalan, the original location where it was established at the latter part of the nineteenth century.

When I returned in 1959, I found the same chief clerk, Madame Andicourt, running the office. We had said a tearful good-bye to her when we precipitously left Bordeaux in the summer of 1940. She was an extraordinary woman, married to a black bank employee, with a wonderful son who became a pharmacist. Whereas my father had been the manager in the 1930s, the manager in charge in 1959 was a Monsieur Roquebert, who was an excellent business manager, aided by an excellent cellar master, a Monsieur Tardieu, who took care of the wine side. It took me little time to get settled. I once more found a room, this time in the best hotel in Bordeaux, the Hotel Splendid. I rented a room on a long-term basis on the top floor, where rooms had been occupied in the past by domestic servants and had been converted into small rooms with a shower instead of a bath. Seemingly, no one wanted showers, so the rent was low and included an excellent continental breakfast. There was one other fringe benefit. The hotel had a superb list of old Burgundies, which no one ever ordered: this was Bordeaux, and the guests of the hotel drank Bordeaux wines, which were represented by an equally great list, alas at market prices and not discounted to lighten the inventory.

The work I did in Bordeaux was very similar to the work I had done in Mainz, except this time I was concerned with the multitude of Bordeaux and other regional appellations. Similar to the process in Mainz, we bought most of our wines in bulk and blended and bottled them. We also bought chateau-bottled Bordeaux as advantageously as we could, a complicated game. Due to our comparatively small business, we did not qualify to buy these wines at the opening prices; instead, we were forced either to buy them through merchants that could buy them at the opening or to take advantage of a second offering, at higher prices, from the chateaus. These top Bordeaux chateau-sourced wines—so-called *grands crus* or great growths—are classed in five levels of ascending quality following the famous 1855 classification, and the chateaus offer their wines in limited quantities to a limited number of wine merchants, known as *négociants*, about six months after the harvest, for delivery about two years later in bottle. The merchants either resell these "futures" or hang on to them. The same chateau may well offer the same wines a little later at increased prices. At that time, not being able to obtain wines at "first offering" did not pose a particular problem because Bordeaux was still in deep crisis, and great wines were available in old and great vintages from these famous *premier grand cru châteaux* at what must seem today ridiculously low prices. Properties were for sale at equally depressed prices, and most properties needed considerable investments to once more make world-class wines.

The main business we had at the time was regional Bordeaux, Burgundy, and Rhône wines, bottled under the Sichel label, as well as Bourgeois and classified growth wines, which we bought mainly from the properties. At the time, unlike today, the properties, including classified chateaux, had great difficulties selling their entire crops yearly and had a rather large inventory of current and older vintages. These were sold at comparatively low prices.

We also handled a certain number of fine Burgundies either under the Sichel label or under the label of the estate from which we bought them. Again, as in Mainz, we had tasting sessions in Bordeaux, often tasting along with executives from our British company who were there to make their purchases. In due course we also visited Beaune in Burgundy and bought wines in bulk and bottle, both for Bordeaux and for London. This was an interesting exercise because England at that time did not respect the *appellation d'origine contrôlée* (AOC) laws of France. These AOC codes had been recently enacted to control and ensure quality wine production on a region-by-region basis. This offered an excellent opportunity: when we decided, for instance, to buy a Pommard, we had the option of buying it either with the appellation we needed for most of our export markets or simply as a non-appellation wine, which would be shipped to England and baptized with its proper name once there. The advantage of price was considerable, and obviously, the merchant could take advantage by baptizing lesser wine with a more prestigious name. If we had a bad vintage, blending wine from the Côtes du Rhône or Algeria would improve the wine considerably. Of course, all this disappeared with the European Common Market, which was established on January 1, 1959, but Great Britain did not immediately recognize the French regulations, and for a while you could buy excellent Burgundies in England at wonderfully low prices.

The region of Bordeaux has roughly the same acreage in vines as Germany, producing an endless variety of wines, both white and red as well as rosé, or as the Bordelais call them, "clairet." Clairet is the origin of the English word "claret," by which word the English identify all red Bordeaux. In addition a good deal of delicious sweet wine is grown in Bordeaux, under such appellations as Sauternes and Barsac.

The city of Bordeaux has been cleaned up and modernized under a series of extraordinary mayors who held high positions in government. French politics enables politicians to be both a mayor of a major city and a minister in the current national government. The city is beautiful, with impressive buildings along the river, beautiful churches, and old patrician residences as well as pretty squares and streets. It is a bustling, busy city with not only the wine industry but also other industries contributing to its successful life.

It was pleasant to find myself once more in Bordeaux. I found old friends from before the war, such as our doctor Otto Hirsch and his wife, who had been so courageous in smuggling my sister out of occupied France in 1940. I quickly made new friends, got to know my British cousins, and set the basis for what would become in time a close relationship to the wine trade and the chateau owners of Bordeaux. I had not forgotten my French in all these years, and I took up once more my interest in French literature and theater.

The two months of "education" in Bordeaux went quickly, and I finally returned to the United States in December, in time to start my six months of familiarization with our import company in New York, H. Sichel Sons Inc., prior to taking it over on June 30, 1960. I had not lived in the United States since 1956 and had not lived in New York since 1942. But I had no problem settling in New York, where I had many family members with whom I had kept up all these years. I also had a number of friends, some of whom had been with me in CIA. I made new friends associated with my business and quickly became acquainted with the movers and shakers in the wine world in New York. I was greatly aided by Uncle Charles, who was quite the man around town.

I was blessed by timing in my return to New York because 1959 turned out to be an extremely hot year, even by today's standards, and was recognized immediately as a great vintage year in almost all European wine-grower districts. Since the last fairly good vintage had been 1955, there was a great deal of press coverage and excitement among the wine-drinking public. For the first time the vintage made the headlines of the daily press, and in one way or another, this helped to raise interest in wine. Consumption was extremely low in the United States, and would continue to be for another twenty-plus years, but a certain segment of the population discovered wine in the 1960s.

CHAPTER TWENTY-FIVE

The Quirky Wine Business

Though I grew up in the wine business, both in Germany and in France, I did not really get involved in it until I joined the family business at age thirty-seven, as the president of a small family import company, H. Sichel Söhne Inc., in New York. This company was established in the late 1930s, to keep the name of Sichel alive on wine bottles and to enable the Sichel cousins, who had to flee first Germany and then Europe, to earn a living. The fact that I had inherited some shares from my father in the British import company, which owned the New York company, and that I was part owner of the Mainz Sichel company when the German authorities returned it to us made this transition easy.

My early youth was spent living in the world of wine. We would regularly visit the family vineyards and winery in Nierstein, where not only grapes of our own vineyards were pressed, fermented, and turned into wine, but also grapes we bought from other vineyard owners, who did not have the state-of-the-art winery we had. Each fall, large baskets of prunes would be delivered to our back door, the harvest from the trees in our vineyards, which were turned into jams and many glass jars of preserved fruit. For lunches we frequently entertained customers from the four corners of the world for lunch, as well as growers from whom we bought wine, either in bulk or in bottle. I learned a lot of the business, just seeing and listening. In 1929, during a general strike, I worked in the packing hall, wrapping bottles of wine into white tissue paper. We continued this practice until I joined the business in 1960 and told our German winery to discontinue it, without telling our customers. Our customers never complained; they might not even have noticed.

Today wine from many countries is sold on a worldwide basis. The quality, by and large, is better, at every level of the market, than it has ever been before. Winemaking, from grape growing to pressing the grapes and making wine to blending and bottling, has improved tremendously during the last forty years. Varieties are married to the proper soil, fermentation takes place under controlled conditions with the proper yeasts, and wines are aged in various selected containers in ideal temperatures and bottled at the right time. As in the past, there are two distinct markets: daily wines, which are often sold under either a brand name or a varietal designation, with the bottler prominently identified, and "fine" or "luxury wines," which come from estates with limited production and enjoy consumer recognition. With the international explosion of wine consumption, these latter wines have often become real luxury products, claiming very fancy prices.

Whereas world wine consumption has not increased markedly in the last few years, it has shifted from the traditional wine-consuming countries of France, Italy, Spain, Portugal, and Argentina to new markets, such as China. In spite of low per capita consumption, China, by the very size of its population, takes an increasing amount of wine. As of 2011, 50 percent of all wine consumed worldwide is consumed in France, the United States, Italy, Germany, and China.

The wine business has changed dramatically since my great-grandfather incorporated the family company in 1857, and yet, in some ways it is still the same. It is still a business in which strong personalities, with clear ideas about what wine they want to make and how to sell it, dominate the market. It might have changed from a business that supplied the elite to one that supplies a broad segment of the consuming population. It might have changed from a hand-selling trade to a modern marketing of a consumer product. It certainly has grown and diversified. A hundred years ago, wine was, in many countries and regions, a local product consumed by the local population. Back then, the main consumers lived right in the regions where the grapes grew and the wine was made. A small part of the business was selling to the elite in countries where wine did not grow, or in wine-producing countries where certain flavors could not be grown, such as Bordeaux-style wines in Germany.

As of 2011, 60 percent of world wine production took place in France, Italy, Spain, and the United States, and another, almost 16 percent, in Argentina, Australia, Chile, and Germany. Because of fashion, some wines are in short supply, and others, equally good, are plentiful. All this is reflected in the price at which the wines sell. Whereas quality has something to do with price, fashion in some cases is even more important. I used to worry, when I was apprenticed, that we would run out of certain types of wine. My father reassured me that "no wine merchant ever went out of business for lack of wine."

One of the early problems of the wine trade was transporting barrels from wine-production areas to wine-consuming markets. Most wine was sold in barrels until the twentieth century, to merchants who bottled the wine for local consumption. Only a small portion of superior wine was shipped in bottles, and even that only in the last one hundred years or so. Because of this problem of weight and bulk, most of the wine merchants were located either near Atlantic ports or near rivers. "Water transport" was essential before the steam engine. With steamships and railroads, the wine trade changed dramatically, enabling sales to just about anywhere where people fancied wine.

Initially, several distinct areas of production were familiar to wine consumers in Europe, Russia, and America: Bordeaux, Burgundy, Rhine and Mosel, Chianti, Rioja, and sherry, port, and champagne. Since initially, in non-wine-producing areas, wine was consumed by the elite, it took some time before other areas became known and popular. Traditionally, the wine-producing countries put little or no restrictions on the sale of wine. They also leveled little if any taxes on wine. This was not so in nonproducing markets, where high taxes and restrictions were common—and still are even to this day. Some of these taxes have been imposed as a tax on luxury products, though most have been so-called sin taxes, intended both to increase revenue and to limit consumption. In some countries, and in some states of the United States, the government has insisted on handling the sale of wine, restricting the number of wines offered and discouraging their consumption. Other countries have prohibited the sale, such as the United States during Prohibition, though the latter still allowed "home production" for political reasons, largely to placate the ethnic vote.

There has always been a complicated set of rules, outside of the old-world wine-producing countries, restricting the shipment and sale of wines, requiring a lot of paperwork to move wine from the area of production to the final consumer. Whereas wine has been always regarded as a food item in the producer countries, in other countries it was regarded as an alcoholic beverage, the sale of which should be restricted. Only slowly is this prejudice disappearing.

From as early as the eighteenth century, the enterprising Hanseatic league of traders, as well as the Irish and British merchants, not only brought wines from producing countries to their home markets but also established their own houses in Bordeaux, Oporto, Jerez, and other places. They then set out to sell their wines wherever a market could be found.

Between 1871 and World War I, commerce prospered, and there were very few restrictions either on travel or on trade. My grandfather and his two brothers not only established a growing business in Germany but also learned languages and traveled widely to sell their wine. By the end of the century, they had established houses in Bordeaux, London, and New York, all run by relatives. They built a worldwide business, sending a salesman twice a year to all major markets in South America and traveling widely in Scandinavia and Russia. World War I destroyed that business, and it had to be totally rebuilt after 1918. World War II posed similar challenges. Trade prospers only in peace.

The US wine market has always been a complex one. Repeal of nationwide Prohibition was possible only because each state was given the authority to impose its own laws and regulations on the sale of alcoholic beverages within its borders. So following repeal in 1933, some of the states and many counties within states remained "dry," prohibiting the sale of any alcoholic beverage. Others restricted the sale to state monopolies, such as Pennsylvania, and some authorized the sale only in wine and liquor specialty stores or limited the sale to one licensee. It is too complicated to enumerate all the difficulties imposed on the wine trade.

Until the 1970s, most Americans did not drink table wine, which is usually drunk with food; the strength of table wine is between 10 percent and 14 percent alcohol. Until 1970 more fortified wine was consumed in the United States than table wine; fortified wine is usually 18 percent to 19 percent alcohol, such as sherry and port or flavored fortified wine brands such as Thunderbird or Richards Wild Irish Rose. These brands often were the cheapest way to get a buzz. In 1970 the per capita consumption of wine per year in the United States was 1.31 gallons, and almost 50 percent was fortified wine; in other words the per capita consumption of table wine was around 0.66 gallons, which is about 3.3 750-milliliter bottles per capita. Things have changed a lot, however, since 1970. As of 2011, roughly 30 percent of the US population drank wine sometimes, another 37 percent drank beer and spirits, and about a third of the US population did not drink any alcoholic beverages.

The per capita consumption in America as of 2011 was around fourteen bottles a year; in comparison, the French consumption at this time was more than seventy bottles a year, and the Italian consumption was only a little less. In other words, although America consumes close to 12 percent of all wine produced worldwide, our relative per capita consumption is still quite small compared to world leaders such as France and Italy. For all the changes and increases in US consumption habits, you still cannot call America a wine-consuming country when only slightly less than 16 percent of the population drinks wine with some regularity: at least once a week. Obviously, wine drinking has a lot to do with lifestyle, and when you are in the wine business, you are really in the lifestyle business.

The wine business is in some ways different from other businesses. It offers enormous variety: it is agriculture and science (both botany and chemistry), it requires the ability to taste and distinguish flavors, and it involves marketing and sales and ultimately an ability to run a business that makes money, and in that latter way, it is no different from any other consumer product business. Since growing grapes and making wine depends on the ability of individuals to produce in many instances products different from their neighbors' products, the industry is replete with strong and colorful individuals. There is also a strong element of collegiality among people in the wine business, on both the production and selling sides. There is a willingness to share experiences and be helpful when technical problems arise. Ultimately, everyone in the wine business is interested in producing as good a product as he or she can. It takes money to produce good wine and a good deal more to produce great wine, though not as much as the price demanded for great wine might indicate.

CHAPTER TWENTY-SIX

My First Important Decisions as US Director

I arrived in the States in early December 1959 and went to Washington to go through the formalities of resigning from the CIA, with the appropriate lunches and dinners with old friends. I arrived in New York shortly before Christmas and moved into the Roosevelt Hotel, which was a couple of blocks from the H. Sichel Sons Inc. offices at 342 Madison Avenue. I stayed in the hotel only a couple of weeks, having found a lovely apartment at 35 West Eighty-First Street, overlooking the Museum of Natural History.

I was fortunate to have both family and friends in New York. The family members were, on one side, the three surviving sisters of my mother and my sister Ruth. On the other side were those members of my family who were involved in the wine business, either the one I was about to join or Fromm & Sichel. This latter company, Uncle Franz had created when the family business was not large enough during the war to provide a livelihood for all the members of the family.

Uncle Charles ran the family business in New York. He was in his midseventies, had remarried in 1952, and was anxious to retire. He and his brother Franz had decided not to invest in the German business when it was returned to us after the war and had taken out their money. Nevertheless, he and Franz had been partners in the British business, which owned H. Sichel Söhne Inc. Having lived in England for many years before the war, Charles had acquired British citizenship and moved to the United States during the war. He was a lady's man, a man of great charm, and a great wine expert and superb salesman. He and Franz had also taken out their money from the British business after the war, and part of the agreement left Charles as the CEO of the New York import company. We agreed that I should work for six months with Charles to learn the business and then take over as the CEO on July 1, 1960.

I had no idea about the workings of the office, of the wine market, or of who did what. The only thing I knew after my months in Germany and Bordeaux was the type of German and French wines our company sold and the quantity. I also knew that besides German and French wines, we sold port and sherries, as well as some Chilean wines. These additions to the traditional Sichel wines had been added during the war to keep the company afloat. I also knew that the company made a profit every year. I must admit that I was confident that I could master the business and make a good living from it. I was not in the least afraid of jumping into a new life and business and was confident that I could learn it and succeed in it.

I started working on Monday, January 4, 1960, reporting for work at 342 Madison Avenue. I spent my first couple of days with Uncle Charles to get briefed on what the business was all about. I learned a lot in a relatively short time. The business was located in about three or four rooms in a nice office building near Forty-Third Street, close to Grand Central in the heart of Manhattan. There were eight to ten employees, including an administrative office manager, a trilingual secretary, two young women who handled all the complex reporting and licensing details needed in the wine and liquor trade, and three salesmen.

Uncle Charles was still the key salesman, selling to the best restaurants and top wine stores in New York. Another salesman was Herbert Weiss, who had worked in Mainz for Sichel before he immigrated to the United States. Herb had then worked for Sichel New York before going into the army and rejoined after the war. He ran the business when Uncle Charles was not in New York. The other salesman was a young Frenchman. These salesmen, including Charles, not only sold wine in New York but also visited other important US markets, selling to top stores and restaurants.

Our New York import company had both an import and a wholesale license. (Then as now, federal and state alcoholic beverage regulations mandated a three-tier sales system as follows: the wine, spirits, or beer producer or importer is known as the "first tier" in this arrangement, the wholesaler or distributor is strategically poised at the so-called second tier, and the retail liquor store or restaurant owner composes the third tier.) The wholesale license permitted our company to sell our wines to wine stores and restaurants in New York. Because we possessed the import license, we also were allowed to try to sell wines in whichever states it was worthwhile for our salesmen to visit. These sales, however, had to be handled through a local wholesaler (at the second tier!) and often required complicated applications for licenses and registration of labels within each state's jurisdiction. All these state and local regulations came on top of a complicated federal licensing and registration procedure. In our office alone, two women were kept busy doing this, and this work included often some additional reporting.

The wines were stored in a public warehouse, from which truck drivers loaded and delivered to shops and restaurants in New York or arranged shipments to our network out-of-state wholesalers. The New York office had almost two hundred separate items (known in the trade as stock keeping units, SKUs) that we were selling: about 40 German wines and 160 French. A lot of wines were prestigious labels in several vintages and often in several sizes, such as half bottles, the standard 750-milliliter bottles, and magnums, the latter containing the volume of two 750-milliliter bottles. Whereas the German wines were bought from our German company, a lot of the finer French wines, such as top Burgundies and Bordeaux, were bought from a multitude of sources, such as Bordeaux and Burgundy global wine-trading firms, known collectively as *négociants*, including our own Bordeaux-based family-run firm, Sichel & Fils Frères, as well as Burgundy Estates.

Uncle Charles would spend a couple of months in Europe during the summer and spend part of that time visiting Burgundy, Beaujolais, Bordeaux, and Germany. He would taste the wines that the German and French companies were going to sell him, often getting involved in blending some of them and haggling over the price. He also would buy fine chateau-bottled Bordeaux and top Burgundies. The latter would be bought from estates and wine companies and sold under the Sichel label. I ultimately would follow his example, though I would not haggle, being a partner in both the Sichel European houses and seeing no reason that they should not make the markup they needed in order to exist.

Uncle Charles briefed me thoroughly on the market and told me that if I wanted to be successful, I had to become a star salesman. He also explained how wines were sold in the New York market. He described to me a complex set of payoffs and illegal deals to bypass, on one hand, the New York liquor laws and to pay off, on the other hand, sommeliers, wine buyers, and whomever. There were also bribes, of one sort or another, to officials. These might be in free goods of fine wines rather than cash. Whatever the terms of such underhanded dealings, this was and is known to this day as the "vig" or vigorish, a Yiddish expression meaning "the take" or a payoff.

At the same time that Uncle Charles was briefing me, he took me to the finest restaurants in New York, where some of these shenanigans took place. Some of these "payoffs" consisted in buying back corks of wine bottles from sommeliers, thereby assuring that the wines were being consumed, resulting in reorders. After being informed about all these illegal payments by Uncle Charles, I decided to have a confidential conversation with both the company lawyer and our accountant. It was clear to me that the system sooner or later would lead to trouble. I also knew that this was not the kind of "business practice" I could or would want to get involved in. Obviously, creating money for the payoffs also involved phony expense accounts, which sooner or later would lead to problems with the IRS.

While I was getting acquainted with the sordid details of the New York and other markets, which were no better, I started to analyze our business. I found excellent sales statistics. I found that many items in stock hardly ever sold, and some items sold mainly to the staff. Though there was a good stock of sherry and ports, their sale was mainly to the staff. I immediately lowered their price and eliminated them from our offering. We had the same problems with Chilean wines. Chile offered inexpensive wines during the war, but once European wines were available, their sales collapsed. The Chilean wines came with another problem. The cases in which they were shipped had half the bottles standing up and half the bottles upside down. Because of the slow sales, half the bottles spoiled because standing up dried the cork and let in air. I closed them out as well. Both Charles and the staff objected, but to no avail.

After my conference with the lawyer and accountant, I also became concerned that it was going to be my duty to sign the tax return for 1960, and there was no way I wanted to do so unless I was the CEO for the whole year. I informed Charles, shortly after I became acquainted with the illegal activities, that I would take over immediately as president and CEO of the company. I continued his salary until June 30 and gave him an increase for the six months and told him that the company would no longer pay for his expenses. He would have to report his expenses on his tax return. After I did all of this, Charles was convinced that I would ruin the business, but he cared little since it was not his to lose.

One morning in June, after I had started worrying about the future, I called my secretary Ruth and informed her that I was going to Jones Beach for a day or two to think and would return once I had decided on the future of the company. It was a brilliant summer day; I spent most of the day walking the beach, took a dip in the frigid ocean, and returned to New York having made up my mind about the future.

I knew the resources we had in France and Germany, as well as the limited resources in the United States. It made no sense to me to have the family act as importer and distributor in the United States. We lacked the resources to engage enough salesmen, let alone to spend money on advertising and promotion. In addition, if we were successful, we would need additional money in

Europe to grow our production facilities. I also thought it was inefficient to sell just French and German wines: we knew that selling in other states was possible only by selling large accounts and then finding a distributor to handle the wines. The distributor rarely bought more than we presold. We had no ongoing business with the distributor, who saw no reason to stock our wines. He was content to make a profit from our presold orders but would have difficulties with his other suppliers if he added wines from an unknown importer. It took me no time to figure out that what we needed was a successful importer, with a national distribution network, where our wines would supplement the importer's offerings. So my task was to find an importer that had a full line but lacked German and French wines.

Having made up my mind, I notified my partner Walter Sichel and told him that I would start looking for an importer, and when I had found one, I would like him to come over to New York and help negotiate a contract. I also advised Charles, whom I had retained as a salesman and consultant. I was anxious to preserve what business we had before passing it on. Charles thought my idea excellent and was more than helpful. He must have realized that I was not made to deal with a corrupt market. He briefed me on potential partners and introduced me to the main players. Charles had joined most of the wine and food societies, including the Confrérie des Chevalier du Tastevin, the Burgundy wine society. Charles knew his way around the trade, and he was a charming old-world roué, a man who enjoyed fine food and good company and had an eye for beautiful women. He considered himself a merchant prince, a man who had rubbed shoulders with the British aristocracy and had sent Churchill every Christmas a couple of bottles of Trockenbeerenauslese, one of the rarest and most sought-after late-harvest dessert wines from Germany. He had also inherited the title of Guatemalan consul from his father, which made him feel the equal or superior of anybody.

I investigated three potential prospects and decided that the one I liked best was an old family company by the name of Schieffelin & Company in New York. Schieffelin had been in the pharmaceutical business for generations. During Prohibition, the company had taken on Hennessy cognac, which could be legally sold on prescription. After repeal they hired a government enforcement agent, Tex Bomba, to build a liquor import portfolio around Hennessy. When I interviewed them, they were handling, in addition to Hennessy, Moët & Chandon champagne, Teachers scotch, Wray and Nephews Jamaican rum, Don Q Puerto Rican rum, and Ruffino and Folonari Italian wines.

The great advantage to me was the fact that it was a family company, not a large liquor distiller. Best of all, Schieffelin's general manager of its wine and liquor division, Tex Bomba, was the kind of person I could work with. As the name implies, he was a Texan, with considerable charm. By the time I met him, he was a well-versed wine and liquor executive who had lived in the New York area for many years and had a large circle of friends both in the business and in New York society. The fact that he could donate champagne, wine, and liquor to charity functions made him very popular in the social whirl. In addition he was sophisticated, and in due course he became a good friend.

Schieffelin's other division, beyond the wine and liquor division managed by Tex, was the pharmaceutical side. Both divisions made their home at 30 Cooper Square, where the company owned a building that was used for offices and some warehousing. I was introduced to the family members who ran the company, Captain William Schieffelin and his son, also William, known as Bill. Bill was my age; he had been a classmate of a close friend of mine at Groton and had gone from there to Yale. He was descended from President Rutherford Hayes and had served as an officer in the Far East during the war, after which he had joined the family business, first running the pharmaceutical business and ultimately replacing his father in 1962 as chairman of the company. Bill was a good-looking member of New York society, attractive and charming; alas, he was a chain smoker and heavy drinker. He also did not fit into the rough world of the wine and spirits trade. But he certainly was the kind of classy individual who could interact with the owners of his supply companies, who were true princes of commerce. He left the running of the business to Tex, and Tex hired the kind of executives who could operate in the rough-and-tumble of the wine and liquor trade.

We negotiated a contract, making Schieffelin the sole importer of Sichel French and German wines and setting realistic sales goals. Though Schieffelin was willing to take over our stock, they insisted on reducing the items they would buy in future, since there was no way that their organization could handle two hundred items. I fully agreed with their demand, since I was convinced that only a small concentrated portfolio had any hope of success. We initially scaled down the combined line to twenty-six items and would continue to refine and reduce it in the years to come. We signed a contract in November 1960 and set the date for transfer of stock and their takeover of sales and marketing for February 1, 1961.

We agreed that they would hire some of the key people of Sichel, including all the salespeople and the operating officer, who were familiar with the past history and the various permits and licenses. I continued H. Sichel Söhne Inc., retaining my trilingual secretary, and was provided offices at 30 Cooper Square by Schieffelin. I was to be the "suppliers' representative," helping to market and sell the wines. Being an owner and having my name on the label offered considerable advantages. The Schieffelins invited me to their Christmas party for their staff at 30 Cooper Square, and I made the acquaintance of the entire New York staff, from clerks to officers of the company. The executives acted as barmen; the staff were the invited guests.

I spent considerable time building the price list before the takeover, and I put all our emphasis on Blue Nun Liebfraumilch. By 1960 Blue Nun was by far the largest-selling single item in our portfolio, and we had started to spend a little money advertising Blue Nun in England. It was also the only item that sold outside the New York market.

CHAPTER TWENTY-SEVEN

Becoming a Wine Personality

Once I had settled into the Schieffelin offices and had a chance to see the operation, it became clear to me that the Schieffelins did not operate any differently than we had at H. Sichel Sons. They were just as involved in the shady side of the business as our little company had been. The only difference was that the officers of the company, such as Bill Schieffelin and Tex Bomba, did not get their hands dirty. They left the "dirty" part of the business to the sales executives, a band of highly successful salesmen with long experience in the rough-and-tumble of the wine and liquor trade. They were no more corrupt than their colleagues in other large distribution and marketing companies; it just happened to be the custom of the trade. The gentlemen who owned or ran the overall businesses pretended not to know what was going on, until ultimately the state decided to clean up the market in the mid-1980s, and then all major companies paid heavy fines, in the millions, to safeguard their licenses and keep out of jail. Looking the other way was certainly no defense, and I was glad that I had decided not to get involved in something that I both knew I could not do and was convinced would lead sooner or later to trouble with the government.

I realized that there were people much more gifted than I in selling and marketing wine. One thing I had learned during my years in intelligence was to know what I was good at and to know what were my weak points. I had also developed over the years a keen understanding of who was more intelligent and able than I was, and I often sought out people who were better than I to work for me. I had learned to build a team that could work together and also learned to diplomatically deal with other agencies and services.

It was therefore not complicated for me to figure out how exactly I would interact with Schieffelin and the general market to promote and grow the market for Sichel wines. I was lucky that I started in the US market just as it started to become wine-conscious and that the marketplace was receptive to listening to wine personalities. By this time, two notable wine importers, Frank Schoonmaker and Alexis Lichine, had become the prophets of the wine world, and I decided that I would try to emulate them to some extent. I had some advantages over them: I was younger, my family had been in the wine business for four generations, and I was not busily traveling the world to sell wine; I had delegated that job in every country of the world or had other members of the family busily engaged in it.

I knew that I could not separate myself completely from the business of selling and promoting, so I had to devise ways of doing so where my time was spent most productively: in addressing distributor meetings and working a limited time with top salesmen, preferably in top accounts. My main functions in the wine business were interacting with the sales and marketing staff of Schieffelin to come up with ideas for marketing and promotion and working with them on product and brand development, as well as making myself available for public relations exploitation. I ultimately ended up traveling to Asia, Australia, and New Zealand, as well as all major markets in the Americas, to implement, more or less, what I had done in the United States.

On the marketing and sales side we were blessed with one of the most creative and unconventional people I have ever met, J. Penniston "Penn" Kavanagh, who started out as an assistant advertising manager at Schieffelin in 1966 and ended up being the president of the company in 1981, after the company was sold to Moët Hennessy, the French champagne and cognac global marketer. I think it is safe to say that you are most successful when you enjoy what you are doing and when you feel the creative juices flowing. Another element is the joy of working with people who are on the same wavelength and who inspire you to do your best. It was that combination that made working with Penn Kavanagh and his staff on making Blue Nun a winning brand an exciting time of my life.

Though most of the work was on selling and promoting Blue Nun, we made many attempts to create other brands, some with success, others with no success at all. For example, we created a rosé from the Loire, calling the wine Amourose, with a modicum of success. I personally created a wine to go with Chinese food, which I called, with the help of Chinese friends, Wan Fu (meaning ten thousand happinesses). I found a Chinese artist who created the label, and I blended the wine in Bordeaux to be slightly sweet, since most Chinese dishes have a pinch of sugar. We launched it in New York, giving out fortune cookies with the message "To eat Chinese without Wan Fu is to eat but with one chopstick." The wine had some success and is still in some markets. To try to animate the market for a reasonably priced red Bordeaux wine, we created My Cousin's Claret, a good, basic Bordeaux, which had a message on the label from my cousin Peter in Bordeaux, telling me that the wine had been specially selected and bottled for me. This was not a success. And finally, we created a premixed mulled wine under the brand name of Après Ski. I am afraid it was a complete failure, but fortunately, we had limited its distribution to the ski areas of the country. I guess flavored wines were not successful at that time, and we should have known it from our failure to sell much May wine.

I joined most wine societies, including the Commanderie de Bordeaux, where I became the *maître* (head cook and bottle washer!) in New York for a long period and where I am still active today. I also joined the Society of Wine Educators and was its president for a couple of years. Elsewhere, I joined the Wine and Food Society and taught its members how to have tutored-tasting events—wherein attendees are instructed by an invited expert or winemaker through a "flight," or selection of eight to twelve wines—instead of cocktail party–type tastings. I also joined the Confrérie des Chevaliers du Tastevin, a Burgundy wine society, and became one of its *officier commandeurs.*

I created the German Wine Society and was its president for a number of years. In subsequent years, I was invited to join the board of the Culinary Institute of America as well as the North American Board of the Institute of Masters of Wine. Over time and in recognition of my growing profile in the wine world, I became an active judge and supporter in a number of notable US and international wine competitions, including the Los Angeles County Fair, where I was the honorary chairman, and the International Wine and Spirit Competition in London, where I was president many years ago and where I am still vice president. I was asked to be a judge in numerous other wine competitions in Oregon, Texas, Virginia, Hudson Valley, and Dallas and in many competitions in Australia. In the latter case, I was asked twice to be part of the panel of judges in the national competition in Canberra, and chair one year the western Australian competition. I also created, with Len Evans, one of the country's most respected and outspoken wine marketers, a wine competition between Australia and California, which was sponsored by Quantas.

One of the reasons for all this activity was the opportunity to present our wines in educational tastings and to get to know the other personalities in the wine trade. The wine trade differs from many other businesses in that we are dealing with a fascinating product that is central to lifestyle. In more recent years other consumer goods that are subject to differences in style and taste have similarly entered the lifestyle marketplace: coffee and high-quality chocolate come to mind, as well as watches.

People in the wine business—particularly those who grow grapes and make wine or blend wine—are forever looking to improve the product and are anxious to learn. Dealing with a nice product, they are by and large extremely nice people and in many cases show an interest in art or the sciences. They are willing to share their experiences and willing to help when asked for advice. Though working hard to sell their wines over others, they also appreciate what others produce and are willing often to help others promote their wines. It can be said that the wine trade is an international fraternity, where all the main players know each other. This includes wine writers as well as producers, restaurateurs, and merchants.

I spent approximately eight months of the year in New York and other parts of the United States, and Canada; two months in the summer in Europe, both in France and in Germany and on vacation; and traveled the rest of the year to the Far East, Australia, and/or New Zealand and to other markets in the Americas. I also visited Bordeaux and Germany in March, when the last year's crop could be tasted, and in November or early December, when the crop was in and either fermenting or finished with its fermentation. Both periods were important, since both the size of the crop and the quality influenced the price of past vintages and the likely price of the new one.

I also edited and brought up to date a classic on German wines: Frank Schoonmaker's *Wines of Germany*, first published in 1956. Frank was a good friend, and we were both in OSS in Algiers and later on in France after the southern French invasion. He was not only a wine importer, selecting fine wines mainly in Germany and Burgundy, but also a great wine writer. Before the war, he had started as a travel writer for the *New Yorker* and developed his wine interests in due course. He had written one of the great books on German wine, but alas, it was badly out of date, and I was forever after him to revise it. Unfortunately, he died without ever doing so. After his death in 1976, his widow asked me if I would undertake the task. It was a work of love: I spent months visiting wine growers on the Rhine and Mosel, researching the past and the present, which was also useful for my business.

Since there was no practical consumer guide to the wines available on the US market, I decided to write a general guide with evaluations of the main wines available in the market. I was ably assisted by Judy Allen, who became my coauthor. The book was published in 1975 by Harper and Row under the title *Which Wine*, and this gave me an opportunity to appear as a TV guest on *Good Morning America* and *The Today Show*. It also gave me the opportunity to meet and get to know Ernest Gallo, the amazing head of the largest US wine company and a man who had thought deeply about the product and its marketing. He commanded a world of his own and was the incubator of many of the great winemakers of our age. I also used the book as a means to appear on many other local TV and radio shows and thereby was able to get a wide distribution for our Blue Nun message, the "wine that is correct with any dish."

It is said in academia, "Publish or perish," and to some extent publishing also serves as an excellent lever in other lines of business. So thanks to my publishing credits, I was then asked to record an LP with Columbia Records called *Wine with Peter Sichel.* The recording had a young couple asking me, the specialist, about wine choices on one side of the record and "music to wine with" on the other side. It was very successful, selling more than one hundred thousand records.

I was fortunate, as the business grew, to have at one time two secretaries working for me: one was Gunda Hogreve, who was trilingual, and the other was Mrs. Wyatt, who was monolingual, and together they kept me organized and up-to-date. Ultimately, I moved out of the Schieffelin offices and into midtown, establishing an office with one secretary and a wonderful personal assistant, John Rapp. John Rapp came from a prominent Philadelphia family and knew a great deal about wine and knew personally a number of the players in the world of wine. He became in the true sense of the word my alter ego and part of the family. Unfortunately, he died young. I also employed Herbert Weiss, who had been with Sichel in Germany and New York and then with Schieffelin. When he retired, he needed an occupation, and there were many loose ends that needed his experience. Herbert ultimately died in his seventies, while still in my employ.

There were many crises in our business: the first was the United States going off the gold standard in 1971 when, under the Nixon administration, we embarked on an era of floating exchanges rates, a flexible monetary regime still in force today. Up to that time world trade worked with a more or less fixed conversion rate between currencies. Suddenly, this was no longer true. Up to that point we had invoiced our German and French wines in US dollars, but with the uncertainty of the new currency conversions, I was anxious to invoice in deutsch marks and French francs, since our expenses were all in those currencies. I negotiated a change in our invoicing, which was far from easy.

The second crisis came with the oil shock in 1973, which coincided with the Bordeaux wine crisis. The oil shock suddenly increased the price of oil dramatically. At the same time a bubble had developed in Bordeaux. The 1970 vintage, which was excellent, had been sold at a reasonable price, and the 1971, a short and decent crop, had sold well. Suddenly, when 1972 came along, there was anxiety in America that there would be a shortage of well-known Bordeaux chateaus, and the trade started speculating with wines before the crop was in—in other words, buying futures of wine from grapes that were still on the vine. The crop came in, and the speculation continued, in spite of the trade knowing by that time that the wine of this vintage was inferior, if not terrible.

The Bordeaux wine bubble was a classic case of speculation in a commodity regardless of the quality. With the 1973 oil shock came a recession, and suddenly, the market for expensive wines shrank. When the wines were tasted ultimately in 1973–74, it soon became apparent that the wine was not worth the price it had fetched in the futures market. Suddenly, Bordeaux wine merchants and American importers were left with large quantities of wine that they could not resell, let alone profitably. In addition the merchants in Bordeaux were saddled with contracts with all the leading Médoc chateaus, which obligated them to buy not only their allocation from the 1972 crop but also the following vintages of 1973 and 1974, which were only marginally better in terms of quality. When the Bordeaux merchants went to the banks to finance these purchases, the banks refused to extend credit.

The resulting crisis touched the entire Bordeaux wine trade, from the chateau owners to the trade in the United States and other large Bordeaux markets. To make matters worse, one of the leading Bordeaux merchants had been found to have labeled ordinary wines with prestigious names of origin, a scandal that was called "Bordeaux-gate." The whole house of cards soon collapsed: a number of old and prestigious Bordeaux merchants and chateau owners went bankrupt, and American importers dumped their inventory, including wines from good vintages, on the market at ridiculous prices, on the principle that the first loss is the smallest. Our family house, Sichel & Co., got into financial difficulties, which caused my British cousin Walter and me to guarantee a major loan, which we had to pay ultimately when Sichel & Co. could not. This, however, did not suffice to save the company, so I negotiated a sale of the Sichel name on French wines to Schieffelin for $1 million, which saved the company. It was indeed an exciting time.

The rapid growth of Blue Nun also necessitated keeping up the supply. This involved making sure we had enough wines to blend to one consistency and the ability to bottle these wines and ship them to the different customers worldwide. In the late 1960s, we first moved the family company in Mainz from where it had been since 1857 to the suburbs of Mainz, where we bought and converted a textile factory into a winery and bottling plant. This, however, was not sufficient, so we bought a piece of land in the provincial town of Alzey, twenty miles from Mainz, and built a modern winery and bottling plant. I rented a small apartment in Mainz, spending at times two to three months a year all told in Mainz. This work involved decisions that could not be handled by mail. It obviously also involved dealing with banks and with wine cooperatives. We had to be sure that we had sufficient funds and sufficient wine. We could not have had better cooperation. Fortunately, I was blessed by two comanaging directors, Riquet Hess on the commercial side and Friedrich Weidman on the administrative and production side. Both had been with us a long time and were excellent tasters who, with the chief winemaker and me, if I was there, would participate both in the buying and the blending of wines.

As Blue Nun grew so rapidly, and as we faced some small crops in the 1970s, there was some anxiety that we could not continue to supply the wine from Germany in the quantities needed and at prices that would leave the wine in the price category at which it was so successful. I went on a prospecting trip to Argentina and Chile, to see if I could source a wine similar in taste from either of these countries. I learned a good deal about the wine industry in both countries, which has evolved dramatically since my trip. I also learned that neither country could furnish a wine close to what we were looking for. This fear of running out of wine was quite widespread at the time, and Seagram's, a large diversified wine and liquor company, developed a line of wine sourced in different countries to forestall possible shortages.

We ran into a major problem when the liquor control board in one of the Canadian markets found glass splinters in several bottles of Blue Nun. It is useless to go into details of our investigation, but suffice it to say that we examined almost one million bottles of wine with a team we sent to New York from Germany, and ultimately, we resolved the problem. It cost us many hundreds of thousands of dollars. We were able to do all this without disturbing the market.

I learned a lot about crisis management, and yet when a crisis comes, it is always different from the last one. It is during crisis that you learn how important relationships are. If you have not built them, you will find it hard to get out of a crisis. If you have built them solidly, you will find that the support of others will get you over almost any crisis. Communicating and telling the truth is essential.

As a result of the Bordeaux crisis, which forced us to face reality, Walter Sichel and I decided to sell half of our German company, H. Sichel Söhne in Germany, to Schieffelin. This enabled us to increase our capital and to handle financially our rapid growth without giving all the profits to the banks in interest payments. It also enabled Walter, my main partner and cousin, to convert some of his shares into cash to be able to ultimately pay estate taxes. I negotiated a sale to Schieffelin, wherein we retained majority voting rights in the German company.

When Schieffelin was sold in 1980 to Moët Hennessy, the latter acquired these shares and accepted the arrangements we had made as to voting rights. Moët Hennessy insisted, however, that anytime the German company had major financial problems, that arrangement would be canceled. Ultimately, Walter and I bought back the German company shares from Moët Hennessy around 1990, when the distribution of Blue Nun, a greatly diminished brand at that time, was abandoned by Schieffelin and passed to its new US importer and marketing agent, Shaw-Ross International Importers of Miami, where the brand still is to this day.

A Falling Trajectory

As Blue Nun went down in sales, in the mid- to late 1980s and early '90s, it became obvious that if this trend continued, we would no longer be able to support the overhead of the new plant or have a reason to maintain it. We first associated ourselves with a group of cooperatives who were our main suppliers, since their interests were identical to ours. As sales plummeted further, I decided that in order to save anything, we had to sell the majority of the company, hopefully associating ourselves with a larger company that could utilize our facilities. We sold in 1995, but it did not completely work out as we had hoped. But then not everything always does.

At the same time or shortly thereafter, it became apparent that the London Sichel import company also was no longer viable. It had become both an agency business and the importer of Sichel German and French wines, but the market had changed, and the company had not. I had gone on the board of the British company in the 1980s and was instrumental, to some extent, in having the company liquidated in time to save enough capital to take care of the family members and the staff.

CHAPTER TWENTY-EIGHT

The Rise and Fall of Blue Nun: A Singular Story

When the Sichel cousins returned from the battlefields of World War I, they felt the family brand needed a shake-up and asked the local printer to design new labels. One of the labels the printer designed was a brown label with blue nuns in the vineyards. In those days and still today, German wine labels often featured religious figures. The church had always been very much involved in growing grapes and making wine on the Rhine and Mosel, and the name Liebfraumilch, evoking the Holy Virgin's milk, invited allegorical images. That particular label was the logical choice for the partners' top Liebfraumilch. H. Sichel Söhne sold many different Liebfraumilch, at different prices and with different degrees of sweetness. This was long before the German wine law's strict regulations on the designation Liebfraumilch, when Liebfraumilch was more or less a generic appellation for Rhine wine. Bottlers used and blended wines from different Rhine regions, which made it easier to blend them consistently from year to year.

The Blue Nun brand has a long history. Its brown label with blue nuns on it was first used by H. Sichel Söhne in Mainz in 1929 on a 1921 vintage Liebfraumilch that was shipped to our sister company in London, H. Sichel & Sons Ltd. It was an immediate success, possibly because 1921 turned out to be the twentieth century's greatest German vintage. But whether it was the wine or the labeling, the Sichels of Mainz decided that their best Liebfraumilch would henceforth be bottled using that distinctive label. Even at that time, when wine offerings were only a fraction of what they are today, a distinctive label could make an enormous difference to distinguish one wine from others.

Something extraordinary happened three years after Sichel started shipping the wine with Blue Nuns on the label. Customers placed new orders, specifically requesting the Blue Nun label, distinguishing it from the other labels that sold Liebfraumilch of lesser quality. Very quickly, it had become Sichel's best seller.

Around 1930, the partners decided to put "Blue Nun Label" on the label and sell the wine as a "branded" item, long before branding had reached the wine business. In those days, the wine business was a great deal smaller and limited to an entirely different customer, who bought his wines either in a specialty store or in a restaurant. There were no self-service stores or restaurant chains. It is a little-known fact that the Blue Nun Liebfraumilch was sold throughout the war in England and the United States. Interestingly, it was impossible to sell German products in England during World War I, which wasn't the case during World War II. It was, in fact, only ten years after World War I that German wines could again be sold in England.

England was initially the Blue Nun's largest market, followed by the United States, with sales increasing gradually. Blue Nun was also successfully introduced into the Scandinavian markets, Australia and New Zealand, Canada, Japan, Hong Kong, and Singapore and various holiday spots in the Caribbean and South America. The wine markets in these countries were tiny compared to what they are today. The increase in wine consumption in the major English-speaking markets progressed steadily, as it did in northern Europe. Increased travel brought about a larger consciousness of types and ultimately brands.

Walter Sichel had lived and worked in the United Kingdom since the late 1920s and promoted the Blue Nun brand there. He was the first to spend money on advertising and public relations and rightly decided that Blue Nun should be promoted as "the wine that goes with any dish." Since the market was small but had burst out of the "snob" category and started to reach a broader and younger consumer, Blue Nun had to signal clearly to the consumer that it could be adapted to any dish and most cuisines. This was a promise it could keep, even if most German wines in this category could also do the same. From the early 1970s, public relations and advertising yielded striking results, especially in the US market.

Due to the nature of the Sichel partnership, the American market had been run during and after the war by Charles Sichel, from an older generation of the family, who had used the Blue Nun Label on a large number of products—four Liebfraumilchs, including a Spätlese, an Auslese, and an extra dry; two Mosel wines, a Bernkasteler and a Bernkasteler Berg; and of course, a sparkling wine. All these wines still featured the blue nun label with the women in the vineyards. These wines were sold at different prices, which was confusing to the consumer, who bought wines featuring the blue nuns without looking for details on the label and ended up with wines of vastly different taste profiles. This situation continued until 1961. With the advice of the marketing people at Schieffelin, we soon eliminated the Blue Nun label on all wines except a Liebfraumilch and a sparkling wine. By taking the word "label" off the brand designation as well, we were able to make "Blue Nun" figure prominently on the label, and a more cheerful nun also helped.

During the late 1960s, as Blue Nun grew both in England and in America, it also started to grow in other markets, including Australia and New Zealand, Scandinavia, Japan, Hong Kong, and Singapore and in lesser markets too. It was never much of a hit in southern Europe. Canada, however, became a very strong market, a mirror image of the American market, closely monitored by me.

It became increasingly clear that assuring its continued success meant supplying the ever-increasing quantities required and assuring the wine's consistency.

Whenever someone bought a bottle of Blue Nun, the wine would have to be similar to the wine bought previously, never mind the year on the bottle or its origin, which by that time was either Rheinhessen or Rheinpfalz, following the new German wine law.

Working together from Mainz, London, and New York, we undertook considerable consumer research to ensure the right blend was not too dry, with enough body to justify its adaptability to various cuisines. Rhine wines with the broadest appeal had a Riesling-like taste, though they were not necessarily 100 percent Riesling. Research showed that a 100 percent Riesling did not do as well as one incorporating other German noble grape types, specifically Müller-Thurgau, Silvaner, and often a little Gewürztraminer. Blending also made for a cheaper wine because these other varieties did not command the same premium pricing as Riesling in the marketplace. The degree of sweetness was important since at that time new wine drinkers tended to prefer wines with a degree of sweetness. We decided on roughly 2.5 percent of residual sugar balanced by 6.2 to 6.4 grams of acidity. Sourcing was also considerably easier and not subject to large swings in supply and price. Due to the large area of vineyards where the designation Liebfraumilch was permitted, we had a plentiful supply of base wines at more or less steady pricing. Blue Nun always carried a vintage year, something considered essential according to consumer research surveys.

Fortunately, excellent marketing executives in both England and the United States handled the daily details, while first-class advertising agencies were in charge of the highly inventive advertising campaigns, first in print and later on radio and television. The leitmotif—or what Madison Avenue advertising types called the brand's "unique selling proposition"—was that Blue Nun worked with any dish. In print, Blue Nun would be paired with Chinese, French, and American dishes. On radio, it might be advertised via a funny sketch, such as the famous advertisement in which a man announces to his host his gift of a bottle of Blue Nun, to which the host replies, "You'd better bring her in out of the cold." The humor and originality of the US advertisements became an important part of the brand recognition.

The combination of a new marketing director at Schieffelin and the Jerry Della Femina advertising firm was a winning matchup for Blue Nun. Comedians Jerry Stiller and Anne Meara, who delivered the radio ads, were brilliant. The radio, print, and trade advertising campaign did as much for the comedy duo as it did for the brand. More importantly, the national advertising campaign had an immediate, positive effect on Blue Nun's sales, rare in any advertising campaign.

Also noteworthy: Blue Nun's advertising campaign was supported by a national wine-by-the-glass program— maybe a first in US wine-marketing history—using for the first time screw-top magnum-sized (1.5 liter) bottles, decades before screw-top closures became widely accepted by American consumers. Blue Nun came in five sizes: quarter, half (375 ml), and standard (750 ml) bottles, one-liter bottles, and 1.5-liter bottles, known as magnums in the wine trade.

The Blue Nun brand reached its high mark in England around 1980, when it sold some 300,000 nine-liter cases. In the United States, it sold around 1,300,000 cases in 1985. Around the same time, the Canadian market topped out around 200,000 cases, and 50,000-plus cases was the high point in Australia. With so many other markets contributing steady sales of 10,000 to 20,000 cases, the grand total in the brand's heyday was close to 2.5 million cases, which qualified it as one of the world's largest-selling wine brands at that time.

Both in England and in the United States, the Blue Nun consumer tended to be young and new to drinking wine or an older consumer who had started to drink wine instead of beer or spirits as an occasional drink or something to order at a bar. In the meantime the US wine market had grown, and other German wines, particularly Black Tower, turned up with innovative packaging and good marketing. Brands from other countries also entered the market, principally Mateus Rosé and Lancers from Portugal, followed by Reunite from Italy. All these brands could claim this particular entry market—that is, younger, legal-age drinkers just getting to know a bit about wine—as well as taste profiles that fit any dish.

There were problems too. Many Germans, particularly those living in the United States and England, denigrated Blue Nun, not recognizing that it was aimed at a broad public and was never meant as a wine for the discerning connoisseur. This went on even after the noted American wine critic Robert Parker had said Blue Nun was an excellent wine. Critics of Blue Nun didn't understand that

German wine designations and labels were a turnoff to the consumer, making it difficult, if not impossible, to sell German wines.

Blue Nun and all the other similar brands started to lose in volume in the late 1980s. In the United States, Chardonnay became the forerunner of the "grape varietal" revolution, becoming a synonym for "white wine." Asking for Chardonnay at a bar, restaurant, or shop meant asking for a white wine. This was followed in due course by whatever the fashion was: Sauvignon Blanc, White Zinfandel, and Cabernet Sauvignon, among others. In effect, the wine's varietal name (or blend of two or more types) had become the brand. Meanwhile, all nonvarietal wines, including Blue Nun, suffered.

We sold the company to a large German wine company, Langguth Erben, that was glad to acquire an international brand. As an antidote to falling sales, Blue Nun's new owners and other proprietary brand owners sought success in line extensions; in the case of Blue Nun, this was a whole collection of white, red, and rosé wines, with varietal designations. We had come back where the label started: as an overall brand for a large variety of wines. One of the designations is Riesling. With the Riesling becoming more widely known and popular, this could become a first step in revitalizing Blue Nun.

CHAPTER TWENTY-NINE

Becoming a Bordeaux Vintner

Since rejoining the family business in 1960, I had spent a lot of time in Bordeaux, both to supervise the blends made for the US market and to buy a select number of chateau-bottled wines for the US market. When I was first involved in Bordeaux in the early 1960s, there were two Sichel companies there; the first, Sichel & Fils Frères, was the French subsidiary company that the German house had established in the 1920s, after failing to come together again with their British cousins after World War I, and the second, Sichel & Co., was the original Sichel *négoce* established in 1896. The latter, Sichel & Co., was owned by Allan Sichel and his family. He was my second cousin, whose grandfather had changed his name to Sichel after marrying a sister of my grandfather and had been asked by his in-laws to head the Sichel company in London. His family, known as the British Sichels, also owned a small import company by the same name in England. Sichel & Fils Frères was owned by H. Sichel & Sons Ltd. of London, a company owned by Walter Sichel and by me; my Sichel branch was called the German Sichels.

Within the family, all these companies made no sense, so my cousin Walter, who was the head of the family and my partner in the different Sichel companies, and I decided to get to know our English cousins Allan Sichel and his son Peter Allan and try to merge the companies and eliminate the confusion they created in the market. We successfully did so in the mid-1960s. This arrangement made a lot of sense: our London company was the larger and more successful of the two, whereas Allen's Sichel & Co. was the larger and more successful Bordeaux company. In addition it was run by Peter Allan, an outstanding expert in the wines of Bordeaux, a successful vintner, and a great personality. So the London companies were merged, with the old shareholders of H. Sichel & Sons Ltd. retaining the majority, and the Bordeaux companies were merged, giving the English cousins a majority in that merged company.

I started to spend more time in Bordeaux, to get a feel for the wines and the culture of Bordeaux. Knowing the wines was not the same thing as getting to know a complex society. I decided that the best way to get the feel of the place was to spend time with my entire family in Bordeaux, get to know the people, and get to know the entire environment. We spent one summer month living in a small house on the property of Peter Allan, Château Angludet; we spent another summer month at Cap Ferret, the nearby seaside resort where a lot of the Bordeaux merchants and proprietors had their summer homes on the

Bay of Biscay. During these vacations, I became fascinated by the plethora of chateau properties available for little money. My wife and I looked, at various times, at a classified property in the Médoc, a property in Fronsac, and finally a property in Sauternes. We got close to buying one or the other but never ended up buying any of them. In due course, we became familiar with many of the principal Bordeaux personalities. Being an active member of the Commanderie de Bordeaux and ultimately the *maître* of the New York chapter helped me to keep in touch with the ever-growing wine world and its developments. By the early 1970s, with the many crises we had lived through, I had given up the idea of buying a property.

I did, however, end up owning a property with friends—and that largely through happenstance. I had a good friend who worked in the financial world in New York by the name of Philip Powers. He was charming, a lover of Bordeaux, and a gifted artist who should have been an architect. He used to invite me to long lunches in the Downtown Club and talk to me about his dream of owning a chateau in Bordeaux. I was on a long business trip in the Orient, Australia, and New Zealand in 1971 when I received a telex in Hong Kong from Peter Morrell, a prominent New York wine retailer and friend. He told me that he was in touch with a young Frenchman, Arnaud de Trabuc, who had an option to buy Château Fourcas Hosten, a property in Listrac, located on the Gironde's left or west bank and just five miles from Margaux, but neither he nor the young Frenchman knew how to attract investors or how to structure a deal. I replied a day or so later, suggesting that he get in touch with Philip Powers.

I arrived four weeks later in New York, and the day after my arrival, I received a phone call from Philip Powers. He had in the meantime structured the acquisition of the chateau and was busy finding investors. He wanted my help in finding investors, and I got busy making calls. In due course, Powers had enough investors, and together they bought the property along with Peter Morrell and Arnaud de Trabuc. They asked me if I wanted to participate, but with all the problems I had in 1971 and 1972 in my own business, I declined, though I agreed to act as a nonexecutive chairman of the venture. Since Philip was a stranger to the wine business, and Peter Morrell and Arnaud de Trabuc were comparatively young, I thought I could help them with their venture.

I had bought some 1961 and 1966 Chateau Fourcas Hosten during my tastings in Bordeaux as part of our "Sichel *Châteaux* Selection," but I had never visited the property in Listrac. I knew at least two vintages of its wines and had found them worthy of my endorsement. The property was sold for the equivalent of $436,000; another $140,000 went into buying over 200,000 bottles of older vintages, which left a mere $100,000 or so for operating capital. Fortunately, the banks were willing to loan enough money to enable the property to not only operate but also make extensive investments in enlarging the planting and improving the vineyards, as well as modernizing the winery. The property was forty-seven hectares (approximately 117 acres), of which roughly half were in production. The winery was old, and the storage consisted mainly of concrete vats and old barrels. Since the wines in good vintages were excellent, an investment in the vineyards, the winery, and the personnel would assure us the ability to improve the wine, even in lesser years, and build a viable business.

We were fortunate that the uncle of Arnaud de Trabuc, Bertrand de Rivoyre, was a prominent wine broker and *négociant* with his own property in the Côtes de Bourg. Bertrand charged himself with supervising the property in return for a small participation and also acted as the main wine merchant selling the wine. It was the custom in Bordeaux at that time, as it is today, that properties sold their wine to a number of wine merchants (*négociants*), who resold the wines both domestically and internationally. Bertrand, who became a close friend over the years, was able to hire the owner of the next-door property, Château Fourcas Dupré, M. Ghislain Pagès, to become the manager of Château Fourcas Hosten. Being next door and facing similar challenges in his own property, he was able to manage the two properties well.

Arnaud de Trabuc, who had established a small importing company in New York handling his uncle's wines, charged himself with distributing the wines in the United States. With a beautiful and charming American wife, he quickly became a popular fixture of the New York social scene. The fact that he was a *comte*, a titled aristocrat, did not harm his selling efforts.

Things went more or less smoothly for a number of years, though the sales in the United States did not quite come up to projections. Fortunately, Bertrand was more successful in France, England, and other European markets, a necessity, as production slowly increased due to new plantings and improvements in the vineyards. Then suddenly, we noticed that sales to the main US importer, Bacardi, had never been paid to the chateau. It turned out that our dear count had asked that the bills be paid to him personally, which Bacardi had done, since Trabuc was the president of the management company. We confronted Trabuc and got him to agree to a repayment over a number of months. But this was not the end of the story. Trabuc had taken out a loan from the Banque Français du Commerce Exterieur for several hundred thousand dollars and also had a loan from one of the partners in Fourcas Hosten. He was not able to pay back either.

Worse was to come. It is customary in the Bordeaux trade to sell the wines of the most recent vintage *en primeur*, also called futures, meaning at a preferential price two years before the wine is bottled and can be delivered to the buyer. These purchases are mainly made on trust, a sign of the honesty of the Bordeaux *négoce*. It turned out that Trabuc had sold several hundred thousand dollars of futures, in wines he did not own. In other words, he was a complete fraud. He had also run up big bills in top New York restaurants, which he never paid. To add insult to injury, he had also rented my house in Southampton with a check that bounced. Finally, he was arrested and sentenced to two years in prison. He asked the judge to give him a week to settle his affairs; the judge asked for his passport and granted the request. Trabuc went straight from court to the French Consulate and reported a lost passport, received a replacement, and flew to France the same day.

The chateau was out a couple of hundred thousand dollars at a time when we could ill afford it. Fortunately, Trabuc had used some of this money to buy an apartment on Park Avenue, which had increased in value, and its seizure by the bank was able to satisfy a number of creditors besides the bank. This was fortunate, since he had given the bank his shares in the chateau as collateral for his loan, shares we were able to retrieve from the bank. Suddenly, we were in financial trouble, and I decided, having asked friends to invest in this venture, that I must take a more active role, to prevent my friends from losing their investment. It was just the right time.

The mid-1980s were difficult times. We had overextended ourselves in our investments in the chateau, and the banks insisted on an increase in capital. At that stage I invested in the chateau and was also active in finding new investors, American, French, and Danish. Ultimately, the American investors, including me, as the second-largest investor in the chateau, controlled the majority of the shares. We not only had saved the chateau but also could finish our investments to produce on all the 117 acres, ferment our wines in temperature-controlled vats, and age them in a mix of new and second-harvest barrels. We had retained Emile Peynaud, the famous French oenologist, as our advisor from the beginning, and when he retired, we retained (and still retain) his assistant Jacques Boissenot and ultimately his son, considered one of the top oenologists in Bordeaux.

We were also able to make the chateau livable, and instead of staying in a hotel in Bordeaux during my visits, I lived in the chateau and even entertained my neighbors there. Philip Powers and I had made friends with many of the other chateau owners. Philip did most of the work during these difficult times and became one of the three managing directors of the chateau, though I helped when and where I could. Alas, he died young, and I was forced to become his replacement, at first as one of the three managing directors and, when Rivoyre also died, as one of two.

I enjoyed the challenges and rewards of being a Bordeaux chateau owner. I spent at least three long periods at the chateau every year. One of these visits was planned after the vintage, when it was possible to evaluate its quality and quantity. Another was in March, when the trade and the press descended on Bordeaux to taste the previous year's vintage. Finally, I went in June, for the madness of the enormous wine fair called Vinexpo, which took place every two years, and in the years when there was no wine fair, I came to attend to business. I got involved in dealing with our largest customers and participated in promotions not only in the United States but also in France.

I gained an enormous respect for the hard work and dedication of my neighbors and their willingness to be always available for advice and help. That respect extended to most of the vintners I got to know over the years. Their devotion to the land, to finding ways to make better and better wines, and to the hard work of selling their wines was most impressive.

I had sold my German business in 1995, when sales of Blue Nun had steadily gone down, and when I figured that if this continued, we would be facing bankruptcy. I was glad to have this second leg, not only financially but also and more importantly to keep me active and busy.

We experienced another crisis in the early part of the new century, and my partners and I decided to put the chateau up for sale. We were all getting older, if not old, and my children were not interested in getting involved. We finally sold the property in 2006 to two brothers, Renaud and Laurent Mommeja, partners in Hermès, who fell in love with the property. They have the means and the devotion to bring Fourcas Hosten to the next level, taking a long view and improving the vineyards, the selection of grape varieties, and the winemaking. They will end up making a great wine. They also happen to be wonderful people. They gave me a banquet after we sold the vineyard, and I told them that I felt like a father giving his daughter in marriage to them. I was sure that they would treat the daughter well, and she would blossom.

Though I am no longer an owner of a chateau in Bordeaux, I have kept up the friendships I have formed over the years and continue to be active in promoting the wines of Bordeaux.

CHAPTER THIRTY

The Wine Community

Over the last fifty years an international wine community materialized. Wine was for centuries the drink of the elite, where fathers would teach their sons what to select. It was the daily accompaniment to food in the areas where wine grew, without much attention given to different grades of quality, except in the case of the elite, who distinguished between different regions and grades of quality.

With more income available for "lifestyle" spending in the developed world, wine consumption increased and created a thirst for more knowledge about wine. Wine, like many other consumer goods, has greatly profited from the revolution in communications. Information on wine is widely available through the daily press, in magazines and specialized publications, through lectures, through wine clubs, and on the Internet. It is safe to say that the international availability of most wine brands has created an international marketplace not only for wine but also for information about wine. At the same time, it has created a class of internationally recognized wine experts, some of whom have used novel ways to look at wine. There are endless Internet sites for information, applications for your iPad, and e-mails sent by the millions, some associated with national or regional wine organizations, others originating with almost every wine producer in the world. We live in a generation of information overload, and wine, like any other subject of possible interest, requires the consumer to make decisions based on the best information he or she can get.

There are outstanding experts who have garnered international recognition and who are followed by wine enthusiasts in every country where wine is consumed. They have written wine atlases and books on specific wine subjects, from grape varieties to vintage years to specific regions and their producers, almost any part of the complicated quilt that makes up the subject of wine. Most wine-consuming countries have also developed specialized magazines on wine, some of which are sold worldwide. In other words it is easy to inform yourself on wine, wherever you live.

Though there are a number of specialized wine magazines, there are only two that are truly international in scope and readership: a British magazine called *Decanter* and the *Wine Spectator*, an American magazine that is part of the publishing empire M. Shanken Communications Inc. of New York City. Marvin R. Shanken, who built this conglomerate, was an investment banker who saw the wine revolution coming and created a newsletter called *Impact*, a business publication for the wine and spirit industry. Being visionary and dynamic, he then in 1979 bought a struggling newspaper called the *Wine Spectator*, which has become in the last thirty-five years the most widely read wine magazine in the world. For thirty years the *Wine Spectator* has hosted a consumer wine extravaganza called the New York Wine Experience, which has become a must for top producers worldwide to showcase their wines. In addition M. Shanken Communications hosts wine and spirits business seminars, where top executives of the international wine and spirits industry present their vision of the market and its future.

Obviously, all of these experts have their own tastes, and what they describe is influenced by their own likes and dislikes. The best of them are consistent, which makes them reliable even to those whose tastes might differ. My cousin Peter Allan Sichel hated to read tasting notes; he thought they were silly since every person has his or her own taste preferences. Nevertheless, a large portion of the discerning wine-consuming public reads avidly every pronouncement of their favorite wine writer.

Probably foremost among these writers is the American critic Robert Parker Jr. Having succeeded in establishing a recognized one-hundred-point scoring system, he has branched out from his original Bordeaux expertise into all major wine regions through a staff of competent specialists and wine tasters. His influence is so pervasive that his ninety-and-above scores feature prominently on price lists, often alongside scores from the two widely read American wine magazines: *Wine Spectator* and *Wine Enthusiast*. In my opinion, Robert Parker is the only American who can claim this international "stamp of approval."

The *New York Times* has had and still has outstanding wine writers, whose articles are widely reproduced in other newspapers around the country: the late Frank Prial was followed by Eric Asimov, who informs his readers about the ever-expanding supply of wines worthy of note. There have been other American wine writers of note, such as Gerald Asher and Alexis Bespaloff, but their influence has been more anecdotal. There also have been writers who were really in the "trade," as importers, merchants, or wine producers, yet they wrote books that were influential in their time. The outstanding ones who come to mind are Alexis Lichine and Frank Schoonmaker.

Perhaps the most consistently original and informative wine experts are British, starting with Hugh Johnson, who, after writing perhaps the most useful introduction to wine, was the first to write a pocket book on wine and had the genius to create a *World Wine Atlas*, explaining geography as well as a lot of other things so essential to understanding wine. He also originated a DVD series on the history of wine. The other remarkable wine writer is Jancis Robinson, who writes a wine column for the *Financial Times* and also publishes articles on her own website and for her subscription-only *Purple Pages*. She is the only real competitor of Robert Parker Jr., with a somewhat worldlier and less magisterial approach.

The granddaddy of all wine writers was André Simon, a Frenchman who lived in England most of his life and represented a champagne house. He wrote *A Dictionary of*

Wines and an excellent basic guide to French wines titled *The Noble Grapes and the Great Wines of France*, as well as many other books, including books on the wine trade.

Other English men or women who are part of the coterie spreading their wine knowledge include

Michael Broadbent, Serena Sutcliffe, David Peppercorn, Nicholas Faith, and many others too numerous to mention.

On top or along all these people are those I would describe as "wine personalities." Some of them are wine producers, others are wine merchants, and every one of them is a personality in the true sense of the word. Probably the most outstanding of this bunch was the late Len Evans, an Australian wine grower, wine writer, organizer of wine competitions, great chef, raconteur, and artist of considerable originality and one of the most charming, accomplished, and generous people I have ever met.

There are other personalities who by their remarkable success and ability and willingness to share their knowledge have had a great influence on both the development of the wine market and the styles of wines made. Robert Mondavi, Paul Draper, Warren Winiarski, and André Tchelistcheff come to mind, as well as Konstantin Frank, who was able to make the Vinifera (the grape species that includes all the great European grape varieties) prosper in the eastern United States, where prior to his arrival wine was made exclusively with native American grapes.

There are also remarkable wine personalities in the international arena; Augustine (Cucho) Huneeus and Marchese Piero Antinori come to mind. I would not do justice to wine personalities if I did not mention Ernest Gallo, who with his brother Julio built the largest and most successful wine company in the United States. Many of the top oenologists and marketers of wine started their careers in his employ. Many new methods of making wine were originated in the laboratories of Gallo. "Ernie," as he was generally called, was a very private man with a sharp mind and endless curiosity.

There are equally remarkable personalities in France, Italy, and Germany and no doubt in other areas. My knowledge includes only France and Germany, and when I write about these two countries, I cover what I know about the personalities who have given areas of production an image, which often depends on people who can act as missionaries.

The wine community consists of growers, merchants, importers, marketers, wine writers, journalists, and just about everyone else who is involved in either making or selling wine or who is seriously interested in wine. It is very special in many ways. Members of this community share a common interest in discovery and quality and a general love of the product. They also like to share information and enjoy interacting with fellow members of this large community. In addition there are very few "bad eggs" in this community. The interest is in a complex and interesting product, which attracts people who tend to be largely honest and not particularly confrontational. It is a remarkable international community.

When I started in the business, before I was a grower, I quickly realized that the function of the merchant was

all-important to the grower/producer. Of equal importance were the retailers, restaurateurs, wine writers, and
journalists because all of these individuals had to transmit
to the winemakers their opinions on the style and taste of
wines in the market. Without these interactions we would
still make wines that are faulty in one way or another.
The style of wine has evolved over the ages, and the fresh
fruity wines of today are totally different from what people
drank thirty or forty years ago. This is a continuous process: today's preoccupation is with high alcohol content
caused by the planet's warming and how to moderate it.
Not only do tastes change, but so do fashions. As more
and more wine is consumed outside of meals, the style and
the types differ more and more. It is the interaction of the
whole community that leads to change. This generation of
better-educated and more enterprising winemakers and
winery owners embraces both tradition and change.

CHAPTER THIRTY-ONE

Some Advice on Wine

These memoirs would be incomplete if I did not write about my love of wine and give some advice on how to find one's way through the confusing plethora of labels in the marketplace. I also want to give some advice on how to find your way through the complexities of German and Bordeaux wines.

Though I have favorites, I generally appreciate wines from almost any region of the world. As a matter of fact, once you start to take an interest in wine, your interest becomes global. You want to try every wine anyone recommends and seek out wines that tickle your curiosity. You would be well advised to try all the basic grape varieties early on. You should also attend some basic wine appreciation courses, available in all the major markets. Retail stores and educational organizations often offer them.

Certain grape varieties will please you more than others, as will certain regions. In spite of that, you will be forever tempted to try different wines, particularly if they are made from grape varieties you like but are grown in areas other than their original home. Examples are the traditional varieties grown in Bordeaux—Cabernet Sauvignon, Merlot, and the other varieties used to make red Bordeaux—and Riesling, the predominant grape variety used in making German wines. In due course you want to try wines made from these grape varieties in other areas of the world. Though the *terroir* (soil and climate) will be different, there is still a basic similarity in taste, at times so similar that it is hard to distinguish one area from the other.

When you travel, you should always try the wines made from grapes grown in the region where you happen to be. Some countries use grape varieties not found anywhere else, particularly Greece and parts of Italy, which gives you an entirely new taste sensation. Variety is indeed the spice of life. There is an old wives' tale that wines do not travel well. By and large that is not true, and in some cases travel can age and enhance the quality of the wine. Today most wines are well made, so that even low-alcohol wines, such as wines from the Mosel, withstand and are often enhanced by travel.

When I started out seriously attacking the American market in the early 1960s, the wine market was considerably smaller, and a lot of wines in the market were not good. There has been a vast change since then. Countries not known for fine wine are suddenly producing them. The better-known grape varieties are planted almost everywhere. Whereas twenty years ago there were faulty and unpleasant wines in the market, today almost all wines are faultless and pleasant. Usually the only difference between inexpensive and expensive wines is the taste: as wines become more expensive, they have more flavor. This is due to many things; smaller production per acre, more care in the selection of grapes at harvest, better *terroir*, more aging in wood, and better control during fermentation are just some of the differences. There is, however, another factor that plays into the price/quality relationship. Some wines demand a higher price because of their reputation and limited production. They have achieved their "snob appeal" through the winemakers' many years of making superior wines and thereby are able to demand a premium. There is also a definite fashion element to wine. Otherwise, the Chinese would not pay so much more for Chateau Lafite than for one of the other first growths of Bordeaux.

I have always distinguished between daily wines and Sunday wines—that is, wines for special occasions. We are starting to distinguish, to some extent, the difference by their closure: daily wines increasingly have screw-top closures, whereas Sunday wines continue to be cork-finished, though even here there are exceptions. I would classify daily wines as those sold for under twenty dollars a bottle. Then there is the large territory of wines between twenty and forty dollars, the no-man's-land that includes daily and Sunday wines. Anything over forty dollars is definitely Sunday, though it might not live up to the billing. As you spend more money, you are well advised to consult one of the many wine guides, or better still, consult a knowledgeable retailer. In many cases vintage is important, particularly in the up-to-forty-dollar category. In good vintages the less expensive wines tend to profit most. It is an old adage that in good vintages all wines tend to be good, whereas in lesser vintages, the more well-known and famous wines tend to be considerably better than their lesser neighbors—because they can afford to disqualify a larger amount of grapes as unripe or unhealthy. This does not mean that wines in lesser vintage years are bad; they just tend to be lighter, with less fruit. In a world where wines are increasingly higher in alcohol than twenty years ago, largely due to fashion and climate change, lesser vintages might well be more suitable. High-alcohol wines often do not blend well with food; the alcohol tends to burn the mouth and palate. Lighter vintages also tend to be ready for drinking earlier. This is more important in red wines but can also apply to whites.

Obviously, selecting wines for personal consumption involves many other elements that contribute to the wine: grape varieties, where one's personal preferences play an important role; *terroir*, the French collective name for soil and climate; degree of alcohol; amount of oak aging or the lack of same (some people appreciate oak aging for Chardonnay, whereas others like their Chardonnay fresh and fruity without contact with oak); and last but often most important, the producer or bottler of a particular wine. Since the majority of wines being sold are blends of wines from the same general region, all from a specific grape variety or grape varieties, the blender or bottler is a very important element.

Over the last thirty years there has been a dramatic improvement in winemaking almost everywhere. Whereas for many years the main emphasis for improving quality was on winemaking, it is now increasingly on producing better and better fruit. It is safe to say that there has been more progress in making good wines in the last forty years than in the previous five hundred.

With the increased production of good wines, the market has become very crowded with thousands of labels, making it more and more difficult for producers to sell their wines and for consumers to choose them. Regions, grape varieties, and price are obviously one way for consumers to choose their wines, and another is vintage year. A little study on the topic of wine or a subscription to either a website or a wine magazine is well worthwhile because a book will never tell you what an up-to-date tasting by an expert will tell you. Remember that the taster has his or her own likes and dislikes, and they may not be the same as yours. If the taster is good, however, his or her recommendations will be consistent and serve as a guide. If you are really serious about wine, you should also find a knowledgeable retailer who can guide you. My father used to say that you need a reliable lawyer, a reliable doctor, and a reliable wine merchant. I would ask why he included the wine merchant. He would answer that a bad one could make you look like a fool to your guests.

Tastes differ. In addition tastes tend to change with time. This is due both to increased sophistication, which comes from experience, and to age: as we get older, our taste preferences often change. In my old age, I increasingly prefer wines lower in alcohol, with less forward fruit and more style and elegance.

There are a plethora of terms used by wine tasters, both amateur and professional. They come down to trying to express in words what your palate and nose experience while you are tasting a wine. The terms used to describe wine hardly qualify as an internationally accepted vocabulary and are often the butt of jokes. Basically, they describe the various flavors you encounter when smelling a wine and the taste sensation you experience when drinking it or swirling it in your mouth to release the various flavors. Descriptions try to define the "weight" of the wine, from light to heavy, as an example. Comparisons with the smell of various flowers or herbs are frequent, but also references to coffee, leather, and other daily smells are often used.

I spent most of my career in the wine business selecting, blending, and selling German wines, as well as growing and making wine in Bordeaux. I also selected, and sometimes blended, Bordeaux and wines from Burgundy and the Rhône. Through my involvement I developed a preference for wines made from the Riesling grape variety and the traditional Bordeaux varieties, mainly Cabernet Sauvignon, Merlot, and Cabernet Franc. But at the same time I learned to appreciate wines made from other varieties and in other regions. Initially, I liked Burgundy equally well as Bordeaux. Then, in my mature years, my preference became Bordeaux. In my old age, I seem to have come around again to hold Burgundies and wine made from the Pinot Noir in equal esteem as Bordeaux. This may well be a sign of a changed palate as I aged.

Though Chardonnay is probably the dominant white

grape variety, I consider Riesling the outstanding grape variety for white wine. This does not mean that I do not appreciate wines made from the Chardonnay grape. If the food I am eating tastes better with a wine made from the Chardonnay grape, I will always pick that wine rather than a Riesling. A good example is oysters, which are ideal with a bone-dry Chablis. It is just that Riesling is made in such a variety of styles. I drink wines made from the Riesling grape more often than wines made from Chardonnay, Sauvignon Blanc, Chenin Blanc, and other white varieties. In addition I find Riesling to be the ideal quaffing wine. It serves well as an aperitif and does not need food to accompany it. Its low alcohol seems ideal for that occasional glass of wine.

The home for Riesling is the Rhine River and its main tributary, the Mosel. Riesling is grown in many other countries as well. There are large plantings of Riesling in both Washington State and New York State, as well as in Michigan and in parts of Canada. There are endless good bottles of "daily" Riesling on the market for fifteen dollars and below, coming from Germany, the United States, and other countries, most of them delightful daily wines.

Riesling is a cold-climate grape variety, a hardy vine that prospers in northern climes. It matures slowly and prospers in dry climates and does not suffer overly in wet ones. Its roots are deep, seeking water where they find it. Its taste reflects the soil in which it grows. It is suitable for dry wines as well as semidry wines, sweet wines, and wines with "dessert"-type sweetness. A little sweetness often balances its high acidity. By and large Riesling wines are lower in alcohol than most white wines, the German wines being usually around 10 percent alcohol, an enormous advantage when most Chardonnays are 14 percent. The low alcohol and many fruit flavors make Riesling the ideal wine to drink without food. One challenge in selecting a Riesling is knowing the degree of sweetness of the wine. Recently, a lot of Riesling producers have adopted a back label, devised by the International Riesling Foundation, with a scale showing the degree of sweetness of the wine.

Another way to establish the degree of sweetness in a German wine is to know that German wines are graded according to the ripeness of the grapes at harvest. In ascending order, going from the lightest to the ripest, they are designated Kabinett, Spätlese, Auslese, Beerenauslese, Eiswein, and Trockenbeerenauslese. The last three are very sweet dessert wines. The first three tend to go from almost dry to quite sweet. If they bear the name Trocken on the label, however, they will be completely dry. There are two other categories: Qualitätswein, which usually has a small degree of sweetness, and a designation called "Classic," which has less sweetness still than Qualitätswein. The sweetness, in both designations, offsets the acidity in the wine. There are also designations for top wines: "Erstes Gewächs" and "Erste Lage," which is similar to the French designation *premier cru*, reserved for top wines from designated sites, and "Grosses Gewächs," which is similar to the French designation *grand cru*, again site-specific for certain top wines. The wines from these designations are all dry. Finally, an association called Charta puts its imprimatur on Rheingau Rieslings that are dry to the palate and have achieved a higher degree of maturity than required by law.

As you can see, it is not all that easy to find your way with the plethora of labels out there. It is no wonder that there are many books trying to educate consumers on the different wine regions of the world. Almost all regions are complex, individualistic, and fascinating. That is why some of us who have spent a considerable amount of our lives in wine have developed expertise in only a few regions.

My other love, Bordeaux, produces as much wine as all of Germany. It is the area that produces more fine wine than any other region in France. It produces red, white, and rosé wine all three, though red predominates. It also produces some of the finest sweet wines in the world, mainly under the appellations of Sauternes and Barsac and various other appellations. Most of these are sold under chateau names, though a small amount is sold by merchants, whose names figure on the label.

The last thirty years have seen a veritable revolution in the quality of white wines made in Bordeaux. The main grape varieties are Semillon and Sauvignon. By restricting the quantity, selecting the right clones, and learning to make wines from healthy grapes under temperature control, winemakers can produce a large amount of good dry white wines, which are mainly sold under merchants' labels. In addition there are a few hundred properties that sell their wines under the chateau labels, wines that are distinctive and of high quality. Most of those come from Pessac-Leognan and Graves, though some also come from a large area called Entre deux Mers, and a small amount is grown in the Médoc, under the simple Bordeaux designation. These latter wines usually bear the label of prestigious chateaux, which have made their reputation by making high-quality red wines.

Bordeaux is famous for red wine, produced from Cabernet Sauvignon, Merlot, Cabernet Franc, and two other grape varieties that are added in small quantity by some properties: Petit Verdot and Malbec. The latter variety is used less and less. Cabernet Sauvignon is the main grape grown in the Médoc, and Merlot predominates in St. Emilion, Pomerol, Graves, and Pessac-Leognan and even more so in the large areas making daily wines under the appellations such as Bordeaux, Bordeaux Superieur, and Côte de Bordeaux. The choice of the variety depends on the soil, as well as on the style of wine the estate owner wants to make. Red Bordeaux traditionally has been blended from a number of varieties, enabling the vintner to follow one style from year to year and also overcome problems with one variety over another, due to vintage variations. Since Cabernet Sauvignon and Merlot ripen at different times, this is very convenient.

There are roughly eight thousand properties in Bordeaux, of which a considerable number bottle their wine bearing the name of the property. These labels reflect the fact that the product was grown, made, and bottled at the property. Though a good two to three hundred of these chateaus are well known, and a goodly number are world-renowned, a vast number are usually known only in certain markets in which they have successfully sold their wines. The well-known belong to the category of Sunday wines, selling to knowledgeable consumers who follow their wines from vintage to vintage. Most of the most famous wines in the Médoc, St. Emilion, Graves, and Sauternes/Barsac have been classified under one classification or another. The most famous is the classification of 1855, when sixty-five red wine properties, all of them in the Médoc, except for one in Graves, Chateau Haut Brion, were classified as first, second, third, fourth, and fifth growth, in descending order of quality. Except for one property, which has been upgraded from second to first, Chateau Mouton Rothschild, this classification has survived to this day, though some of the lesser-classified chateaux are today judged to make better wines than some of their more highly classified neighbors. Graves produces about double as much dry white wine than red, and the classification in Graves encompasses both red and white. Sauternes and Barsac were also included in the 1855 classification.

Most of the well-known wines—including just about all of the 1855 classified wines—are Sunday wines. Some of them have become so expensive that they qualify for investment portfolios. Their prices are quoted like shares in the stock market, and their price has gone up steadily in the last few years, due to a large demand in China and, as in the stock market, due to speculation. These wines are subject to fashion and often to politics. Since the initial writing of this book, China has ceased to be a large buyer of the fanciest wines, and indeed, circumstances might change the market again by the time you read this paragraph.

Obviously, with thousands of properties, you need help in selecting "your" Bordeaux. There are endless tasting notes on Bordeaux by Robert Parker and Jancis Robinson and in magazines such as the *Wine Spectator,* the *Wine Enthusiast, Decanter,* and many others. Ultimately, you must have a reliable retailer, who not only offers a large selection of Bordeaux but also can guide you.

It would be wise to establish your taste preference between the Médoc and its parishes that bear their own appellation—(Margaux, St. Julien, Pauillac, St. Estèphe, Moulis, and Listrac (on the so-called left bank of the Gironde) on the one hand and the wines of St. Emilion, Graves/Pessac-Leognan, and Pomerol (on the so-called right bank) on the other—since these two principal areas differ in style. (Confusingly, the Graves/Pessac-Leognan appellations are on the left bank, but because their wines are rather more dominated by the Merlot grape, these wines I would group tastewise in with right bank appellations, which are also chiefly dominated by Merlot; on the left bank, Cabernet Sauvignon is the dominant grape variety of the greatest wines, though Merlot, Cabernet Franc, Petit Verdot, and Malbec are also grown and vinified, depending on the property.)

You should also try the lesser appellations as well

as regional bottlings of reputable merchants. They offer wines at reasonable prices for daily consumption. It will take time to get your bearings, but the time is well spent. More importantly, the wines are very accessible and are ideal with food.

CHAPTER THIRTY-TWO

A Look Back

When you write your memoirs, you face the challenge of what to write and what to leave out. You write for your children and friends but hopefully also for a wider public that might be interested in parts of your life. My life has been influenced by the violent history of the twentieth century. It is a life that could be of interest to a wider public. At best I have covered what seemed important, but I feel that so many elements of my life that were important to me personally, I have either mentioned in passing or totally left out. Those elements are what I want to mention here, since they are important to me and form an important part of my life. Without them I would not be the happy person I am today. They also maintained my sanity and motivated me every day.

I have covered, probably adequately, my youth and the happy home I grew up in, and obviously, the web of friends and contacts I established over these last fifty or so odd years, since I joined the wine trade, continues, as does the web of old friends from my life in intelligence. New friends have been added, and the many activities that were on the periphery in the past occupy a more important part of my life today. In later years life becomes a little more leisurely; the pressures of the past disappear. It is as well to describe what has occupied me over the last few years, years that have been personally rewarding, because they have provided me an active life yet have afforded me more time to learn and think.

Obviously, a lifetime spent in wine does not disappear; neither does a long career in intelligence. So I have continued my interest in wine. This involvement has many facets. As I mentioned previously, I got involved, early on, in many wine competitions. They included such diverse areas as Oregon, New York, Virginia, and Texas and international wine competitions associated with the Los Angeles County Fair and the International Wine and Spirit Competition in England. Whereas I was a judge in most of them, in some cases I ended up being on the board of directors or serving as honorary chairman.

I have been a judge over the years in three major wine competitions in Australia and helped organize the Quantas wine cup, which was a competition of Californian and Australian wines. I visited Australia even after retirement to participate in a major wine competition. I must have visited the country six or seven times. I gained a good knowledge of Australian wines and made friends with the most amazing and charming vintners and wine experts I have ever known. I also was a main speaker, some thirty years ago, at a conference in Australia that tried to define how Australia could be successful in the world market. The Australian wine industry was guided by that conference, and the industry's success is partially due to the advice some of us gave at the time. I visited every wine region in Australia, except for Tasmania, and was greatly impressed by what I saw and tasted. I have never seen such generosity and hospitality.

Another field in which I have been active—and still am active, to some degree, even today—is education in wine. I was on the board of that other CIA, the Culinary Institute of America, for many years, and I lectured there on wine and got involved in many other activities, including finding the institute the old Christian Brothers winery, which established the institute's presence in California. I was, until recently, on the board of directors of the Institute of Masters of Wine North America, an organization that helps, in the best sense of the word, to make the wine business a proud profession.

Having spent so much time in the wine industry, I have also been involved in name-of-origin disputes between the United States and the European Common Market and have represented the United States at the Office Internationale de la Vigne et du Vin (OIV), an intergovernmental agency that coordinates technical, regulatory, and social problems involved in the international wine scene.

I made friends with many people in the wine industry, both in the United States and elsewhere. One thing led to another, and I ended up helping find key people for various key jobs in the wine industry, somehow fitting the right people to the right jobs and pleasing both parties. Many of these people have become lifetime friends who even today keep in touch with me. My connections also led to an involvement in mergers and acquisitions in the wine and spirit industry. All this has made my life more interesting.

A friend from my days in the OSS and the Seventh Army, Lucius Eastman, got me involved in the World Monuments Fund (WMF), of which he was chairman at the time, when the fund was small and had one or at most two employees. That one employee, Bonnie Burnham, grew with the organization and is today running an extraordinary cultural resource. I became a trustee in the 1980s and, though no longer active on the board, am still involved. Stella and I have traveled with WMF in Europe, China, and the Middle East. What we have seen has enriched our lives and our knowledge. We have also, through WMF, reestablished ties with my old British public school, Stowe, which has been the recipient of major funds to bring it back to its original glory. I was also helpful, through my contacts in Germany, in establishing a partnership between a German foundation and the World Monuments Fund, which has been instrumental in preserving many sites, mainly in East Germany. So much in life can be accomplished through a wide circle of friends and acquaintances.

I had from early childhood an interest in music. I had a speech impediment as a child, and our family doctor diagnosed it as a breathing problem and suggested to my mother that I be given singing lessons to overcome the problem. Singing became one of my great loves. I took singing lessons up to my time in Hong Kong, where I had an Italian singing teacher. I sang in choirs in England and also in chapel services. To this day I sing German Lieder. Singing is a liberating experience.

As children, my sister and I were taken at a rather early age to the opera. Our piano teacher usually explained the main themes and the story of the opera before we went. I developed a lifetime love of opera and as a child even dreamed of becoming an opera singer. As a matter of fact, my father once asked me what I wanted to be when I grew up, and I told him that I wanted to be an opera singer. He replied, "You are a baritone-bass; they are a dime a dozen. Now if you were a tenor, it would be quite another thing." I abandoned the idea immediately. I joined the Metropolitan Opera Club shortly after I moved to New York. I was actively involved in the club for many years, both as a director and as president, as well as one of the organizers of the Metropolitan Opera Ball, which for years was a major fundraiser for the Metropolitan Opera Association. I regularly visit opera houses in Europe or wherever I travel and have been to Bayreuth as a guest of the German government. I cannot imagine a life without music and regret to this day that I did not practice my piano as a child. My mother's prophecy, that I would be sorry someday that I did not practice, became so true.

I continue to be hugely influenced by my British and German education and background. I constantly quote the poetry and whistle and sing the songs I learned as a child. Above all, I am apt to quote the German proverbs, used daily in Germany, to express a truth or two. Though fluent in French, I never lived long enough in France to have the easy use of the vernacular, as I have in German and English. I am also less well read in French than in English and German literature.

The Enlightenment fascinates me. My heroes are Spinoza and Diderot, not Voltaire. I consider myself a child of the Enlightenment and abhor religion being used in politics. I do not believe that there is a God or higher being. It is my sense that this feeling or belief is shared by many but stated only by few. There is a societal fear of questioning the existence of God.

Ever since my career in intelligence, I have had a keen interest in politics, both domestic and foreign. My political convictions could best be described as those of a social democrat, in the meaning of the term as used by Tony Judt, the late and distinguished professor of modern European history at New York University. I abhor the extremism of both the right and the left. I am a strong believer in secularism. I abhor the denial of scientific evidence. I believe in compromise, both in politics and in life. I abhor the immense gulf between the rich and the poor and consider it dangerous for society. I believe in socialized medicine; life is too unpredictable to abandon those struck by illness.

I have a number of regrets, and foremost is my regret that I will never be able to read all the books I want to read or inform myself about the many questions for which I seek answers. Never having gone to college or university, I had to "catch up" by reading. I largely have limited myself to nonfiction reading for the last ten years or so, though not completely. That would be impossible. Nevertheless, the world is still becoming more understandable the more I read, with my being disciplined enough to read what I consider important for my education.

I took Russian lessons in Heidelberg and then in Berlin after the war, but due to lack of time, I abandoned them. I regret that I will never be able to read the great Russian authors in their original language.

I sometimes wonder whether the world is more complicated today than when I grew up and have come to the conclusion that the speculation is useless. The complications and challenges today are different, but as we are better informed, we should be able to adapt better than our parents.

ACKNOWLEDGMENTS

I thought about my memoirs for years and made various attempts to write them, each ending in frustration. The main problem was having enough discipline to devote the necessary time without interruption. Martin Sinkoff, an old friend in the wine world, suggested that I retain David Lincoln Ross to help me. David had written and edited many wine-related publications and had the necessary cultural background to understand what I was trying to do. It turned out to be the solution to the problem. He helped me to structure the memoirs, made appropriate comments when my prose became hard to understand, and more importantly, kept my nose to the grindstone. It turned out to be a happy and constructive relationship.

Katharina Otto-Bernstein, an extraordinarily gifted filmmaker and writer, gave me advice on the structure and style. Alas, this was in the later stages, when I could not adopt all her ideas, being afraid of running out of time: in my nineties, the clock is ticking. Had I consulted her earlier, this book would be considerably better.

Many people helped me remember various segments of my life, as well as put them in historical context. During the writing, I fortunately still had some friends and relatives whom I have known since childhood and others who became friends in subsequent years and could serve as living witnesses. The only relative from my childhood who was still alive during the writing of this book, Anne Sichel, was extremely helpful in memories of my Mainz childhood and our subsequent residence and flight from France. She unfortunately died recently.

Professor Alain Ruiz, from the University of Bordeaux, who has made a major study of the Jewish refugees in the Gironde after the German occupation, was invaluable in providing details of the internment camps of Libourne and Gurs and the fate of their detainees.

Various people in Mainz who were involved in researching the Jewish contribution to Mainz, both economically and intellectually, gave me a considerable amount of other information on Mainz before, during, and after the Nazi times. Some of this research was done for the Verein für Sozialgeschichte Mainz (an association for the study of community history) and partially financed by MAGENZA-Stiftung für Jüdisches Leben Mainz (a foundation established to study the Jewish society in the Mainz area—Magenza is the Latin name for Mainz). The city of Mainz has kept contact with survivors, wherever they may be now, and has invited every survivor to visit Mainz at the city's cost. Some of these outstanding citizens, some of whom have helped me in reconstructing the past, are Dr. Hedwig Brüchert, Dr. Tillmann Krach, and Reinhard Frenzel, each of whom has published a number of monographs, as diverse as the history of the Jewish students in the (female-only) high school during my youth, a history of the new Jewish cemetery and the history of its most prominent dead, a history of the brewing industry in Mainz, and various biographies and other studies.

I was fortunate enough to have four survivors from

my OSS/CIA days with whom to discuss various elements of my intelligence career chapters. They have all died in the meantime. They were Thomas Polgar, William Hood, John Hadden, and Clair George.

Thomas Polgar served with me in Berlin after the war and went on to a prestigious career in the CIA. He had thought deeply about the function of intelligence in helping government policy, and I thank him for reminding me that nations do not have friends, but interests. He was helpful in my chapters on Berlin and Germany, as well as acting as a sounding board for my critique of the CIA.

William Hood was another friend whom I had known since the 1940s. Though we never served together, we did work together on various challenges. He helped Dick Helms write his memoirs and wrote some good books himself, among which was *Mole*, based on an actual espionage case involving a high Soviet intelligence officer. Since he lived in Amagansett, Long Island, where I have a house, we spent many a Sunday breakfast together discussing our careers and the function of intelligence.

John Hadden was an officer who worked with me in Berlin. He was a West Point graduate who brought a knowledge of military strategy and history to his various, ultimately high-level jobs in the agency. He read and criticized part of the manuscript and gave me information, some of which I could not use for security reasons. He was a close and dear friend.

Last but not least, Clair George had served as a young Chinese-language officer with me in Hong Kong and would ultimately rise to be DDP, head of the clandestine services. He helped me remember Hong Kong and put some of the other incidents of my intelligence life in proper perspective. He became blind after retirement, and I would visit him in Washington, where we reminisced about the "good old days."

Dr. Jonathan Clemente, who is writing a book on physicians and OSS, was invaluable in guiding me to access old OSS records in the National Archives and in finding sources for other information. He was always available and willing to share his extensive knowledge.

I am sure there are many other people who were helpful, but none who were as helpful as those mentioned here.

I was also helped enormously by various publications: The yearbooks published by the Leo Baeck Institute were invaluable as I mined the Jewish past in Germany, as were various special studies distributed throughout the year. Carol Kahn Strauss, the director in New York, and Dr. Frank Mecklenburg, head of research, were always available to help and give wise counsel. The various publications of the German Historical Institute were invaluable for background of German history in the twentieth century. *Studies in Intelligence*, a publication covering unclassified articles, published periodically by the CIA Center for the Study of Intelligence, proved useful. The publication also covers books written on the subject.

Fortunately, a lot of the people who were in the wine trade with me are still around and have been helpful in many ways. They have provided details of trends and markets, which were most useful. They are too many to mention, but foremost were Riquet Hess and Friedrich Weidmann, who were joint managing directors of H. Sichel Söhne in Germany.

Allan Sichel was instrumental in giving me many details to make the Bordeaux chapter more interesting.

Ronald Sichel and David Hunter provided details on the Sichel companies and their activities, which proved most useful.

Last but not least, I want to thank my patient wife for proofreading various drafts, making constructive comments on how to make my writing more accessible, and correcting grammatical and other mistakes.

BIBLIOGRAPHY

Amos, Elan. *The Pity of It All.* New York: Metropolitan Books, 2002.

Anonymous. *A Woman in Berlin: Eight Weeks in the Conquered City.* New York: Henry Holt, 2005.

Bamford, James. *The Puzzle Palace: Inside the NSA, America's Most Secret Intelligence Organization.* New York: Penguin, 1983.

———.*The Shadow Factory.* New York: Anchor Books, 2009.

Bissel, Richard, with Jonathan E. Lewis and Frank T. Puldo. *Reflections of a Cold Warrior.* New Haven, CT: Yale University Press, 1996.

Blake, George. *No Other Choice.* New York: Simon and Schuster, 1990.

Brown, Anthony Cave. *Treason in the Blood: H. St. John Philby and the Spy Case of the Century.* New York: Houghton Mifflin, 1994.

Calvi, Fabrizio. *OSS La Guerre Secrète en France: Les Services Speciaux Americains, La Resistance et le Gestapo 1942–1945.* Paris: Hachette, 1990.

Chavchavadze, David. *Crowns and Trenchcoats: A Russian Prince in the CIA.* New York: Atlantic International, 1990.

Colby, William. *Honorable Men: My Life in the CIA*. New York: Simon and Schuster, 1978.

Critchfield, James. *Partners at the Creation: The Men behind Postwar Germany's Defense and Intelligence Establishment*. Annapolis, MD: Naval Institute Press, 2007.

Cutler, Richard. *Counterspy*. Omaha, NE: Potomac Books, 2004.

Delattre, Lucas. *Fritz Kolbe, Un Espion au Coeur du IIIe Reich*. Paris: Denoel, 2003.

Dulles, Allen. *The Secret Surrender*. New York: Harper and Row, 1966.

Fisher, Louis. *In the Name of National Security*. University Press of Kansas, 2006.

Ford, Corey, and Alastair McBain. *Cloak and Dagger*. New York: Random House, 1945.

Friedländer, Saul. *Nazi Germany and the Jews*. New York: Harper Collins, 1997.

Friedrich, Otto. *Blood and Iron from Bismarck to Hitler: The von Moltke Family's Impact on German History*. New York: Harper Collins, 1995.

Gaddis, John Lewis. *George F. Kennan: An American Life*. New York: Penguin, 2011.

Gup, Ted. *The Book of Honor*. New York: Anchor Books, 2001.

von Hassel, Agostino. *Alliance of Enemies*. New York: St. Martin's Press, 2006.

Helms, Richard, with William Hood. *A Look over My Shoulder: A Life in the Central Intelligence Agency*. New York: Random House, 2003.

Hersh, Burton. *Old Boys*. New York: Scribner's, 1992.

Karlow, S. Peter. *Targeted by the CIA: An Intelligence Professional Speaks Out on the Scandal That Turned the CIA Upside Down.* Paducah, KY: Turner Publishing, 2001.

Kellerhoff, Sven Felix, and Bernd von Kostka. *Hauptstadt der Spione: Geheimdienste in Berlin im Kalten Krieg.* Berlin: Berlin Story Verlag, 2012.

Kloman, Erasmus. *Assignment Algiers.* Annapolis, MD: Naval Institute Press, 2005.

Knightley, Phillip. *The Second Oldest Profession.* New York: Norton, 1986.

Macdonogh, Giles. *Berlin.* London: Sinclair Stevenson, 1997.

Mann, Golo. *Deutsche Geschichte des 19 und 20 Jahrhunderts.* Frankfurt/Main: Fischer Taschenbücher, 1992.

Mauch, Chistof. *The Shadow War against Hitler: The Covert Operations of American Secret Intelligence Service.* New York: Columbia University Press, 1993.

Miller, Roger. *To Save a City: The Berlin Airlift 1948–1949.* Washington, DC: Air Force History and Museums Program, 1998.

Murphy, David E., Sergei A. Kondrashev, and George Bailey. *Battleground Berlin.* New Haven, CT: Yale University Press, 1997.

Priest, Dana. *The Mission: Waging War and Keeping Peace with American's Military.* New York: Norton, 2003.

Smith, Bradley. *The Shadow Warriors.* New York: Basic Books, 1983.

Smyser, W. R. *From Yalta to Berlin.* New York: St. Martin's Press, 1999.

Vaughan, Hal. *FDR's 12 Apostles*. Guildford, CT: Lyons Press, 2006.

Waller, Douglas. *Wild Bill Donovan*. New York: Free Press, 2011.

Weiner, Tim. *Legacy of Ashes: The History of the CIA*. New York: Doubleday, 2007.

Weiner, Tim, David Johnston, and Neil A. Lewis. *Betrayal: The Story of Aldrich Ames, an American Spy*. New York: Random House, 1995.

Winks, Robin W. *Cloak and Gown*. New Haven, CT: Yale University Press, 1987.

Wolf, Markus. *Man without a Face*. London: Jonathan Cape, 1997.

WWI   14—18
Hitler   32
WWI   39—45

CPSIA information can be obtained
at www.ICGtesting.com
Printed in the USA
FSOW01n1905220116
16063FS